THE LION AND THE SPHINX

By the same author

A Good Dusting – The Sudan Campaigns 1883–99
The Fists of Righteous Harmony – The Boxer Uprising 1900
Remember with Advantages – History of the 10th, 11th and Royal Hussars
Soldiers of the Nile – British Officers of the Egyptian Army 1882–1925

The Lion
and the Sphinx

*The Rise and Fall of the
British in Egypt, 1882–1956*

HENRY KEOWN-BOYD

M
C

© Henry Keown–Boyd, 2002

First published in 2002 by
The Memoir Club
Whitworth Hall
Spennymoor
County Durham

British Library Cataloguing-in-Publication data
A catalogue record for this book is available from the British Library

ISBN 1 84104 061 4

Designed and typeset by Carnegie Publishing, Lancaster
Printed in the UK by Bookcraft, Bath

To the Memory of my Parents

'He that undertaketh the story of a time, specially of any length, cannot but meet with many blanks and spaces which he must be forced to fill up out of his own wit and conjecture.'

Francis Bacon – quoted by P. G. Elgood in *The Transit of Egypt*

Contents

Acknowledgements

IN A VARIETY OF WAYS, the help and co-operation of the following have been invaluable: (alphabetically) Clare Brown, Michael Brunt, Colin Campbell, Patrick Cunningham, Ian de Sales la Terriere, Sir Douglas Dodds-Parker, Thalia el Nakeeb, Hugh Farey, Tim Fisher, Charles Fitzgerald, Peg Forbes, Elsie Vernon Hart, Tom Hartman, Francis Henn, Jane Hogan, Archie Hunter, Andy Hurst, Lillian Ireland, Alwyn Jennings-Bramly, David Keown-Boyd, Jeannette Keown-Boyd, Sir Anthony Kershaw, Tony Kirk-Greene, Theo Klat, Michael Lee, Sarah Searight Lush, David Mackenzie, Sybil Magar, John Maudslay, Michel Michailides, Caroline Mieczkowska, Hallam Mills, Laura Morris, Patricia Nashaat, Jackie Nimr, Edward O'Farrell, Dan Parsons, John Pollock, Samir Rafaat, James Reynolds, Sally and Jasper Scovil, Peter Sekuless, Jennifer Thorp, John Udal, Ian Weston-Smith and Allan Woodliffe.

I should also pay tribute to those no longer with us whose anecdotes and experiences, recounted to me in days gone by, appear in these pages. They include my parents (to whose memory this book is dedicated), my aunt and godmother Ruth Maudslay, her son Rennie, Nanny Talmage and three stalwarts of the Egyptian Police, 'Uncle' Walter Lucas, George Naldrett-Jays and Dick Giles.

Foreword, by Leo Cooper

HENRY KEOWN-BOYD has written a most unusual book. He tells me that it was not easy to find a publisher for it, so he has finally decided to publish it himself. A brave but, in my view, the only sensible decision to make. Henry is well qualified to write this book as his father, Sir Alexander Keown-Boyd, served in the Egyptian Government for many years and part of Henry's early life was spent in the highly charged atmosphere of British rule.

Dealing with Egypt has never been easy and this book, written with much inside knowledge, is a valuable contribution to the history of Britain's diplomacy at work in one of the most challenging parts of the world, which many of us came to know so well during the Suez crisis or on National Service in the Canal Zone. Henry, however, goes further back to produce a dramatic and well-documented picture of life in that turbulent country from 1882 to 1956.

While having to deal with the Egyptian political scene, which of course is no easy job, there is another theme running through the book, that of Egyptology, the world of discoveries, pyramids and the sandy activities of Howard Carter. One suspects that people were more interested in Egypt for its antiquities than almost anything else but of course the building of the Suez Canal changed world history and all this is recorded with great skill and not a little humour.

I urge anybody interested in the Middle East to get hold of this book which, knowing the book trade as I do, will be a difficult task – not unlike finding treasures in the desert – but they will be rewarded by the immaculate prose and the very obvious first-hand knowledge of the subject.

I have had the privilege of publishing Henry's books in the past, including *A Good Dusting* and his book on the Boxer Rebellion, both of which revealed a high standard of scholarship and fine writing. Anything written by Henry is worth attention – not least his day-to-day correspondence! I recommend this book highly.

Background

ALTHOUGH the description has been contested by some recent scholarship, Mohamed (or Mehmed) Ali Pasha has often been called the Founder of Modern Egypt. His dynasty survived under lesser, indeed usually pretty inadequate, successors for over a hundred years after his death, largely because the British decreed that it should. Once their protection had been removed the dynasty fell and, with it, British influence in Egypt. So, we may conclude that, although neither 'partner' was much enamoured of the other, they were locked together in an embrace of mutual interest.

When we refer to the 'Mohamed Ali Dynasty' it should be borne in mind that most of his successors were descended from Mohamed Ali's stepson, Ibrahim, and therefore not a drop of the founder's blood ran in their veins. In return for a handsome bribe, the Sultan of Turkey had granted a firman to Ibrahim's son Ismail, the first ruler of Egypt to be known as Khedive, that the succession should descend through his personal line and not that of the eldest surviving male descendant of Mohamed Ali.

As far as the British officials of the Egyptian Government were concerned, their policy of dynastic support was carved in tablets of stone. As late as 1952, nearly seventy years after the British invasion and occupation of Egypt, one such official, long retired but still resident in Egypt, wrote to a Minister of the in-coming British Conservative Government urging him to go to almost any lengths to support King Farouk, to all intents and purposes the last of the dynasty. The alternative, he believed, was Communism (in the event it was Nasser's 'Arab Socialism' which prevailed) and 'the pashas in the Mohamed Ali Club ... all trembling in their shoes ...' were right when they predicted the downfall of 'first the English, then all foreigners, then the Copts, then us!' [1] His warnings were in vain. Indeed, by this time there was probably little or nothing the British could have done to save the monarchy, and within a few months Farouk had been deposed and within a few years

1

the British and many of the foreigners, Copts and Pashas had been dispossessed and deported or fled the country.

Mohamed Ali, an Albanian born at Kavalla (Greece) in about 1769, came to Egypt as a junior officer of irregular Ottoman cavalry in 1799 as part of a force to defy and, with the help of the British, to defeat the French.

By a combination of extraordinary political acumen and lethal ruthlessness (he probably arranged the murder of his own commanding officer and managed to depose the Sultan's appointee as Governor of Egypt) he had established himself as Viceroy or Wali of this Ottoman province by 1805. A few years later he consolidated his power by his notorious massacre of the Mamlouks, the previous governing military caste, after a banquet at the Cairo Citadel.[2]

Although he was a moderniser who took great interest in all forms of technological advance, who dug canals and built factories and, above all, introduced the production of long-staple cotton which for decades was the mainstay of the Egyptian economy, his principal interest was in military adventure and conquest. With the aid of his step-son and heir, Ibrahim Pasha, an able general but, according to Cromer, 'a half-lunatic savage',[3] he waged a series of campaigns until British alarm at his threat to the already enfeebled Ottoman Empire caused them to curtail his expansionism and force him to hand back to the Sultan, theoretically his liege-lord, the territories he had conquered.

Ultimately from the British point of view, the most important of Mohamed Ali's conquests was the Sudan, which remained in Turco-Egyptian hands until the Mahdist uprising of the 1880s. Re-conquered by Anglo-Egyptian forces under Kitchener in 1898, the history of the Sudan was inextricably linked with that of Egypt throughout the period of the British Occupation.

In the early years of his reign Mohamed Ali relied mainly on volunteer recruits from the various subject races of the Ottoman Empire, princi-pally Albanian, Bosnian and North African, to fill the ranks of his army, but, as his ambitions widened, so these sources became inadequate. For centuries, slaves from the Sudan had been imported into Egypt, many of them from the warlike tribes of the upper Nile and Nuba Mountains and Mohamed Ali realised their military potential. Thus the Sudan was to be conquered for its 'Black and White Ivory' – slave-soldiers and elephant tusks – its cattle, its camels and its elusive mineral wealth.

After a series of campaigns, prosecuted with extreme brutality by various of the Viceroy's sons and, in particular, his son-in-law, the infamous Defterdar Mohamed Khusraw, most of the northern (Arab)

The birthplace of Mohamed Ali at Kavalla, Greece.

Sudan was in his hands and by the late 1820s razzias (slave-raiding expeditions) were pushing into the far south and Nuba Mountains. The problem here was that, although many thousands of potential soldiers were captured, owing to the appalling conditions under which they were marched or transported by river northwards, only small numbers reached the training depots in Egypt alive and the Viceroy therefore sought yet another source of recruits.[4]

The Egyptian *fellah* (peasant) was, and is, strong, hardy and usually docile. However, luckily for him, he had not, since ancient times, been regarded by his rulers as fighting material. Mohamed Ali, however, would have none of this and, despite the loathing and fear with which military service was regarded by the fellahin, embarked upon a programme of conscription. Perhaps surprisingly, under Ibrahim, these unwilling warriors fought well in the Viceroy's campaigns in the Hejaz, Syria and Greece, successes which alarmed the British by their threat to the survival of the Ottoman Empire – a cherished counter-balance to Russian power.[5]

Ironically, it was to be the descendants of these men under a native Egyptian officer who, half a century later, were to pose the first great threat to the Mohamed Ali dynasty and, unwittingly, to bring the British into Egypt.

CHAPTER I

Enter the British

MOHAMED ALI died, senile, in 1849 and was succeeded by the 'half-lunatic' Ibrahim who had held the regency for a time but succumbed to cirrhosis of the liver (or, according to Cromer, of pneumonia after drinking two bottles of iced champagne!) and soon followed his stepfather to the grave.[1]

Many instances of Ibrahim's terrifying and unpredictable cruelties are recorded. On one occasion, we are told, he sliced off the head of a groom, who was also his foster-brother, for harnessing his horse with too mild a bit; on another, he decided to drown his entire suite while sailing from Istanbul to Alexandria. However, in a marathon session lasting eleven hours, his Armenian secretary Nubar, a future Prime Minister of Egypt, by dint of much flattery, managed to keep Ibrahim talking about his successful campaigns and his genius as a general until they reached Alexandria and the opportunity for the mass drowning was lost.[2]

Of the next two Viceroys, Abbas I Hilmi and Mohamed Said, both direct descendants of Mohamed Ali and the last of his bloodline to rule Egypt, there is little to be said which has much relevance to this history, except that they were both cruel, capricious and greedy. It was during the latter's reign that Egypt's financial position started to deteriorate and when he died in 1863 he was succeeded by his even more profligate nephew Ismail, the first Viceroy to bear the title Khedive and, for all his shortcomings, perhaps the first of the line to possess at least a veneer of civilisation. This, of course, did not inhibit him from extracting punitive taxes from the fellahin with the aid of the kourbash (rawhide whip) and spending the proceeds on himself, nor from murdering his Finance Minister for the crime of knowing too much. At the same time he was in many ways childlike. Cromer quotes an English member of his domestic staff. 'Ismail and his brother Mustapha, when they were in Paris, used to buy whatever they saw: they were like children, nothing was fine enough for them; they bought carriages and horses like those of Queen Victoria or the Emperor and let them spoil from want of shelter and cleaning ...'³

However, not all their expenditures were wasted on self-indulgence and it should be remembered that it was under these rulers that the Suez Canal was dug (and, incidentally, the Cairo Opera House hastily built to celebrate the opening of this great waterway) and hundreds of miles of canals and railways constructed.

This is not the place to delve into the highly complicated financial problems which faced Egypt and her creditors in the 1870s. Suffice to say that by 1876 Egypt could no longer service her debts and an international board known as La Caisse de la Dette (the Commission of the Public Debt) was formed to administer her finances. Among the commissioners appointed was a British artillery officer, Major Evelyn Baring, with some experience of financial administration in India and a banker by breeding and instinct if not by profession.

In 1879, under pressure from the Powers, the Sultan officially deposed Ismail and appointed his son Tewfik in his place. Ismail was, comparatively speaking, a nicer man than any of his predecessors and there were those who regretted his departure, including General Charles Gordon who had served as his Governor in the southern Sudanese province of Equatoria and who, perhaps naively, believed that Ismail genuinely wished to abolish the slave-trade.

But Tewfik's appointment solved few problems and created others in that he was a weak and vacillating man, lacking the ruthlessness and cunning sense of self-preservation, which characterised his predecessors.

From the early years of the nineteenth century the Egyptian Army had been officered principally by the Turks, Albanians and Circassians and their descendants who had come to Egypt with Mohamed Ali. To these were added from time to time French and American (usually ex-Confederate) military advisers. Some native Egyptians were commissioned but were usually denied promotion and senior rank. When foreign pressure forced military expenditure cuts upon Tewfik, it was the Egyptian officers who felt themselves most vulnerable to redundancy as they were the least well-connected in ruling circles.

The political, diplomatic and military drama which led to the British invasion and occupation of Egypt was spread over a period of approximately eighteen months. In January 1881 a petition was presented to the Prime Minister, Riaz Pasha, demanding the promotion of some Egyptian officers and the reinstatement of others. It also required the removal of the War Minister, Osman Rifki Pasha. The prime movers behind this petition were the commanding officers of two regiments of the Cairo garrison. Ahmed Orabi Bey (later Pasha) and Ali Fehmi Bey, the latter being the lieutenant-colonel (kaimakam) of the 1st or Guard Regiment, responsible for the security of the Khedivial palaces.[4]

This petition was regarded with grave disfavour by the Khedive and his ministers, so much so that the arrest and Court Martial of the two colonels was ordered. The trial was convened at the Ministry of War on 1 February but it was interrupted when men of the two regiments concerned broke into the courtroom, roughed up the Minister of War, smashed the furniture and removed their colonels. Uncertain of the reliability of the remainder of the army, the Khedive and his government were in a quandary. Should they stand up to the rebellious colonels and order their re-arrest, thus risking full-scale mutiny, or should they accept humiliating defeat? When a third regiment, stationed outside Cairo, marched on the city they chose the latter course, sacked the War Minister and appointed the colonels' nominee, one Mahmoud Baroudi Pasha.

There then followed a period of intrigue and counter-intrigue involving the representatives of the Powers, especially the French, the Khedive and his Prime Minister trying to re-establish their authority, the Sultan and, of course, the Egyptian officers determined not to lose the initiative and the concessions they had already gained. Not only were they convinced of their patriotic duty but also they knew that the cost of failure was almost certainly death. Then, in an unexpected show of defiance, the Khedive dismissed Mahmoud Baroudi; at about the same time a regiment sympathetic to the colonels was ordered to move from Cairo to Alexandria and a rumour spread that the Khedive was planning the assassination of the colonels.

On 9 September, Orabi marched on Abdin Palace at the head of a large force with artillery. For the first time the Khedive appealed for British help, in the shape of Sir Auckland Colvin, an experienced Indian Civil Servant, who had recently taken over from Baring as Controller-General of La Caisse de la Dette. With the Acting British Consul-General, Sir Charles Cookson, and an American officer of the Egyptian Army, Stone Pasha, Colvin persuaded the Khedive to confront Orabi in the square in front of the palace. The dramatic scene which followed was later described by Colvin:

> The square was entirely occupied by soldiers drawn up round it ... The Viceroy (Khedive) advanced firmly into the square towards a little group of officers and men ... I [Colvin] said to him 'When Arabi [sic] Bey presents himself, tell him to give you his sword and then give them the order to disperse. Then go the round the square and address each regiment separately and give them the order to disperse.' Arabi Bey approached

on horseback; the Viceroy called on him to dismount. He did so and
came forward on foot ... and saluted. I said to the Viceroy 'Now is your
moment.' He replied. 'We are between four fires.' He took council of a
native officer on his left and repeated to me, 'What can I do? We are
between four fires. We shall be killed.' He then told Arabi to sheathe his
sword. The order was obeyed; then he asked Arabi what all this meant;
Arabi replied by enumerating three points [see below], adding that the
army had come there on the part of the Egyptian people to enforce them
and would not retire until they were conceded. The Viceroy turned to
me and said 'you hear what he says.'

To this Colvin replied that it was not fitting for the Khedive to negotiate
with a colonel in public and that he should retire to the palace, leaving
Colvin and Cookson to continue negotiations.[5]

The points demanded by Orabi were that the Government should
resign; that a parliament should be convoked and that the strength of
the army should be raised to 18,000 men. Presumably on Colvin's
advice, the Khedive agreed to the first point and. against his own
inclination, a candidate acceptable to all parties, Cherif Pasha, was
appointed Prime Minister with Mahmoud Baroudi reinstated as Minister
for War.

The other two points were referred for decision to the Sublime Porte
(the Ottoman Government in Istanbul), presumably as a delaying tactic.
The idea of a parliament was anathema to Tewfik as it smacked of
democracy and a diminution of his autocratic power, while an increase
in the size of the army was unacceptable to Colvin and his fellow
commissioners on the grounds of expense.

It would be wearisome to catalogue every twist and turn in the
struggle between Khedive and Colonel over the next six to eight months.
This has been dealt with exhaustively by Cromer in his *Modern Egypt*
and included the appointment of Orabi as War Minister, his dismissal
and reappointment.

The Porte ducked the decisions which were required of it: an impasse
was reached and civil disturbances in which a number of Europeans
and other Christians were killed broke out. By the summer of 1882
Britain and France had decided that armed intervention to save the
Khedive and their own interests in Egypt was almost inevitable. The
British in particular were concerned to safeguard the route to India and
the Far East through the Suez Canal (a 44 per cent interest in which
had been acquired by Disraeli in 1876), although, at that stage, the
British Government, under the anti-imperialist Gladstone, was less
warlike in its intent than the French.

An Anglo-French fleet gathered off Alexandria and further serious
rioting broke out in the city during which the British Consul, Sir

Charles Cookson, was injured and a considerable number of other foreigners killed. An ultimatum was issued to Orabi (who was by now the de facto ruler of Egypt) to dismantle the defences of Alexandria, but when it was ignored the British fleet opened fire on 11 July 1882 and a heavy bombardment forced the withdrawal of the Egyptian garrison which paused only to set fire to the city.

The French, in a characteristically unexplained and incomprehensible change of policy, had sailed away the night before – an act which they never ceased to regret and which gave their traditionally greatest rival on the international stage, Britain, virtually unfettered control over Egypt and ultimately the Sudan and the Nile waters for the next three-quarters of a century.

The rioting continued but the landing of marines and sailors was delayed by several days on the insistence of Gladstone who objected on the grounds that it would have been an 'assumption of authority' and 'grossly disloyal in the face of Europe'. Whatever he may have meant by the latter phrase, the normally restrained Cromer commented later that 'It is difficult to conceive of the frame of mind of anyone who considers that firing several thousand shot and shell into Egyptian forts did not involve "an assumption of authority", whereas landing some men to prevent a populous city being burnt to the ground did involve such an assumption.' [6]

When the naval landings were approved a few days later they were quickly reinforced by two battalions of infantry from Cyprus under General Alison. While General Sir Garnet Wolseley ('Our Only General'), who had been appointed to command an invasion force, completed his plans, Alison was instructed to keep the Egyptians busy in the area of Alexandria and rumours were spread to the effect that all British operations would stem from that city. On 19 August, with the dateline Alexandria, the *Egyptian Gazette* published the following announcement by Wolseley (in French):

> The Commander-in-Chief of the British Army wishes it to be known that the Government of Her Majesty has sent troops to Egypt with the sole objective of re-establishing the authority of the Khedive; in consequence the army will take action only against those who defy this authority.
>
> All peaceable inhabitants will be treated with due consideration and they will not suffer any act of violence; their religion, their mosques, their families and their goods will be respected.
>
> All supplies for the army will be paid for and citizens are invited to present tenders for such supplies.
>
> The Commander-in-Chief will welcome with pleasure all those invested with authority who will use it to assist him in repressing the rebellion

against His Highness the Khedive, who, alone, governs Egypt by virtue
of the Firmans of His Imperial Majesty the Sultan.

> G. J. Wolseley
> Commander-in-Chief of the British Army in Egypt [7]

In fact, Wolseley intended to seize the Suez Canal and launch his drive
to Cairo along the railway from Ismailia via Zagazig and the Sweetwater
Canal. Having lain at anchor off Aboukir for some days, he sailed for
Ismailia and started to disembark his 40,000 British and Indian troops
on 20 August.

Eight days later his advance guard fought a successful action at
Kassassin, some twenty miles west of Ismailia, which included a much-
vaunted moonlight charge by the Household Cavalry, forcing the
Egyptians to withdraw to a well-constructed defensive position at Tel
el Kebir. It was here that the main action of the campaign was fought
in the semi-darkness of the small hours of 13 September.

This battle has been described by, amongst others, the journalist
Charles Lowe with splendid Victorian hyperbole. The brunt of the
fighting was borne by the Highland Brigade, the 'shock' troops of the
time, who suffered the heaviest casualties (45 killed out of a total of
57). The Guards, under one of Queen Victoria's sons, the Duke of
Connaught, had been held in reserve, causing Lowe to comment rather
improbably that they '... almost died of grief at the thought that they
had never got a chance to die of wounds'! [8]

Orabi's conscripts were no match for Wolseley's regulars and the
outcome was predictable. By 7 a.m. it was all over and the broken
Egyptian army was in full retreat having lost some 2,000 killed and an
uncounted number of wounded.

The following day British and Indian cavalry entered Cairo. Within
a few days the remnants of the Egyptian army had been disarmed and,
no doubt to their astonished delight, allowed to go home, while Orabi,
who had taken no part in the Battle of Tel el Kebir, had surrendered
to the cavalry commander, Drury-Lowe. [9]

It is difficult not to sympathise with Orabi. He was probably a genuine
patriot, not simply a self-seeking adventurer, but he had bitten off more
than he could chew. He lacked the killer instinct, political skills and
perhaps even the physical courage of a successful revolutionary. He was
no Mao or Castro, not even a Gamal Abdel Nasser, another obscure
colonel who, three-quarters of a century after Orabi, was to rise up and
sweep away the Mohamed Ali dynasty and the last traces of British
dominance in Egypt.

The desire of the Khedive and the Turco-Egyptian ruling class to
have Orabi and his friends summarily executed without trial was

unacceptable to the British authorities, already conscious of murmurings at home, led by the influential anti-imperialist Wilfred Blunt, against the whole Egyptian enterprise. Neither the British Government nor its leading men-on-the spot, Lord Dufferin, British Ambassador to the Porte, the Consul-General in Egypt, Sir Edward Malet, and Colvin, wanted martyrdom for Orabi. Blunt raised a substantial fund for his defence and a leading British barrister, A. M. Broadley QC, was briefed to defend him.

Even Cromer admits that the trial was carefully stage-managed. Orabi was to plead guilty to rebellion and be sentenced to death, which sentence would be immediately commuted to perpetual exile, and that is what happened.[10]

Orabi and six of his closest confederates sailed for Ceylon on 26 December 1882. About 150 other people were sentenced to various lesser punishments and all others charged were amnestied on 1 January 1883.

But not all those involved were so lucky. Presumably condemned in a separate trial, the colonel held responsible for the riots and killing of Europeans in Alexandria and two police officers were hanged, which macabre events were witnessed by Charles Coles, the recently appointed Chief of Police.

> I had never seen a Turkish execution and was very perturbed at what I was about to witness ... I was still more nervous when on enquiry I was told that all that was necessary was to seat the condemned man on a chair mounted on a small table and pull both from under him ... The poor devil (Colonel Suliman Daoud) was in an abject state of terror, and after swallowing something offered him in a glass by the Levantine doctor, which I imagine was a very strong narcotic or perhaps poison, he swooned, and was swung off in an insensible condition.
>
> The hanging of the two police officers was even more dramatic ... on this occasion there were two gallows facing each other. The condemned men were to arrive on foot from two different prisons and one was late. We waited a few minutes and it seemed to me to be brutal to keep the first man in suspense; I therefore begged the Governor not to allow any further delay. Unfortunately the second prisoner arrived on the scene just as his brother officer was swung off and was still struggling, as with the system adopted it was more or less a case of strangulation. But I never saw a man (the second officer) die more pluckily. He mounted the table almost without assistance and it was soon over.[11]

Orabi returned to Egypt less than twenty years later in 1901. He had been well treated in Ceylon and had been allowed to receive visitors, many of them British. On his return home, he irritated his former supporters by declaring that the British were doing a pretty good job

in Egypt. He died in obscurity in 1911 and to-day there are a few
streets named after him in Egyptian towns but it is doubtful if many
Egyptians know why.[12]

CHAPTER 2

The Early Days

'IL N'Y A QUE LE PROVISOIRE QUI DURE,' say the French. The British invaded Egypt ostensibly to crush a military coup, stabilise Khedivial rule and sort out its chaotic finances, promising to leave as soon as these objectives had been achieved. They stayed for three-quarters of a century.

Direct rule was never attempted, not even during the Protectorate period from 1914 to 1922, and British power was exercised unofficially through a diplomatic representative known innocuously as the British Agent and Consul-General, later re-designated High Commissioner and, finally, Ambassador. In theory these gentlemen had no more authority in what was, legally, until 1914, a province of the Ottoman Empire and, from 1922, an independent monarchy, than the representatives of the other Powers. However, in practice, as they controlled the army, the police and, through ministerial Advisers, most of the other organs of government, in their hands lay the ultimate reins of power.

The first official to occupy this anomalous and ill-defined position was Sir Edward Malet, a career diplomat who was *in situ* at the time of the invasion but about a year later he was replaced by Sir Evelyn Baring, the former Director-General of La Caisse de la Dette, later elevated to the peerage first as Baron then Viscount and finally as the Earl of Cromer. To avoid confusion from now on he will be referred to as Cromer.[1]

Before his arrival, another Evelyn had already appeared in Egypt. The reconstruction, reform and control over the Egyptian Army were obviously a vital priority for the British occupiers, especially as trouble was brewing in the Sudan, and, under a Khedivial decree of 20 December 1882, this task was begun. A former British officer in the Ottoman service, Colonel Valentine Baker, was originally chosen for the post of Sirdar or Commander-in-Chief, but, probably under pressure from Queen Victoria, the British Government refused to confirm the appointment and Major-General Sir Evelyn Wood, VC, replaced him.[2]

The story of Baker's disgrace, imprisonment and removal from the British Army is quite well known but may bear repetition here.

In the spring of 1875, Baker, a former commanding officer of the 10th Hussars, was asked to organise a Review at Aldershot in honour of the Sultan of Zanzibar and on 17 May was returning from that garrison town to London by train. In those days first-class railway compartments, three to a carriage, were separate from each other with no corridor on either side. He boarded the train at Liphook and found there to be a young woman, a Miss Rebecca Dickinson, already in the compartment. She was alone. As Baker refused to offer any defence at his trial we have only her version of the events which followed. The two started to converse in a friendly way but according to Miss Dickinson, at some point after Woking. Baker tried to kiss her. She made a dive for the alarm bell, which apparently did not go off, and started to scream and, having started, did not stop. Then, despite a terrified Baker's frantic entreaties, she opened the door and tried to get out, falling backwards as she did so. At this point either Baker grabbed her or she grabbed Baker and his clothing became 'disarrayed' – although in precisely what way is not clear, but apparently around his 'waistband'.

The extraordinary spectacle of a girl half hanging out of a railway carriage with a middle-aged man clinging on to her was witnessed by a platelayer who managed to signal to the driver. The train stopped at Esher station where officials placed Miss Dickinson and Baker in separate compartments for the remainder of the journey to London.

Attempts to settle the matter privately failed and when the affair hit the headlines public opinion, led by the Queen, swung against Baker who was charged with rape, indecent assault and assault.

His trial at Croydon Assizes was a travesty. Upper class Victorian convention forbade Baker from contradicting Miss Dickinson's evidence against him, nor would he allow his counsel to cross-examine her. Although acquitted on the first charge of rape, for which there was no evidence whatsoever, he was sentenced to twelve months imprisonment and a fine of £500 plus prosecution costs on the two assault charges. He was also dismissed from the army.

We may speculate that such harsh punishment for a single stolen kiss based on uncorroborated evidence is unlikely to have been inflicted at any other time in British history – except, perhaps, our own, when political correctness might cause a judge to echo the words of Mr Justice Brett at Baker's trial: 'If a man kisses a woman against her will, and with criminal passion and intent, such an act is indecent assault ...' adding, 'The mere laying of a man's hand on a woman amounts to criminal assault.'[3]

Lord Cromer (seated second left) with his long-serving Oriental Secretary Harry
Boyle to his right, *c*.1900.

Although Baker was to serve the Ottoman Empire with distinction,
the remainder of his life was dogged with ill-fortune. Appointed to
command the raggle-taggle Egyptian Gendarmerie, he led this untried,
untrained and unwilling rabble to its destruction against the Mahdists
at the first Battle of El Teb in 1884.

He and his wife and two daughters lived on a *dahabia* (houseboat)
on the Nile at Cairo and here both his wife and elder daughter Hermione
(reputedly Kitchener's fiancée) died, Baker himself following them to
the grave two years later at the age of sixty.[4]

Evelyn Wood, a prominent member of the celebrated Wolseley Ring
of imperial campaigners, brought with him an initial cadre of about
twenty-five carefully selected British officers and a similar number of
NCOs. Of these officers, including Wood himself, three were to reach
the rank of Field Marshal and three others that of full General.

Egyptian service was an attractive proposition, particularly for officers
with small private means and little social influence. The pay, starting
at £E450 per annum for subalterns, was good, promotion automatic as
all officers stepped up at least one rank and none ranked lower than
Bimbashi (major). Thus there was no shortage of recruits and, in due

course, there were to be about a hundred and fifty British officers serving in the Egyptian Army at any one time.

After the trauma of the Orabi experience, the Khedive and, to some extent, the Turco-Egyptian ruling class were, at least at first, happy with this arrangement. 'What,' wrote Cromer, 'could be more perfect than the presence in Egypt of a thoroughly disciplined force, commanded by young men who took no interest in local politics and who occupied themselves exclusively with polo and cricket?'[5]

Among the more exotic of these officers was one Lieutenant Harry Stewart, known for some reason as 'Bimbash'. An impecunious Gordon Highlander, Bimbash had commanded the Mounted Infantry contingent of his regiment in the Gordon Relief Expedition of 1884–85. According to his friend Percy Marling he had left Cairo with nothing but the clothes he stood up in, but by the time he reached Assouan he had filled two kitbags with all the equipment he had stolen from his brother officers. On his return to Cairo after the campaign, in the hope of improving his fortunes, he proposed to the daughter of the Prime Minister, Nubar Pasha (an Armenian Christian), but his suit was rejected when he admitted that he had nothing but a castle in Scotland and a claymore.[6] The decision was a wise one as when he died in 1904 he left the lady, a Miss Romilly, who had been rash enough to marry him, penniless.[7]

As the entire cost of the employment of British officers (who were under contract to the Khedive. a contract which Bimbash did not complete) and NCOs was borne by Egypt, the British Treasury was also pleased, as the size of the relatively expensive British Army of Occupation (later described by Kitchener as the Army of No Occupation) could be reduced to a mere three battalions of infantry, two cavalry regiments, a couple of artillery batteries and a few sappers and L of C troops, Later, especially in times of tension, the British garrison was considerably increased, rising to hundreds of thousands during the two World Wars.

Initially the British intended to restrict the size of the new Egyptian Army to 6,000 men consisting of two infantry brigades, one squadron of cavalry, an artillery battery and two companies of Camel Corps. One of the brigades was to consist of Albanian volunteers but a mutiny (see Appendix B) among the first intake of these men (it is by no means certain that they were either Albanians or volunteers) led to the abandonment of the idea. In any case, with the rise of the Mahdi in the Sudan, which more or less coincided with the arrival of the British in Egypt, it soon became clear that a much larger force would be required and the army eventually grew to three times its originally intended strength.

Like Mohamed Ali before them, the British were confident that fellahin conscripts could, with the right treatment and training, be turned into reasonably good soldiers. Similarly they quickly realised the admirable fighting qualities of the southern Sudanese troops of the old Egyptian Army, some of whom were to be found unemployed and destitute in Egypt while others were trickling back from the Sudan into Massawa and Suakin on the Red Sea as, one by one, the garrison towns fell to the Mahdi.[8]

From 1882 to 1925 nearly eleven hundred British officers (and a smaller number of British NCOs) served at various times in the Egyptian Army. Their contracts were for two years and could be renewed up to ten years, although a small minority served for much longer periods.

Early attempts to bring the Sudanese troops mentioned above under British command were inauspicious. Many had never seen a European and English as a language was entirely unknown to them, nor had the British officers had much time to learn Arabic. The result was bitter resentment against the newcomers, not only on the part of the men but also the 'native' officers, a mixture of Turks, Egyptians and some Sudanese promoted from the ranks.

Initial endeavours at Suakin early in 1884 to form a Sudanese battalion failed after the senior native officer, the Saghkolagasi (Adjutant-Major), attacked his British CO with a sword. Eventually and with great difficulty these troops were brought to Cairo and officially designated the 9th Sudanese Battalion (the first eight battalions of the new army consisting of Egyptian conscripts), but trouble erupted again when an attempt was made to exchange their old Remington rifles with Martini-Henrys. The British were obliged to disband the battalion and reform it with a nucleus of a hundred men of proven loyalty to the new regime. This worked, partly as a result of a substantial pay increase from one (1p) to two and a half piastres per day, plus a marriage allowance of one piastre per day (Sudanese troops were notably uxorious and extremely loath to be separated from their womenfolk). By August 1884 the battalion was considered reliable enough to be sent to the Sudan frontier at Wadi Halfa where it was to spend most of the next decade.

Gradually more 'Black' battalions were formed. In January 1886 the 10th was raised at Abbassiyeh Barracks near Cairo with a nucleus of fifty-seven NCOs and men from the 9th and later that year the 11th was formed out of what was described as a battalion of 'gendarmes' (possibly survivors of Baker's disastrous first Battle of El Teb in 1884) under the later famous Hector MacDonald. In November 1888 the 12th was raised on Gezira Island (now a suburb of Cairo) and the 13th was born at Assouan in Upper Egypt in 1889. The 14th did not appear until 1896, most of its men being deserters or prisoners from the Mahdist army during the Dongola campaign of that year. Finally, the 15th was converted from Egyptian (Reserve) to Sudanese at about the turn of the century.

However, the building up and training of the Sudanese battalions was not as smooth a process as this simple chronology implies. Having to manage on a financial shoestring, the army was short of equipment and 'job security' for the men precarious. From Bimbashi Mitford of the 9th we learn that his battalion boasted only twenty-seven pairs of boots for 1,000 men and when the Egyptian Treasury ran short of money military growth was the first to be pruned. At one point the newly formed 10th and 11th Battalions were abruptly, if temporarily, disbanded and their men discharged without pension or gratuity. When fresh funds became available a few months later there was no difficulty in reforming the battalions as most of their men were to be found eking out a miserable existence in makeshift villages around the Abbassiyeh cantonment, some existing on occasional baksheesh (hand-outs) from their British officers who were in no way responsible for their predicament and had themselves accepted pay cuts.

Despite its early trials and tribulations the new Egyptian Army developed rapidly into a viable fighting force. Although mainly employed on the Lines of Communication during the Gordon Relief Expedition of 1884–85, small detachments of Egyptian Army troops under British officers were present at various actions against the famous Mahdist emir Osman Digna in the eastern Sudan. Then, in December 1885, at the Battle of Ginnis on the frontier some Egyptian and Sudanese battalions took part as complete units and acquitted themselves creditably.[9]

Bimbashi Haggard (brother of the author H. Rider Haggard), who commanded the 1st (Egyptian) Battalion at the Battle of Ginnis, was able to write a few years later of the Egyptian conscripts:

> The young soldiers of the present army are well fed, well paid and well clothed. They get a periodical furlough to see their friends; are allowed ... to travel by train or steamer at greatly reduced rates; are given medals for active service; and if discharged from the service on account of wounds or sickness, they are sent home with a gratuity and a complete set of clothes ... Malingering by self mutilation (a common occurrence in the old Egyptian Army) has entirely ceased. The young soldiers themselves ... have frequently behaved with distinction in the field.[10]

Paradoxically it was an outbreak of cholera in the summer of 1883 which did much to create confidence and even affection between the Egyptian conscripts and their British officers. In the these early days the Egyptian Army Medical Department was still in its infancy and the duty of nursing the highly infectious sick fell to some of the British officers led by Bimbashi Wingate (later Sirdar and Governor-General of the Sudan) who was appointed director of the army cholera hospital. Despite their lack of anything but the most basic medical knowledge, Wingate and his colleagues managed to aid the recovery of those who survived and ease the passing of those who did not. One officer, Bimbashi Turner, contracted the disease by drinking medicine from the same bottle as his patients. However, he recovered only to drown while swimming in the Nile.[11]

By 1896 the Egyptian Army, some 14,500 strong, had reached a state of readiness and efficiency which enabled it to embark, virtually unaided in the initial stages, upon the re-conquest of the Sudan. Once this had been achieved, its principal occupation became the maintenance of law and order in the Sudan, especially in the south (see Appendix E).

The histories of Egypt, the Sudan and Britain being so closely linked during this period we should turn our attention briefly southwards to el Bilad el Sudan (the Land of the Blacks) which, as related in the Background to this book, had been conquered by Mohamed Ali with ruthless brutality in the 1820s.

Since then Turco-Egyptian misrule, in later years exacerbated by British-inspired attempts to stamp out the slave trade, an important element in the Sudanese economy, gave rise to serious discontent in the Sudan, a catalyst for which was sooner or later bound to appear. As virtually the only unifying factor among the northern Sudanese Arab tribes was Islam, perhaps it was inevitable this should take religious form and in the shape of a Messiah.

The Mahdi, Mohamed Ahmed, was born near Dongola in the 1840s, the son of a boat-builder who claimed descent from the Prophet. His rise to power was rapid and his military and political success phenomenal. Between 1881, when he first appeared on the scene as no more than an unusually charismatic *fiki* (holy man), and 1885, he had overrun the demoralised Egyptian garrisons in the Sudan, annihilated a British officered force under Hicks Pasha, and captured Khartoum, slaying one of Victorian England's most celebrated heroes. General Charles Gordon, in the process.

Thus, no sooner had they taken up the reins of power in Egypt, than the newly arrived British were faced with an immediate and unexpected crisis, their initial reaction to which was to pretend that It had nothing to do with them, a policy which did not survive the destruction of Hicks in November 1883.

Desperate to destroy the Mahdi, the Egyptians re-conscripted about 8,000 of Orabi's disbanded army and asked the British to supply officers, a request politely refused. However, Valentine Baker was authorised to help the Egyptians to recruit half-pay or redundant British and other European officers and, according to one source, the applicants' names were picked out of a hat.

When Wood took it upon himself to point out to the Egyptian War Minister that many of the conscripts were unfit for active service, especially in the harsh environment of the Sudan, the reply was a hearty laugh and an assurance to the effect that if the men were so old and infirm they would not be able to run away! In the event many of them were dispatched to the Sudan in chains.[12]

As for the officers, they were a second-rate lot. Colonel William Hicks himself, a half-pay colonel of the Indian Army, was fatalistic about the prospects of success but, like his subordinates, he needed the job. In the event they were all to perish, not without honour, in the heat and horror of the massacre known as the Battle of Sheikan, deep in the waterless scrubland of Kordofan. Only a few hundred out of a force of some 11,000 survived to be enlisted in the Mahdi's own army.

It was this catastrophe above all, and the clamour aroused by it in the Press, which forced a reluctant Gladstone and his Liberal cabinet to allow the dispatch of Gordon to the Sudan, against the instincts and advice of Cromer, to whose orderly mind Gordon's chaotic brilliance and indiscipline was anathema.

The story of his heroic defence of Khartoum, the failed attempt to rescue him and finally his martyr's death is too well known to need repetition here but these events, following so quickly on her invasion of Egypt, were to draw Britain ever more inextricably into the politics and history of the Nile valley. Anxious though Gladstone, and to a lesser extent his Tory successor Salisbury, were to withdraw from Egypt as soon as practicable, the Mahdist threat from the south was an added reason to stay. In fact, any direct threat was more perceived than real as the Mahdi, who died only six months after the fall of Khartoum, and his successor, the Khalifa Abdullahi, never had the military or logistical capability to invade Egypt. The one serious attempt, under the Emir Wad Nejumi, ended in total defeat when his ill-equipped and half-starved horde was crushed by the new Egyptian Army at the Battle of Toski in Upper Egypt in the summer of 1889.[13] Nevertheless, of more realistic concern was the fact that the Nile flowed through the Sudan and therefore any actual or potential interference with its waters was a matter of life or death for Egypt. Therefore, in a later chapter, the vexed problem of the Sudan and its effect upon Anglo-Egyptian relations will be dealt with more thoroughly.

Bähler Mr Peel Lady Grenfell. Sir F. Grenfell Mrs Peel
Edward Major Maxwell. Miss Grenfell
Mrs A. Grenfell

General Grenfell, Sirdar of the Egyptian Army, with a family group at the Pyramids.

Another important but virtually moribund organisation to which the British had to turn their attention was the police, and responsibility for the reconstruction of this corrupt, incompetent and brutal force was given, in addition to his role as Chief of the Gendarmerie, to Valentine Baker. Unfortunately neither he nor his brother Charles, a VC of the Indian Mutiny, who succeeded him, showed the organising ability or imagination required to carry out the necessary reforms and it was not until Kitchener, by that time Adjutant-General of the Egyptian Army, had been asked by Cromer in 1891 to try his hand at this challenging task that results began to show.[14]

Throughout his career Kitchener was to exhibit an unusual understanding of and sympathy with Middle Eastern methods and customs. Unlike many westerners, he did not swim against the current but used it and adapted it to get the results he wanted. During his brief term as Inspector-General of Police he managed to reduce serious crime by half and double the conviction rate. It is highly unlikely that he achieved this by kid-glove methods and the probability is that he allowed his Egyptian subordinates to continue with their traditional means of obtaining evidence and confessions, merely refining their implementation. He was, however, responsible for one humanitarian reform. In order to avoid the brutal scenes at executions as witnessed by Charles Coles in the previous chapter, Kitchener designed a 'mobile' gallows with a proper drop thus ensuring instantaneous death. This contraption was kept at police headquarters and sent around the country as required until, some years later, Coles, as Director of Prisons, arranged for a special execution room to be constructed in each prison.[15]

Be that as it may, by the time Kitchener handed over to his successor, another Sapper, Settle Pasha, the Egyptian Police had been transformed into a reasonably efficient force, although, like all police forces, it was constantly subjected to political interference and its structure and control remained a serious bone of contention throughout the period of the British Occupation. Remarkably, however, its two largest divisions, Cairo and Alexandria, remained under British command until 1946.

In the early days the British Inspectors of Police or Constabulary, as it was sometimes known, were mostly army officers (although some like Charles Coles were drafted in from the Indian Police) temporarily detached from the Egyptian Army. Two of these, Hector MacDonald and Herbert Jackson, were to distinguish themselves in the Sudan in later years, MacDonald as the Hero of Omdurman and Jackson as OC Troops during the Fashoda Incident and, as a long serving provincial governor, deputy to the Governor-General.

At around the turn of the century a policy of recruiting young British civilians was put in place and among the first entrants was one Thomas Russell. later to become perhaps the most famous policeman of the British Imperial era. We will hear more of him later.

To deal with an influx of foreign criminals attracted by Egypt's new prosperity, a policy of increasing the number of European, mostly British, constables in the Egyptian police was also implemented. Wrote a senior British police officer many years later:

The arrest of foreign delinquents at the request of Consuls [see Appendix C] was assuredly one of their [the European constables] primary functions, together with general supervision of the lawless element amongst the constantly increasing numbers of Italians and Greeks who were, at this time, beginning to settle in Egypt.

From the year 1890 onwards, Egypt began to attract a number of lawless persons who had probably found their own countries both unprofitable and increasingly risky to live in. Opportunities were brighter in a country where wealthy tourists were plentiful and where the upper classes appeared to have plenty of money to spend ... and so pick-pockets from Naples, tricksters from Marseilles, pimps and white-slavers from Corsica, specialists in safe-breaking from Vienna and others of their kidney began to take advantage of the regular maritime communications now opening up between Egypt and Mediterranean ports. Passport regulations at this time were practically inexistent and certainly inadequate to check the flow.[16]

CHAPTER 3

A Place in the Sun

THE LEFT LIBERAL CONSENSUS which, since the Second World War, has dominated comment on the British Imperial era, has persuaded itself and, presumably, its readers and listeners that the British in Egypt ruled from the summit of Mount Olympus, seldom, if ever, descending into the world of the mortals below. This is far from the truth.

British administrators, provincial and irrigation inspectors, lawyers, businessmen and officers of the Egyptian Army and Police had no choice, even if they wanted one, but to live and work in reasonable harmony with their Egyptian colleagues. There were no British or European residential quarters as such. Egyptians, British and other foreigners lived where they could afford to live and there were no barriers other than the ability to pay.

Even at times of extreme tension and danger, friendship and mutual loyalties remained firm. While British policy often clashed with Egyptian national aspirations, this had little effect on individual relationships. An example of this occurred after the Second World War when a senior British diplomat records that 'It was customary to hold an annual Oxford and Cambridge Dinner at the Mohamed Ali Club. However in the autumn of 1950, the political atmosphere was so strained that doubt was felt about the likely response from the Egyptian side. Nevertheless it was decided to go ahead and a record attendance was the gratifying result. It seemed as though the Egyptian members wished to demonstrate that whatever the political differences between our governments, between us as individuals there was a great fund of goodwill'.[1]

Also shared was a remarkably similar sense of humour and the ability to laugh at themselves and one another. Egyptian jokes, often at their own expense, can be among the funniest and translate readily into English.

It has been said that the British would not allow 'natives' into their clubs. While it is true that there was one club, the Turf (which had nothing to do with racing), the members of which were exclusively

Typical interior of a British residence in Alexandria.

British and often businessmen, the same can be said of the other foreign communities.

The Turf Club was, it seems, originally a privately owned gambling den belonging to a certain Monsieur Casse whose establishment in the early 1880s was encouraged by both the commander of the Army of Occupation, General Stephenson, and the Chief of Police, Baker Pasha, presumably in the hope of keeping junior officers out of mischief even more serious than losing a month's pay in one night. However, and it is not entirely clear how or why, in 1893 it was decided to convert the club into a members only institution with no gambling allowed, no doubt to the chagrin of Monsieur Casse and some of its previous patrons. This had the support of Lord Cromer and the Sirdar, Kitchener, but the driving force behind the plan was the Principal Medical Officer of the Egyptian Army, Colonel (later Sir Thomas) Gallwey, a popular Irishman who later distinguished himself in both the Sudan and South Africa.[2]

However, a glance at the membership list of the Khedivial Sporting Club, forerunner of the Gezira Sporting Club, sometimes misleadingly cited as a bastion of British 'colonialism', for 1905 reveals that the Patron was the Khedive himself, three of the Vice-Patrons were Egyptian, four British and one Greek. Of the ordinary membership at least half-a-dozen nationalities were represented.[3] However, the club itself was a British creation. The racecourse, around which grew the polo grounds, golf course and other sporting facilities, was originally laid in the 1880s and one of the first to use it to exercise his horse was a certain Captain Humphries.

His story, tragic and brief, is a curious one. The son of a gamekeeper he was commissioned from the ranks of the Royal Inniskilling Fusiliers and rose to command, with distinction, a Mounted Infantry company at the Battles of El Teb and Tamai in the eastern Sudan. One day in May 1884, riding round the newly created racecourse, he was thrown from his horse and broke his neck. The doctors feared to move him, eased a waterbed under him and erected a small tent over him. There he lay until he died three days later. Clearly he was a man who inspired devotion, even among his unruly and aristocratic subalterns. 'We never quite found out whether he had any people ... he was a very good friend to me and I was fearfully cut up by his death,' wrote Colonel Sir Percival Marling, VC, in his memoirs.[4]

The 'Old' Turf Club, Cairo.

Returning to the theme of Anglo-Egyptian relationships, there was more snobbery and standoffishness within the British community than ever there was between British and Egyptians, particularly amongst the womenfolk – 'She's all right, I suppose, but she's not really a lady, you know,' or 'My dear, they say the Loamshires are taking over from the Coldstream at Kasr el Nil – why, one won't know a soul!'

Many prominent Britons preferred the Mohamed Ali Club, Cairo's equivalent of White's membership, which was open to anyone of sufficient importance, to the Turf. Here they could meet and hobnob with equally senior Egyptians and engage in serious discussions and/or badinage (the two are by no means mutually exclusive in Egypt) in a relaxed and informal atmosphere, while at the Turf there was always the danger of being cornered by 'a chap who hadn't been to a decent school'.

Incidentally, it was at the Mohamed Ali that the famous notice appeared which read: 'Members are reminded that they may not bring their lady friends into the Club unless they are the wives of other members.'

While there was no social barrier between educated British (and other Europeans) and their Egyptian equivalents, the British working-class, as represented principally by the soldiery of the Army of Occupation, was openly and cheerfully racist. To them, in early days, an Egyptian, regardless of class, social standing or even colour, was a 'nigger', graduating in later years to 'wog' or 'gyppo'. Their officers, while not above using the same pejoratives themselves, were, at least in public, mildly remonstrative as demonstrated by the following exchange said to have taken place at the Court of Enquiry after an accident between King Farouk's car and a British Army lorry during the Second World War:

> President of the Court: Now Driver Jones, tell us in your own words what happened after the collision?
>
> Jones: Well, sir, the car stops and I stops and out of the car gets two fat wogs ...
>
> President: Look here, Jones, you can't use such expressions when referring to His Majesty King Farouk! Please re-phrase your answer.
>
> Jones: Sorry, sir. Well, out of the car gets King Farouk and another fat wog ...
>
> Collapse of President.

The point should be made that during the Second World War, King Farouk was a special target of ridicule and obloquy among the British from the Ambassador, Lord Killearn, down to Driver Jones, and nor was he held in much higher esteem by his own subjects, although to some extent they resented the British attitude towards him.

On the other side of the coin, the Egyptian, aware of Tommy Atkins' lowly social status, regarded him with contempt, at least when he was off-duty, and was concerned only to relieve him as quickly as possible of his 'shilling a day' (relative wealth in Egypt) in the souks, brothels and bars of Cairo, Alexandria and Port Said.

The British Army of Occupation was strictly disciplined and crimes against the civilian population were severely punished. Soon after his return to Egypt as GOC in 1897, the former Sirdar General Grenfell recorded in his diary '... saw a man who had shot a native in cold blood for which he was tried by Court Martial [and] ... although a large number of names were collected for a petition to me to annul the death penalty I felt it my duty to leave the man for execution, the punishment which he so richly deserved ...'. The soldier, Private Walker of the 21st Lancers, was hanged at the Citadel at 7 a.m. on 5 November 1897. 'I'm glad to say he confessed his crime and agreed in the justice of his sentence,' wrote Grenfell.[5]

However, on duty, British troops, especially kilted ones known as 'Escotch', inspired fear and respect. Used as a last resort when police crowd control efforts had failed, the appearance of a small detachment of British infantry with fixed bayonets would usually calm the most volatile and riotous of mobs. C. S. Jarvis tells the story, probably apocryphal but illustrative of the point, of the Guards picket under a corporal marching across Kasr el Nil Bridge to the barracks on the other side at dinner-time. Oblivious to a demonstration blocking the middle of the bridge, the guardsmen tramp steadily forward, 'Left, right, left, right.' The mob, which has been chanting anti-British slogans and working itself into a patriotic frenzy, gradually falls silent as the picket approaches, then, making way for the troops, raises a cry of admiration, '*Aish el Ingleez!*' 'Long Live the British!' until the gates of Kasr el Nil Barracks close behind the hungry guardsmen.[6]

Intermarriage between British and Egyptians was rare but by no means unknown, religion rather than race being the barrier. Nevertheless, several prominent Egyptian Moslems, including the courtier and diplomat Hassan Nashaat Pasha, the industrial magnate Ahmed Aboud Pasha, and the politician Amin Osman Pasha married British women, the latter's wife being described by Gerald Delaney, the Reuter's agent in Cairo, 'as a girl with an Irish name but a strong cockney accent [who] had been a waitress in a cafe in Lancashire'. There seem to be some contradictions in this description but Delaney adds rather patronisingly, 'She was not a bad sort,' and when her husband, already a Pasha, received a British knighthood, she was heard to exclaim, 'Now I'm a

The staff of the Egyptian Army War Office in Cairo, 1888. The massive figure seated in the centre is that of El Ferik Sir Francis Grenfell Pasha, the Sirdar.

Lady at both ends!'[7] However, the poor woman was widowed when her husband, a great anglophile, was assassinated in 1946.

While a handful of Englishmen married Egyptians, usually Copts, many British soldiers married girls from the Greek, Italian and Syrian communities, sometimes without even the advantage of a common language! The Copts were the most anglophile section of the population, feeling themselves protected against the Moslem majority by the British presence. Many spoke perfect and almost accentless English.

As for the British officers of the Egyptian Army, several, particularly those who served for long periods in the Sudan, had 'native' wives or mistresses. Archibald Hunter, who rose to be second-in-command of the Egyptian Army, has left an amusing account of taking his Abyssinian mistress with him on leave to Cairo from Suakin in the 1890s – '... otherwise it means hunting round town with the other chaps and I always get the clap ...' When she visited the polo ground with another Abyssinian concubine, 'two bundles of white gauze with red parasols ... when all the elite and fashion were there ... [It] caused quite a commotion,' but nobody seems to have been particularly shocked.[8]

However, when General Sir Herbert Jackson Pasha, Governor of Dongola Province and the Governor-General's deputy took some of his harem to Khartoum, Lady Wingate, who was somewhat straight-laced, was appalled, threatening to remonstrate with him personally until her husband took on that responsibility. When the subject was broached

Jackson is alleged to have replied, 'Present my compliments to Lady Wingate and notify her that the Ladies Jackson will be at home on second Tuesdays.'[9] Jackson had several offspring by his 'wives', one son becoming Chief of the Alexandria Fire Brigade and a grandson, known as Jacksa, playing football for Omdurman!

On the other hand, Jackson's fellow Gordon Highlander and Hero of Omdurman, 'Fighting Mac' MacDonald, preferred boys and came to a sticky end as a result. Accused of pederasty while GOC Ceylon in 1903, he blew his brains out rather than face Court Martial and ruin.[10]

However, the British officers of the Egyptian Army were not concerned solely with sex and sport. Francis Grenfell, who was to become the second Sirdar, was not only a sportsman but also an accomplished artist, musician and linguist – some of his diary entries being written in Arabic or French – with a strong interest in Egyptology. While commanding the garrison at Assouan in 1886 and finding that his troops had little to do he set them to work excavating some tombs which turned out to be those of provincial governors of the Old and Middle Kingdom periods. Although Napoleon's archaeologists had apparently discovered these ninety years before, they became known as 'Grenfell's tombs'.

He was on friendly terms with professional Egyptologists of note such as Petrie and Sayce and was appointed to the committee of the Egyptian Antiquities Department, which was under French control. He made no bones about using his position to export antiquities to England, thus avoiding customs inspection. Many of these items are now in museums throughout the country but he retained his own collection until 1917 when it was auctioned at Sotheby's. At an advanced age he had had three children by his second marriage (both his wives predeceased him) and felt that this should be done for their sake. The 479 lots fetched £2,600, no great sum even in those days, and one of these items, an oolitic limestone head of the Pharoah Ammenemes III, is one of the masterpieces of the Egyptian Collection at the Fitzwilliam Museum, Cambridge.[11]

On arrival in Egypt many British were pleasantly surprised to find an extraordinarily low cost of living, even by Victorian standards. J. E. Marshall, arriving there in 1890 to seek his fortune as a young lawyer, had only to pay his clerk £E1 per month (and considered him overpaid at that). A good *suffragi* (man-servant) could be obtained for half that wage; fourteen eggs cost a piastre (1p) and six chickens twenty piastres. Land prices and construction costs were low and large profits could be made, even by small investors, as real estate values rocketed over the next twenty or so years of the British Occupation. In the Cromer years and during the First World War Egypt boomed but so did prices. By 1928 Mrs Gladys Peto, an army officer's wife, found that her monthly household budget amounted to £E46, probably many times the cost of living of the Marshall family in the 1890s.[12]

Perhaps inspired by the example of their maternal grandfather, John Wingfield Larkin, who had spent many years in the Consular Service in Egypt in the days of Mohamed Ali, two other early arrivals in 'British' Egypt were the brothers Wilfred and Alwyn Jennings-Bramly, the former appearing in 1892 hoping to take up the post of private secretary to the Khedive Tewfik.

Unfortunately, his intended employer died before Wilfred could take up the position but he seems to have supported himself in a variety of ways including a spell as a customs official and in an unspecified capacity at the Cairo Zoo.

However, by 1905 we find him employed by the Egyptian Government as an administrator in Sinai where he became involved in a border dispute which might have led to war between Britain and Turkey. In 1906, to the annoyance of the British and some Egyptians, the Sultan decided to occupy the whole of the Sinai Peninsula (which legally at that time he probably had the right to do) but, according to one account, was thwarted by Jennings-Bramly who occupied the port of Aqaba, where the Ottoman force intended to land, with a handful of policemen – although the intrepid Wilfred may have had a little help from the British Government which had assembled a fleet at Piraeus with obviously aggressive intent causing the Sublime Porte to back down speedily.

Nevertheless, Wilfred's role was not forgotten by the Turks who demanded that he be removed from Sinai, whereupon, presumably as a gesture of good will, he was posted to distant Kordofan in the Sudan, in what capacity we do not know. Back in Egypt after a decent interval, although a civilian but perhaps as a result of the knowledge he had acquired of the nomadic tribes of Sinai, he was put in charge of the Recruiting Department of the Egyptian Army. The Bedouin living within Egypt's borders were exempted, since the time of Mohamed Ali, from conscription – indeed they were often used to catch runaway fellahin deserters – but although the Bedouin population was estimated at only 20,000, at least 600,000 men were claiming exemption through Bedouin descent!

G.W. Murray, writing in *The Times* after Wilfred's death, tells us that 'while investigating their claims, Bramly amassed heaps of Arab genealogies which he later put at my disposal when I was compiling my book on the Egyptian Bedouin. Characteristically, he repeatedly refused to allow his name to appear on the title page as the joint author.'

First World War service with the Egyptian Expeditionary Force earned him an MBE and an MC and he was later appointed Governor of the Western Frontier District.

On retirement he built himself a remarkable 'castle' in the desert littoral to the west of Alexandria. Here he was regarded by the local Bedouin, the Aulad Ali (the Sons of Ali), as a kind of *omdah* or headman and around his castle there sprang up a thriving community, including a carpet factory. He lived there with his wife for many years until in 1956 at the age of eighty-five he was brutally and senselessly expelled by Nasser following the Suez debacle. For the remaining years of his life he lived with his daughters in Florence where he died in 1960. As his *Times* obiturist put it, he was 'among the last romantic eccentrics of the Arab world where now nationalism allows no time for such men to work their good.' His castle today is used as an occasional Presidential residence, a large industrial complex has sprung up around it and holiday development has sprouted along the coast.

His younger brother Alwyn also spent much of his life in the Anglo-Egyptian service, although his career and character were perhaps less unconventional than Wilfred's. Commissioned into the 1st Dragoons (Royals) in 1895, he soon transferred to the 20th Hussars with whom he served in India and the Boer War. After two years in Uganda with the King's African Rifles, in 1904 he joined the Egyptian Army as a Bimbashi (Major) and served with the 4th Cavalry Squadron at Shendi on the Nile north of Khartoum.

In the following year he was seconded to the Sudan Political Service as an Inspector in various provinces. While serving in Mongalla Province he made a valuable study of the Bari whose tribal territory overlaps from the Sudan into Uganda and the Congo.

In 1913 he was appointed Governor of Sinai, no doubt having learnt a good deal about the peninsula and its people from his brother. During the First World War he occupied several staff appointments with the Egyptian Expeditionary Force and was, for a time, re-engaged by the Egyptian Army, mostly in an Intelligence capacity, and was awarded the DSO. Few details of his subsequent career are available, other than mention of the appointment as Director of the Cairo Police School, a position for which he does not seem to have had any special qualification but which he may have held until the first stage of 'Egyptianisation' under the 1922 Treaty. He died in England in 1936 aged sixty.[13]

Under the Capitulations (see Appendix C) Egypt was a paradise for the foreign entrepreneur who paid virtually no taxes and was protected from almost all interference on the part of the Egyptian Government by his own Consul. But the native population prospered too. One Egyptian writes: 'The British-dominated civil service, however criticised, provided the badly needed umbrella enabling foreign and local talents to develop.'[14] At the same time, the worst tyrannies of the Turco-Egyptian ruling class were curtailed by Cromer and his Advisers, and the fellahin benefited from the abolition of the corvee and indiscriminate use of the *kourbash* (rawhide whip) to exact taxes and debts, although it was retained for judicial punishment.

The corvee was a particularly pernicious evil, described by Colonel Sandes as 'a legalised system of forced and unpaid labour, designed to affect the clearance and repair of Government canals. It was objectionable from an engineering point of view as being a clumsy, wasteful and inefficient instrument. From a philanthropic standpoint it could be regarded only as a deplorable form of slavery. Thousands upon thousands of men were dragged from their villages and sent to work in distant places, unfed, unpaid and unlodged. They supplied even their own tools.' Quoting Sir Colin Scott-Moncrieff (Inspector-General of Irrigation and Under-Secretary for Public Works 1883–90), he adds, '... none of the large landowners ever sent a man to the corvee. They kept their tenants and serfs to weed their own cotton fields and do the irrigation. The work had then to be done by the peasants. The village sheikh was required to find a certain number of men from his village. Those who could afford to do so bribed him. The poorest were driven off, perhaps 100 miles, to work for several months while their fields remained untilled and their families were perpetually on the road, taking food to them.'[15]

Of course, the country had its drawbacks for the foreign resident as well as its advantages. Disease was rife and many children died in infancy. The summer heat was fierce but most wives and children returned home for the summer and many husbands were able to take leave during the hottest months.

At the top end of the social scale large domestic staffs were employed. The typical household of a senior official or successful businessman would consist of two or three *suffragis*, usually Berberin from Upper Egypt or the northern Sudan, a cook and kitchen-boy (known as a *marmiton*). The master of the house would have a valet, often an ex-Egyptian Army NCO or policeman, and his wife a Greek, Italian or Slav lady's maid.

Outside there would be a chauffeur (in the early days a coachman). a gardener (the fellah is a superb gardener often with an extraordinary eye for border lay-out and flower arrangement) and garden-boy. Sometimes a *boab* (watchman), usually Sudanese, would sit at the gate and a *sayes* (groom or car-washer) would be employed in the stables or garage. An Egyptian woman (*ghassala*) would come in to do the laundry and a man (*makwagi*) the ironing (never the other way round). It seems that Cromer's loyal and long serving Oriental Secretary, Harry Boyle, learnt his fluent colloquial Arabic from his *makwagi*.[16]

A mainstay of any such household of any nationality with children would be the nanny or governess, sometimes French or Swiss but usually English or Scots. Even for the relatively impecunious Mrs Peto, with a cook and only one *suffragi*, an English nanny was indispensable.

The present author, delving into the recesses of his memory, recalls trotting through the (then) quiet streets of Zamalek with Nanny Talmage to the paddock of the Gezira Sporting Club racecourse where, on non-race days, the nannies would foregather for a tea of lemonade and sandwiches under the shade-trees and the beady eye of the ubiquitous Egyptian kite ('Now be careful, Henry, that nasty bird might swoop down and take your nice sandwich!'). As their charges whooped and squealed around them, playing Cowboys and Indians or French and English, they would exchange the latest gossip current within the British community ('Have you heard about Captain X and Mrs Y ... disgraceful, she's old enough to be his mother!' 'Well, dear. I always said she was no better than she should be!').

Sometimes a donkey called Telephone with a trusted driver would be brought to the house and ridden to the Club with Nanny watchfully bringing up the rear.

One such pillar of the British Empire was a Miss James from Cardiff. Described as 'companion to a Turkish Princess' she was probably nanny or governess to one of the great Turco-Egyptian families. In the 1880s she married a divorced Belgian lawyer practising in Egypt, Maître Carton de Wiart, who had a young son, Adrian. With the determination and single-mindedness of her kind, she transformed the little Belgian into a large Englishman and moulded one of the most highly decorated and heavily wounded British soldiers of the twentieth century, Lieutenant General Sir Adrian Carton de Wiart, VC, hero of four wars and colonial campaigns. The former Miss James outlived her older husband by many years and, as his fortunes had crashed before his death, she became the responsibility of her stepson, a duty he did not shirk although the reader of his memoirs gains the impression that he regarded her with respect and gratitude rather than affection.[17]

Memorable diversions for British children growing up in Egypt in the 1920s and 30s included bathing at Sidi Bishr in Alexandria; donkey and camel rides at the Pyramids; and the feeding of Said, an ancient hippo long resident at Cairo Zoo. For a piastre a bundle of *berseem* (lucerne) could be purchased from his keeper and thrust into Said's near toothless and cavernous mouth.

Less agreeable, at least for the boys, were the so-called dancing classes at the YWCA. 'Swing, Swing. like a pendulum [with the emphasis on the um]!', would cry the Australian instructress at which command the children, mostly female with a sprinkling of sulky males, would go through various motions which had little to do with dancing but which were perhaps forerunners of today's aerobics.

Many British residents laboured under the delusion that their servants did not understand English and felt it undesirable that they should. Thus wives and children conversed with their domestic staff in what was known as 'Kitchen' Arabic, consisting principally of singular nouns, adjectives and verbs in the imperative. The military equivalent of this lingua franca, 'Bimbashi' Arabic, was spoken by most short-term British officers of the Egyptian Army, who had to pass a very basic test in it. Some senior officials, Lord Cromer for example, never learnt Arabic at all, carrying out all their official business in French, the language favoured by the Turco-Egyptian ruling class, often themselves ignorant of Arabic.

Other British officers, officials and a few businessmen were proficient Arabic speakers, especially those who had served in the Sudan or who had been born in Egypt. Examples of the first category were the Sirdar and, later, High Commissioner, General Sir Reginald Wingate, and his former Private Secretary, Sir Alexander Keown-Boyd of the Ministry of the Interior, while El Lewa George Naldrett-Jays Pasha of the Police, born in Egypt of a British father and a Greek mother, was fluent in five languages including Arabic. However, his Irish colleague, El Lewa Thomas Fitzpatrick Pasha, who had been commissioned from the ranks of the Royal Irish Regiment for gallantry in 1914, was also fluent in the language but quite incomprehensible to the listener. One Egyptian minister politely enquired of another police officer, no doubt with his tongue in his cheek, why Fitzpatrick Pasha always insisted in addressing him in Erse!

British and other tourists had been coming to Egypt, especially in the winter months, for decades before the Occupation. That precursor of mass tourism, Mr Thomas Cook, had opened Upper Egypt and its ancient marvels to the well-to-do of Europe and America with his comfortable steamers and hotels. The British Occupation, however, brought with it The Fishing Fleet, an annual winter migration of well bred young ladies from England in search of eligible husbands from the Cairo garrison or from among the relatively affluent officials of the government and staff of the Residency or even the business community.

One neglected aspect of the Egypt of the later nineteenth and early twentieth centuries was its personal security for European women. Even at times of political violence, for example the period from 1919 to 1924, women were never the targets of terrorist attack. Some may have been injured inadvertently but, in the main, victims were carefully selected and, unlike today, did not include women or children. The highly unusual, perhaps even unique, rape and murder of a Mrs Crosland, an Englishwoman living alone in Heliopolis (a residential suburb of Cairo) in 1926, by her Sudanese servant, was a purely domestic affair without political motive.[18]

European women could walk or travel by public transport almost anywhere in Egypt in perfect safety and be treated with almost exaggerated courtesy. Wrote Mrs Peto in 1928, 'The unescorted lady finds herself treated with the greatest kindness by all Egyptians – both rich and humble ... I have made sketches at street corners, and ridden forever in trams that are little used by Europeans and have always been treated with courtesy and pleasantness ... Some kindly, tarbooshed gentleman will always give an Englishwoman his seat in a tram-car.'[19] Such good-mannered behaviour often extended to men as well as women – indeed, somewhere along the line, the Egyptians even went so far as to invent a special greeting for the British, '*Saieeda*', which, to the best of the author's knowledge, was never used among the Egyptians themselves or even to greet another kind of foreigner.

But not all British visitors or temporary residents were as enamoured of Egypt as Gladys Peto. Another army wife, Daphne du Maurier, who spent two years in Alexandria where her husband, 'Boy' (later Lieutenant General Sir Frederick) Browning was commanding the 2nd Grenadiers in the late 1930s, loathed the place. The Egyptians were 'filthy' and 'don't speak English' while the British community were 'horrible Manchester folk'. When she visited Cairo she found the bazaar (Han Khalil or Muski) 'an inferior Burlington Arcade' and the pyramids 'just like a couple of slag heaps on the Great Western [sic] Road'.

It is extraordinary that such an intelligent, well-bred woman should have made remarks of such vulgar inanity even in private correspondence. Even so, it is a measure of her genius as a writer that, despite intense heat, pregnancy and hated surroundings, she was able to produce her family history *The Du Mauriers* and, after a false start, the first quarter of *Rebecca* while she was there.[20]

However, there was one feature of life in Egypt which was particularly upsetting to the British, especially to the women, and that was the treatment – or rather mistreatment – of animals. The owners and drivers of beasts of burden, though often themselves struggling for a bare existence, were the particular targets of British outrage. The donkey staggering under a back-breaking weight with its owner perched on the top, the half-starved, broken-kneed *ghari* (cab) horse, the exhausted mule dragging a huge cartload of stones were – and to a lesser extent still are – common sights in Egypt.

At some imprecisely recorded date in about 1883, a group of distinguished personages, including the Turco-Egyptian statesman, Nubar Pasha; two future Sirdars, Grenfell and Kitchener; and a number of clergy, met at Shepheard's Hotel to 'promote' the formation of a Society for the Prevention of Cruelty to Animals so we may assume that some form of animal welfare existed from about that time.[21] However, in 1908 we find a Cairo newspaper reporting a parliamentary question put to the Foreign Secretary, Sir Edward Grey, by Mr John Robertson, the MP for Newcastle, who had evidently just returned from a visit to Egypt. Would Sir Edward bring to the attention of the British Agent (Sir Eldon Gorst) the plight of the animals of Cairo and elsewhere, especially since the retirement of Bimbashi Jarvis from the Animal Protection Society (at that time managed by the police)?

The Foreign Secretary replied with the time-honoured formula that he had no official information on the subject but that the matter would be brought to the attention of the British Agency. We do not know who replaced Bimbashi Jarvis, who was also Head of the Traffic Department of the Cairo City Police. Nor should we imagine that the Foreign Office memo ever reached the desk of the British Agent himself. It is more likely to have been filed away by a junior official, a copy having been despatched to Mansfield Pasha, Commandant of Police.[22]

Before continuing with the theme of animal protection, perhaps we should glance at the career of Bimbashi Vernon Jarvis, who was a fairly typical example of a long-serving British officer of the Egyptian Police. As a boy, probably exaggerating his age. he had enlisted in the Army Medical Service (forerunner of the RAMC) and had taken part in the Gordon Relief Expedition of 1884–85, in the course of which he had been present at the ferocious little battle of Abu Klea when the 'unbreakable' British square was broken by the Mahdist *ansar*. After further active service in the Sudan, including the capture of Tokar for which he received the Khedive's Star, he joined the Egyptian Police in 1896 and continued to serve with the force until his retirement in 1932 as a Miralai (Brigadier). He was twice married, on both occasions to Italian ladies, never left Egypt and died there in 1958 at the age of ninety.[23]

One of his exploits as Head of Traffic gave rise to a splendid outpouring of purple prose in the foreign language Cairo newspapers.

On 9 and 10 March 1908 a car race or rally was held at Heliopolis on the outskirts of Cairo – probably the first event of its kind in Egypt

– attended by the Khedive and the visiting Duke and Duchess of Connaught. On the second day disaster struck. According to the *Egyptian Gazette*:

Miralai Vernon Jarvis Bey, who served in the Egyptian Police from 1896 until 1932.

> ... the Brazier car (M. Ferdinand de Martino), which was in front, was coming round a corner at about sixty miles an hour when it swerved and a cushion [sic] became detached falling on the track just before the grandstand was reached. A policeman, who was behind the ropes guarding the course, received the order to pick up the cushion.
>
> While he was in the act of doing so, a De Dion car came round the bend at an enormous speed, caught the policeman who was hurled several yards and killed.
>
> The effect of the shock was sufficient to cause a deviation in the direction the car was taking, causing it to leap into the crowd near the side of the grandstand. The chauffeur (M. Ugo Fenderi) was thrown to the ground but was only slightly injured. Another policeman and a fireman were killed.
>
> Immediately the accident occurred Major Jarvis of the police seized a white flag and, rushing to the corner, succeeded in stopping the other cars which were arriving, thus preventing further mishap.

Reuter later reported the casualties as three dead and fourteen injured and considerable litigation with which we need not concern ourselves. However, 'Onlooker', writing to the *Egyptian Gazette*, waxed lyrical in his praise of Bimbashi Jarvis and the British race as a whole. Finding himself 'not yet recovered from the mental shock which renders me totally incapable of sustained attention to my professional duties' he goes on to say, 'the nation to which he [Jarvis] belongs is honoured by the connection for never did man show greater coolness and courage ...

those of us who are not of the English race ... begin to comprehend why it is that "Britannia rules the waves" and such a very large portion of the habitable globe into the bargain.'

'Onlooker' continues in this vein of several more lines, but 'Anti-Motorist', writing to the same editor, though praising Jarvis, is less complimentary to the drivers, organizers and government. The drivers, 'owing to their overwhelming conceit, which is proverbial, are often carried away and show off regardless of consequences ... the British Government [sic] in Cairo is sleeping and has adopted the Egyptian motto '*Maalesh!*' (Never mind).' More attention should be paid, says Anti-Motorist, and more appreciation shown to the likes of Bimbashi Vernon Jarvis.[24]

Returning to the subject of animal welfare, one which may not have featured high on the agenda of the British Agency or of the Egyptian Government and people but which was a serious preoccupation for many of the ladies, and some of the gentlemen, of the British community.

As we have seen, in pre-First World War days the protection of animals was the responsibility of the police but their enforcement abilities were limited and facilities for the treatment of sick or injured animals inadequate. For example, constables of the Mounted Section of the Cairo City Police were, in theory, supposed to check the convoys of donkey carts which flowed into the city's markets at dawn every day loaded with vegetables. But it was common practice for each driver to slip a tarifa (½ piastre) down the gleaming riding boots of the splendidly mounted but poorly paid officers as his cart trundled by, thus avoiding inspection of animal or vehicle. And even were a suspect cart to be stopped, what was to be done with donkey or driver? The fellah's livelihood was at stake; the stopping of the cart would cause a traffic jam and the constable would be faced with all the formalities of bringing a minor charge against the offender and in the meantime what was to happen to the donkey? So, unless the condition of the animal was desperate, nothing was done.[25]

However in the aftermath of the First World War, public attention, both in Britain and Egypt, became focused on the plight of the old war horses, 22,000 of which were sold off by the War Office at the victorious conclusion of Allenby's Palestine campaign in 1918. Some Diggers (Australian cavalry troopers), hardly the most sentimental of men, were so outraged by this policy that they risked Court Martial by shooting their horses rather than allowing them to suffer the inevitable fate of ceaseless toil, hunger and thirst on the streets of Egyptian towns and villages or in the quarries. One of them wrote a poem on the subject entitled 'The Horses Stay Behind', the last verse reading:

> I think I'd better shoot him and tell a little lie;
> He foundered in a wombat hole and then lay down to die,
> Maybe I'll get Court Martialed; but I'm damned if I'm inclined
> To go back to Australia and leave my horse behind.[26]

In 1930 Mrs Dorothy Brooke, the wife of a British cavalry general, 'rescued' her first old war horse in Cairo. 'An army brand shaped like an arrow was clearly visible on his shrunken near quarter. His size, his huge swollen legs and enormous exposed ribs, hips like hat racks, were not those of the usual Egyptian horse. She called him Old Bill. It was clear he should never be allowed back to work; the kindest solution would be to destroy him. So she bought him for the equivalent of £9 sterling, the cost of a replacement. After two days of good food and tender loving care she had him destroyed.'

This episode marked the birth of what is now the Brooke Hospital for Animals (originally named the Brooke Hospital for Old War Horses). Mrs Brooke died on a visit to Egypt in 1955 and, mercifully, the old warhorses are long gone but have been replaced by their 'civilian' successors, as much in need of rest, care and kindness as they were. Today branches of the hospital flourish not only in Egypt but elsewhere in the Middle East and the Indian sub-continent, perhaps fittingly, one of the few lasting memorials to the British Occupation.[27]

But let us conclude this rather grim topic on a more cheerful note. In 1956 an old ex-British Army mule, purchased in 1918 by the Alexandria Sporting Club, was still in good health and kicking (literally) while grudgingly carrying out its duties in maintaining the greens on the golf course!

CHAPTER 4

The Anglo-Egyptian Sudan

A S WE HAVE SEEN, the histories of Great Britain, Egypt and the Sudan during the period with which we are dealing are inextricably linked.

Borrowing something of the style of *1066 And All That* and blending it with his own caustic wit, in the 1930s C.S. Jarvis summed up the situation with ironic accuracy in these words.

> The Sudan used to belong to the Sudanese then the Egyptians took it away from them, misgoverned the country and massacred the Sudanese; after that the Sudanese took it away from the Egyptians, misgoverned themselves and massacred themselves and everyone else; and then in the end England helped win it back for Egypt or Egypt helped England win it for England and we have been arguing about which occurred exactly ever since.[1]

In the early years of the British Occupation of Egypt the home government's policy, which Cromer strongly supported, towards the Sudan was one of containment. The attempts by Hicks and Gordon to save the Sudan for Egypt had been disastrous and political fingers had been burnt.

Two British expeditions to the eastern Sudan in 1884–85 and subsequent skirmishes in the area may not have been spectacular successes but they ensured the maintenance of an Anglo-Egyptian toehold at Suakin, the Sudan's principal port, and tenuous control over the Red Sea littoral. Similarly, Anglo-Egyptian victories at the Battles of Ginnis (1885) and Toski (1889) in the northern Sudan and Upper Egypt had ensured Egypt's safety from Mahdist expansionism. Thus for eleven years after the fall of Khartoum the British were content to leave the Sudan in a state of isolated vacuum.

The reasons for the Conservative Government's sudden change of heart and mind, under Lord Salisbury, in March 1896 are manifold and complex so, to avoid tedium, we will deal with them in the most basic terms.

It had been known for some time to the Foreign Office, over which Lord Salisbury himself presided, that the French were planning a military expedition to the White Nile, which, since the Egyptian evacuation in the 1880s, they had regarded as a No Man's Land there for the taking. Then, on 1 March 1896, an Italian army, advancing from their colony of Eritrea bordering the Sudan, was crushingly defeated by the Emperor Menelik of Abyssinia at the Battle of Adowa. Weakened and demoralised, the Italians, fearing a Mahdist attack on their outpost at Kassala in the Sudan and possible incursions into Eritrea, pleaded with the British to make some diversionary move in the north.[2]

Salisbury, probably influenced by Cromer, had never relished the prospect of military involvement in the Sudan and, according to Grenfell (former Sirdar and current GOC Egypt), had even harboured hopes that 'the Sudan could be squared by entering into commercial relations with the dervishes'.[3] But, however little sympathy Salisbury may have had with Italian discomfort, these events raised the spectre of some strange and potentially dangerous alliances, perhaps between Menelik and his old adversary the Khalifa Abdullahi or between Menelik and the French. In either case the consequences, though unpredictable, were likely to be inimical to Egypt and Britain's position there. Furthermore, Salisbury's personal attitude to the Khalifa's regime in the Sudan had been much influenced by the accounts of its brutality brought out by the two Austrian escapees from Omdurman, Ohrwalder and Slatin, skilfully exploited by Wingate, the Egyptian Army's Director of Intelligence.

Thus it came about that Cromer, whose financial priorities did not include an expensive military operation in the Sudan, reluctantly found himself, at short notice, passing on London's instructions to the Sirdar Kitchener to retake and occupy the northern Sudanese province of Dongola with the Egyptian Army – a first step in the re-conquest of the whole of the Sudan which began on 18 March 1896. Neither the British Government nor Lord Cromer seems to have deemed it necessary to consult the Khedive Abbas Hilmi 11 (his father Tewfik had died in 1892), in whose name the campaign was to be undertaken.[4]

The story of Kitchener's Nile campaign has been told many times, perhaps most vividly by its most famous participant, Winston Churchill, and will not be repeated here. Suffice to say that, for better or for worse, the British were to find themselves drawn into a considerable new commitment, the governance of the largest country in Africa.[5]

After Kitchener's bloody and conclusive victory at Omdurman on 2 September 1898 he was almost immediately confronted with the problem of dealing with the long-expected French White Nile expedition which had arrived at Fashoda under Commandant Marchand in the previous July and was laying claim to the Upper Nile and Bahr el Ghazal provinces. Due principally to the firm but tactful diplomacy adopted by Kitchener, Wingate, Jackson (OC Troops), and, indeed, the heavily outnumbered Marchand himself, an explosive situation was defused and the French eventually persuaded to withdraw with dignity.[6] The British in Egypt had considerable sympathy and respect for Marchand. Grenfell wrote in his diary, 'I liked him very much, a very sympathetic man, well-spoken and very civil, ... telling me that he had never advised an advance to Fashoda ... He thanked me for the civility and kindness of all the English officers he had met who had treated him like a comrade.' As for Marchand's men, they were 'the most splendid blacks I had ever seen' (they were Senegalese).[7]

But the Gallic nose had been severely disjointed and the affair was to rankle for decades, despite, in deference to French sensibilities, the change of name from Fashoda to Kodok.

The emphasis now moved from military and diplomatic to constitutional matters. The Sudan had been re-conquered in the name of the Khedive of Egypt (ultimately and theoretically on behalf of the Sultan of the Ottoman Empire) by an Anglo-Egyptian force. However, it was clear, probably at that stage even to the Egyptian Government, that the Sudan could not be handed over to Egyptian rule, which, in the light of previous experience, would have been intolerable to the Sudanese and would have led inevitably to widespread unrest and a possible resurgence of Mahdism. Therefore a compromise had to be reached and this was achieved in masterly fashion by Cromer, the Khedive's Chief Legal Adviser, Sir Malcolm McIlwaith, and the Egyptian Foreign Minister, Sami Boutros Ghali Pasha – who, incidentally, was to pay for it with his life (see Chapter 6) – in the form of the Anglo-Egyptian (or Condominium) Agreement of 19 January 1899.[8]

This remarkable – and probably unique in terms of international agreements – document enabled the British to maintain the polite fiction of Egyptian partnership while governing the Sudan without interference from the other Great Powers (who constantly interfered in Egypt, especially on financial matters). The all-important Article III of the Agreement read, in part, '... the Governor-General of the Soudan, ... shall be appointed by Khedivial Decree on the recommendation of Her Britannic Majesty's Government, and shall be removed only by Khedivial Decree, with the consent of Her Britannic Majesty's Government.'

The key words are, of course, 'recommendation' and 'consent' which ensured de facto British rule for the next fifty-seven years.

Until 1924 the position of Governor-General was synonymous with that of Sirdar of the Egyptian Army. Also, although the recruitment of British civilian officials to the Sudan Political Service (SPS) began in 1901 (in fact one civilian, James Henry Butler, was officially transferred from the Egyptian Government to the Sudan Government in 1899), most of the Provincial Governors and Inspectors (later re-designated District Commissioners) were British officers of the Egyptian Army until well into the new century. Under them served Egyptian '*mamours*' (District Officers) who were also seconded from the Egyptian Army and who played an extremely important role, particularly as they shared a common language with the northern Sudanese. However, the lack of opportunities for promotion quite naturally caused resentment among these officers and, with the rise of Egyptian nationalism in the immediate aftermath of the First World War, they were phased out and a policy of 'Sudanisation' implemented (see Chapter 9).

The SPS was recruited, at least in its early days, almost exclusively from Oxbridge graduates with good degrees, often in oriental languages, and some athletic prowess, thus acquiring the well-known soubriquet of 'Blues ruling Blacks'. There was no written examination and, apart from the above qualifications, candidates were accepted or rejected entirely according to the impression they gave to their interviewers, usually former distinguished Anglo-Egyptian civil servants such as Sir Colin Scott-Moncrieff of the Irrigation Department. Of course such a process and basis of selection would be entirely unacceptable and regarded as 'elitist' today and, although it worked very well in practice, it gave rise to much (fairly) good-natured mockery from their brethren north of the Egyptian border.[9]

Again Major C. S. Jarvis of the Egyptian Frontiers Administration has his pennyworth. In comparing the Sudanese service with that of Egypt, he wrote ironically, '... but the Sudan method is so perfect and works so marvellously that one instinctively bows from the waist whenever one meets a member of the paragon service and respectfully uncovers at the mention of the sacred word "Khartoum" where all the super cock-angels [sic] nest and breed.'[10]

The British official who represented the Sudan Government in Cairo was, usually if not always, a member of the SPS and known as the Sudan Agent.

The first of these was, rather improbably, a cousin of Queen Victoria, Major Count Gleichen of the Grenadier Guards. Gleichen had seen a good deal of service in Egypt and the Sudan, having taken part in the Gordon Relief Expedition of 1884–85 with the Guards Camel Regiment and in the Dongola campaign of 1896 on the Staff.

After the Boer War, in which he won a DSO, he returned to Egypt as Sudan Agent and Director of Intelligence of the Egyptian Army from 1901 to 1903. When German titles became unfashionable during the First World War he styled himself Lord Edward Gleichen and after his retirement as a Major General achieved some distinction in a second career as a painter and art dealer.[11]

One of his successors as Sudan Agent, Brigadier Maurice Lush (1935–38), described his role and duties in his memoirs.

> After my first few months in Cairo I concluded that what was expected of the Sudan Agent was, first to give information and advice about every aspect of the Sudan to the High Commissioner (Sir Miles Lampson, later Lord Killearn) and the Chancery at the Residency. All of them appeared eager to be informed if not advised. Secondly my duty lay to the Egyptian Government, which did not seem eager to know ...
>
> Thirdly, I was expected to keep the Governor-General (Sir Stewart Symes) and Government in Khartoum fully posted on the situation in Egypt ...
>
> Fourthly. I was really the Sudan Consul in Egypt for Sudanese (nationals) and British officials ...
>
> Fifthly, to enhance the name of the Sudan and its peoples in the eyes of the Egyptians, the British and the large international community of which Egypt was composed.

Lush also observed, 'Egyptian sovereignty over the Sudan was a great cry for the Wafdist politicians but not so great for Egyptians when they were posted there.'[12] To the ordinary Egyptian the Sudan has always been regarded as a kind of sweltering Siberia – a place of banishment and lingering death – which indeed it was during the decades of Turco-Egyptian rule. The present author recalls being driven to Cairo Airport *en route* to Khartoum in the 1970s. The taxi-driver asked his destination and when told murmured with all sincerity, 'May God help you!'

Nonetheless, the future of the Sudan was to remain one of the principal bones of contention between Egypt and Great Britain up to the eve of Sudanese independence in 1956 and Egyptian discontent with the state of affairs in the Sudan did not take long to manifest itself.

With the outbreak of the Boer War in 1899 Kitchener, who, as Sirdar of the Egyptian Army, had been appointed the Sudan's first Governor-General, left for South Africa and with him went a number of the experienced British officers of the Egyptian Army.

Kitchener, though at that stage of his career unloved by most of his subordinates, British and Egyptian, had been feared and respected and his word was uncontested law. However, on his departure, his successor, Wingate, enjoyed no such automatic authority. Thus, almost immediately on his arrival in Khartoum, he was faced with a crisis in the shape of a mutiny affecting elements of two Sudanese battalions based in Omdurman, the 11th and the 14th, the latter consisting largely of deserters or prisoners from the disbanded Mahdist army.

Heavy-handedness on the part of at least two British officers was probably the direct cause of the trouble, but this had been fomented by junior Egyptian officers dissatisfied with their field allowances which Kitchener, the most parsimonious of men, had reduced before his departure.

Apparently the rumour had been spread that Sudanese troops were to be sent to fight in South Africa where the British had been suffering serious reverses. The Sudanese did not mind fighting, in fact they enjoyed it, but if it meant separation from their women this was a hardship which they were not prepared to endure for any but the shortest periods. There was no violence but some ammunition was hidden and officers' orders defied. Wisely, Wingate summoned the much-respected former CO of the 11th, Herbert Jackson, from Berber where he was Governor. Working with the senior wife of the battalion (*el sheikha el harem*) and some old Sudanese 'ranker' officers, Jackson reassured the men and arranged for the ammunition to be returned. In due course the mutineers of the 14th fell into line. Only one Sudanese corporal was punished and discharged, but seven Egyptian officers, following a Court of Enquiry presided over by Jackson, were deported to Egypt and cashiered. Others were forced into premature retirement.[13]

Relations between the Khedive and Cromer were bad, the former detesting the latter and the latter despising the former. This had been the state of affairs since an incident at Wadi Haifa in 1894 when, in the course of an inspection of the frontier garrison, the Khedive had openly criticised various officers, British and Sudanese, and the general condition of the garrison, infuriating Kitchener who threatened to resign.[14]

Eventually the Khedive was forced into a humiliating climb-down and made to sack his Deputy War Minister, who, it was thought, had instigated the incident. All this inflamed his Anglophobia and he never forgave either Cromer or Kitchener. Curiously Kitchener bore no such grudge (perhaps because he came out on top) and merely regarded him with ill-disguised contempt. When one of his staff remarked how much he disliked the Khedive he looked surprised and simply murmured, 'Naughty boy! Naughty boy!'[15]

Cromer believed, without much evidence but quite possibly on information received from Princess Nazli (see Chapter 7), that the Khedive had been behind the Omdurman trouble and forced him to denounce the offending officers of whom he almost certainly approved even if he had been unaware of their intentions, thus adding a further humiliation to the many which he believed he had had to suffer at the hands of the British.[16]

Nearly quarter of a century was to pass before another mutiny exploded in the Sudan. By then there was no Wingate or Jackson to soothe the rebellious soldiery and, as we shall see, the outcome was bloody and far-reaching.

All Egypt's rulers, up to and including Nasser, endeavoured to assert their sovereignty over the Sudan but in the face of both British and Sudanese resistance, none succeeded. This is probably as fortunate for Egypt as it is for the Sudan.

CHAPTER 5

Sporting Egypt

THE BRITISH introduced most sports to Egypt. These included cricket (which the Egyptians never took to), football (which they did), rugby (played principally by the British Army), tennis (a naturalised Egyptian, Jarislav Drobny, was Men's Singles Champion at Wimbledon in 1954), squash (Egypt has produced some of the finest squash players in the world), athletics and golf. The Mamlouks had played polo and this became the favourite sport of the British cavalry regiments stationed in Egypt and of the Egyptian cavalry, which was under British officers until 1925.

But for some polo was not enough and in 1901 the 11th Hussars, stationed at Abbassiyeh Barracks near Cairo, imported a small pack of foxhounds.[1]

The story of the short-lived Abbassiyeh Hunt is not only quite amusing but of some historical interest as it contains in it a rather sinister portent of a tragedy which would occur some five years later and which deserves a chapter to itself.

On Sunday 21 July 1901 at 4 a.m. the pack sallied forth from the barracks with Captain A.E.W. Harman of the Army Service Corps 'carrying the horn' and Lieutenant Rome and Private Bradley, both 11th Hussars, as his 1st and 2nd Whips. The Field consisted of five other officers, the senior of whom was Major (later Major-General Sir) William Rycroft, Acting Commanding Officer of the 11th, who spoke some Arabic having served in the Gordon Relief Expedition and with the Egyptian Army.

According to his account, at about 5 a.m., the hunt arrived outside the wall enclosing the property of Wilfrid Scawen Blunt, the prominent supporter of Egyptian nationalism (he had organised the defence at Orabi's trial), known as the Sheikh Obeyd Estate. Blunt would spend the winter months there, indulging in his favourite pastimes of baiting the British authorities, both civil and military, seducing their wives and breeding Arab horses. For the summer he would return to England

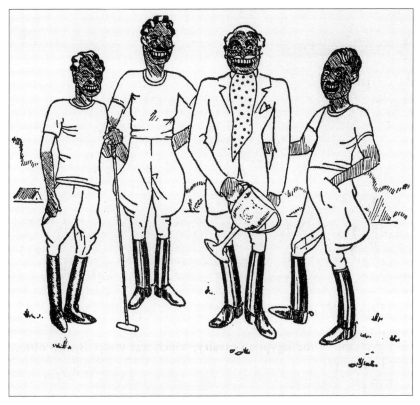

British Army polo team as seen by Roly in the 1930s. 'All polo teams look exactly alike,' according to the original caption.

leaving the security of his property and his valuable stable of (equine) brood mares in the vigilant hands of his numerous outdoor staff under his stud-groom, an Arab called Moutlak.

Finding a fox, the pack streamed over the low wall into Blunt's garden followed by Harman and his two Whips. According to Rycroft, Harman's intention was to call off the hounds and withdraw them from the enclosure. However, he wrote in his report, before this could be done he saw '... a Bedouin, whose name I afterwards ascertained to be Moutlak, shouting to them to stop and striking at them with his stick.' He called upon Moutlak in Arabic to desist, then, entering the enclosure himself with some of the Field, he 'found that both Captain Harman and Lieutenant Rome had been surrounded and mobbed, their hats knocked off, they struck at and their horses severely struck on heads and flanks, the ring-leaders being Moutlak and a powerful grey-bearded ghaffir by name Mohamed.'

The fracas continued for some time, more officers and estate workers arriving on the scene until eventually the appearance of Blunt's *wakil*

King Edward VII's Birthday Parade on the Nile at Cairo in 1901. The 11th Hussars are in the foreground. (*Royal Hussars Museum*)

(estate manager) added to Rycroft's restraining influence upon the other officers and calmed the situation. The upshot was that, although there had been no serious injuries on either side, three of Blunt's men were arrested and charged with assault. Tried before a Native Court, the three, including Moutlak and Mohamed, received prison sentences of several months each, which were later reduced on appeal.

The incident developed into a minor *cause célèbre*, involving the Foreign Secretary, Lord Lansdowne, and the Secretary of State for War, Mr Brodrick. Blunt himself made the most of it, writing to the British press in sarcastic terms and questioning both the courage and the integrity of the officers concerned, who, he said, instead of gallantly fighting off their assailants, had resorted to law – imputations of cowardice which he later withdrew. Like many rich upper-class liberals. Blunt was a snob and made particular reference to the fact that Moutlak had called Harman, not a member of a smart cavalry regiment but a mere Army Service Corps officer and perhaps of dark complexion, 'a Soudanese Sayes [sic]'!

Blunt's men had a reputation for violence and, probably with encouragement from their master, had beaten up several Greek and Italian 'poachers'. Blunt claimed that he regarded his property as a kind of bird and animal sanctuary and insinuated that it was only because British officers were involved that his men's conduct had been regarded as criminal. Doubtless there was an element of truth in this and that the matter should ever have come to Court showed poor judgement on the part of the British authorities, perhaps due to the absence from Egypt on leave of both Lord Cromer and the GOC Egypt. However, warnings were issued to the Army of Occupation that in future care should be taken not to trespass on private property for sporting purposes, warnings which were not always heeded.

What became of the Abbassiyeh Hunt we do not know and we hear no more of it – nor, indeed, of any further attempts to promote foxhunting in Egypt. The climate, particularly in summer, hardly lent itself to the wellbeing of the hounds and the best we can hope for is that they were returned whence they came.

As we have seen in a previous chapter, motor rallying made its disastrously spectacular debut in 1908, but this may have been an initiative of the Italian rather than the British community. Later, in the 1920s, motor-cycle competitions seem to have enjoyed a brief vogue under the auspices of the Cairo Motor-Cycle and Light Car Club (see Chapter 12).

The racing of horses and camels existed, in one form or another, before the arrival of the British but, as already recounted, it was the British who laid out the first 'formal' race course on Gezira Island and others followed at Heliopolis (a Cairo suburb) and in Alexandria (Sporting Club and Smouha).

Writing in 1938, Prince Mohamed Ali, heir presumptive to the throne of Egypt, describes his love of horses, which he had inherited from his ancestors. Apparently Abbas I would pay up to £3,000, a colossal sum in the 1850s, for a mare of the Saglawi Jedran strain from what is now Saudi Arabia and eventually built up a stable of six hundred horses.

Prince Mohamed Ali himself employed an English head groom (as did many of the leading Turco-Egyptian families), Stillwell, 'a stableman second to none', and an Iraqi horse-breaker called Abdallah whom he 'dressed in a beautiful Oriental uniform, brocaded with gold, and some beautiful Oriental saddles, inlaid with silver, were made for him.' It seems that this man could break and ride any horse, however vicious, but was addicted to drink![2]

Most of the leading race-horse owners of the British era were of the Turco-Egyptian 'Bashawat' class, but there were a number of foreign owners, including British. There were also British trainers and jockeys, the best remembered of the latter being Barnes who rode in Egypt for many years in the 1940s and 50s. Another, called Mann, riding in the 1890s, was accused by General Grenfell of being drunk and offensive![3]

But perhaps one of the most famous figures of the Egyptian turf was Lieutenant Colonel Herbert Milward, starter at the Gezira and Alexandria Sporting Club courses. Milward, a former commanding officer of the Sherwood Foresters with a DSO and bar, was celebrated for his fiery temper and command of soldierly language in several tongues; indeed the only Arabic words he ever bothered to learn were expletives. On one occasion, having difficulty communicating his wishes to a young apprentice at the start of a race, he bellowed at a senior jockey, 'Spinotoli! Tell that little f ... if he doesn't line up I'll f ... him!' Spinotoli duly passed the message, calling out in French, '*Eh! Mon petit! Monsieur le Colonel veut coucher avec toi!*'

He did not like Egyptians (nor, indeed, most other 'foreigners') and is reputed never to have had one in his house, even as a servant. Nevertheless, when the majority of British subjects were kicked out of Egypt after the Suez crisis of 1956 and all their property expropriated, 'Herbie' was allowed to stay and died there in 1966. Unfathomable are the ways of the East!

There were at least two attempts to introduce greyhound racing to Egypt, one in Cairo and the other in Alexandria. The first, in the 1930s, seems to have been a British endeavour which was eventually closed down by the police when, for the umpteenth time, the groggy-looking favourite staggered in last and a crowd of outraged punters burst onto the track waving their betting slips and shouting '*Où est la justice britannique?*'

The second, in the 1950s, was an Italian enterprise which did not come up to financial expectations whereupon the promoters did a midnight flit, abandoning their starving hounds to the care of the Alexandria branch of the SPCA.

Aquatic sports were also practised, both on the Nile and at sea. Egyptian students were encouraged to row and scull on the river but there may have been an element of compulsion in this as one oarsman was heard crying out to his British coach, 'I can no more! I am exhaust!' [4] Yachting at Alexandria and other seaports was also popular and King Farouk himself owned the magnificent vessel *Mahroussa* in which, in due course, he was to sail away into exile.

One of Egypt's leading yachtsmen and deep-sea fishermen was Sir Edward Peel, the Alexandrian cotton magnate. His 142-foot steam yacht *St George* was often used for fishing in the Red Sea where the catch was chiefly grouper (rock-cod) and jack. She was regularly sailed to England and based at Scarborough for several weeks' tunny fishing. In 1932 Sir Edward caught a 798 lb fish and in 1934 one of 815 lbs, then a world record for a rod-caught tunny. [5]

The leading cotton broker, Sir Edward Peel (centre left) with Admiral Sir Roger Keyes (centre right) and others, c.1938.

For all the foreign communities and for the Egyptian upper and upper middle classes, sports clubs featured prominently in their lives. For example, in the early years of the twentieth century, an Anglo-Jewish company, Delta Land, developed the residential suburb of Maadi near Cairo and by 1921 the residents had formed their own golf club, a year later to mature in a full-blown Sporting Club with 200 members – some 'country' or non-resident in Maadi – of many nationalities, covering some 150 *feddans* (acres) in addition to the 18-hole golf course.[6]

For some years between the two world wars, an English sportsman by the name of Hubert Martineau would tour the sporting clubs of Egypt with a strong team of amateur cricketers. He was a rich man with an even richer American wife (known to impolite society, perhaps due to her dusky complexion, as the Coal Black Mammy). A keen shot with an impressive grouse moor of his own in Yorkshire, on non-cricketing days Martineau would be invited to some of the great duck shoots of Egypt.

Duck shooting was the most spectacular sport available in Egypt, probably unrivalled in any other part of the world. Vast numbers of duck of many species, breeding in eastern Europe and Siberia, migrate to Egypt to winter on the rich feeding grounds provided by the mainly shallow, brackish, lakes of the Nile Delta and oases such as Wadi Natrun and the Fayoum. The best of these shoots was Ekiad. a string of lakes or large pools covering about 3,000 acres near Tel el Kebir, leased from the Crown by the British Embassy in the 1930s.

From relatively small beginnings the bags achieved at Ekiad reached their zenith during the Second World War when breeding rates in Poland and Russia doubled or trebled. Before the war huge numbers of duck eggs were collected for the photographic film production industry but with battles raging in these areas this activity was curtailed. Also the breaching of dykes flooded previously dry land and improved breeding habitat, thus many more ducklings were hatched and reached maturity.

Lord Killearn's diary records a bag of 646 in December 1935, the best to that date, but on 28 November 1943 15 guns between dawn and midday shot no fewer than 2,298 duck and 12 snipe and some startling individual scores were achieved, six of the guns reaching treble figures, the highest of which may well be a world record.

Peter Stirling (a diplomat on the Embassy staff)	481
Miralai Richard Giles Bey (Cairo City Police and shoot manager)	420
Lord Killearn	357
Captain Coats	205
Dr Halter (a Swiss businessman)	136
General Sir Maitland Wilson (C-in-C Middle East)	131 [7]

It is unlikely that such figures will ever be reached again (even if it were desirable that they should be) as many of the lakes where these migratory duck used to winter have been drained. Also, no doubt the collection of eggs on the breeding grounds was resumed after the war and by the late 1940s the bags had returned to their 1930s levels – the present author's game book recording 575 on 23 December 1949 and 449 on 6 January 1950 'plus 20–30 snipe'.

Few who took part in these shoots will ever forget the experience.

Woken at dawn in the tented camp with a cup of hot, sweet tea, peering through the flap across a near freezing desert towards the first glow of the glorious Egyptian sunrise before dressing and swallowing a hurried breakfast. Butt numbers having been allocated at dinner on the previous evening, each gun, accompanied by a *ghaffir* (game-keeper or watchman), a couple of 'picking-up' boys and a donkey loaded with wooden decoy ducks, marches off in the half-light to his allotted number, either to be rowed or carried on stalwart shoulders, according to distance from the shore, to the butt. The decoys are then placed in the water, the nearest roughly within gunshot.

Not long to wait for the first whistling of wings and soft cackling in the rapidly brightening sky, then little time to think as the numbers of duck flying in builds up; the first hour or two the busiest, shooting with only one gun, load, fire, load; boys scurrying and splashing round the fringes of the pool collecting the dead and wounded with the speed and efficiency of well-trained Labradors. Around ten, perhaps mercifully as gun barrels and sun are by now roasting hand and head, duck numbers begin to slacken. By noon it's all over, a few duck circling higher and higher, finally abandoning the lure of the decoys and setting course for more peaceful feeding places. Back to camp for drinks, lunch and the count. Tips for *ghaffirs* and boys and the swapping of much modesty, false and otherwise, over individual bags and personal performances. Then home to Cairo, dozing in the back of the car, the boot loaded with the tastier species – mallard, teal, widgeon and perhaps a few snipe. Unforgettable and now never to be repeated.

Richard (Dick) Giles was one of the best shots ever to hold a gun. He had been brought up in Cyprus where he had learnt to shoot bats with a 4/10. On one occasion at Ekiad he is reputed to have shot a hundred duck with a hundred cartridges (the Swiss, Dr Halter, celebrated the event with a little poem in English but using the German word Hundert for Hundred!). During the First World War Giles was stationed in East Anglia with the Royal Flying Corps and by chance, perhaps as a stand-in for a more senior officer, was invited to shoot partridges at Sandringham. So brilliantly did he perform that King George V personally summoned him to shoot again the following week.[8]

As C. S. Jarvis discovered while languishing as District Commander of the remote Kharga, Dakhla, Baharia and Farafra Oases in the 1920s, prowess with a gun could be a valuable career qualification. During a visit by his chief, Miralai George Hunter Bey, Inspector-General Frontier Districts Administration, Jarvis organised a small shoot. However, Hunter, who had not brought his own gun, declined to take part but insisted that Jarvis did while he watched. Miraculously, Jarvis, who regarded himself as a pretty average shot, pulled off some remarkable rights and lefts at teal and shoveller and brought down a brace of difficult snipe.

At dinner that evening Hunter remarked to Mrs Jarvis on her husband's expertise, adding, 'I had no idea we had anything in his class on the Frontiers ...' A few months later Jarvis was promoted to the sub-governorship of Sinai![9]

When Giles left Egypt in about 1950, the British Embassy itself took over the management of Ekiad with disastrous results. The individual concerned knew no Arabic and had no understanding of the local people and conditions. The head *ghaffir*, Mohamed Gerbaish, probably at the behest of the *omdah* (headman) of Ekiad village with whom he had been at loggerheads for years, was sacked without compensation; poaching and predatation increased and, in due course, Ekiad was 'confiscated' by the Nasserite regime. Appeals by former guests at the shoot on behalf of Mohamed Gerbaish were refused by Albion, in the shape of a senior Embassy official, at her most perfidious ... 'This man's a beastly nuisance ... and, anyway, he isn't liked by the Regime ...' Thus were the old servants of a once Great Britain so often treated by their former master.

King Farouk himself was a keen shot and Killearn's diary records that, despite their mutual dislike, he was a guest at the King's shoot at Dahshour (more famous for its pyramids) on 6 February 1944 when 437 duck, out of a total of 852, 'fell' to Farouk's gun. However, remarked Killearn, His Majesty had '... a friend in the butt shooting with him and I do not doubt that many ghaffirs were operating in his vicinity!' Sour grapes perhaps on the part of the Ambassador who claimed 135 of which only 117 were picked up. Owing to the climate, gun dogs were seldom, if ever, used in Egypt but the ghaffirs and their assistants, usually small boys, were expert retrievers so he had probably miscounted.[10]

One of the other guns on this particular occasion was Abdallah Wad Nejumi Pasha (only 17 duck and 3 snipe!), a Sudanese with an interesting background. His father, the Emir Abderrahman Wad Nejumi, was the only Mahdist leader to cross the frontier into Egypt with an army but was heavily defeated at the Battle of Toski (Tushki) on 3 August 1889 in which he himself was killed. As was their custom, the ansar (Mahdist warriors) were accompanied by a horde of camp followers: women, children and slaves, most of whom surrendered to the Anglo-Egyptians. Among the many children brought into camp was a year-old baby boy, the son of the great emir. This child was taken to Cairo and given into the care of the British nurses at Kasr el Aini Hospital. Eventually he was commissioned in the Egyptian Army and joined the staff of the Royal Household, serving for many years as an aide and bodyguard to King Farouk.[11]

He was fiercely loyal to the King and, according to one account, was the only member of Farouk's entourage to put up any resistance during the notorious Abdin Incident of 1942 (see Chapter 14).

As early as 1876 the Marquess of Ripon, regarded by some as 'the greatest shot in British game shooting history', visited Egypt and 'brought back 44 varieties for stuffing'. Bearing in mind the Marquess's game book recorded the slaying of no fewer than 556,813 head of game to his own gun, the wildlife of Egypt got off pretty lightly! [12]

Although duck were the principal quarry during the winter migratory season, plenty of snipe lurked on the reedy fringes of the lakes and. as they sprang into their twisting, jinking flight, the beaters would cry '*Abou! Abou!*' – a corruption of the French '*A vous!*'. Quail, although huge numbers were netted commercially as they crossed the Mediterranean coast, wintered in the cultivated areas and were easily 'walked up', with occasionally disastrous results when the sportsman, throwing up his gun to shoot at one, found himself firing directly at a fellah (or fellaha) suddenly popping up from the dense *berseem* (lucerne). The usually superficial wounds healed rapidly with the application of an on-the-spot cash settlement. Some of these injuries were self-inflicted as it was not unusual for a woman or girl to be punctured with thorns before breaking cover and exposing an apparently peppered bosom. But genuinely serious damage could lead to interminable litigation.

Presumably the Prince of Wales encountered no such difficulties when, on 4 April 1890, he and the Sirdar, General Grenfell, accounted for 408 quail at Ayat on the Nile south of Cairo, one of the General's favourite shooting grounds where he achieved some other remarkable bags, including one of thirty-one and a half brace of snipe and a hyena! [13]

In another area rich in game, Mansurieh to the north-west of Cairo, after a successful day's shooting on which Grenfell and his party bagged 170 duck, 5 geese, 65 snipe and a flamingo (!), he witnessed a remarkable spectacle. 'Prince [later Sultan of Egypt – author] Hussein's nephew', he recorded in his diary, 'demonstrated how hawks were trained for hawking gazelle. A large piece of meat was put on the head of a stuffed gazelle and, with a long line attached to a mounted Arab, was dragged very quickly over the desert, the Arab galloping hard. The hawks were then let loose and swooped down on the stuffed gazelle. After several flights the meat on the horns of the gazelle was given to the hawks. They are then taught to fly in front of the gazelle ... and attack the eyes with their beaks, this impedes the gazelle and rough looking greyhounds [presumably a type of saluki – author] are then loosed and course the gazelle until it is taken, the hawk working together with them.' [14]

When in his Foreword to J. Wentworth Day's *Sport in Egypt*, published in 1938, King Farouk wrote: 'Sport is an ambassador which knows no politics, no frontiers,' he had forgotten the role played by a particular sporting (or perhaps unsporting) event in a drama which had seized the attention of the world some thirty-two years before and was to have an enduring effect upon Anglo-Egyptian relations.

CHAPTER 6

Denshawi

I F THERE WAS A TURNING POINT in Anglo–Egyptian relations it came over twenty years after the British had installed themselves in Egypt with the Denshawi Incident of 1906, an episode from which no one, from Lord Cromer downwards, emerges with much credit.

The Mounted Infantry was an arm of the service, which had been created during the last quarter of the nineteenth century and had operated successfully in a number of campaigns. Its companies were made up of officers and men from different units who, having completed their tour with the MI, would return to normal duty with their regiments.

On 13 June 1906 one such company was on 'flag-showing' patrol in the Nile Delta when its officers were invited to lunch by a local dignitary, Abdel Magid Bey Sultan, the lunch to be followed by a dove shoot near the village of Denshawi, a few miles from the large town of Tanta. A similar invitation had been extended to a group of MI officers in the previous year and had passed off without incident, despite complaints from villagers. However, on this occasion, for reasons which have never been adequately explained, disaster overtook all concerned.

In the early afternoon the five officers took up their positions in the date-palm groves around the village and started shooting. The question is, what were they shooting at? Did they confine themselves to the wild doves (*gimri*), which flitted amongst the groves, or were they also blazing away, either out of ignorance or insensitivity, at the tame pigeons (*hammam*), which were a valuable crop to the fellahin, raised in cotes and on the roofs of their houses? The motives for the assault on the officers which followed do not appear to have been very carefully examined so we do not know. As. either by coincidence or design, a fire broke out on a nearby threshing-floor at the same time, they might equally have been blamed for that. Whatever the case, they were soon surrounded by a mob of infuriated villagers led by two notorious 'bad hats', Hassan Mahfouz and Dervish Zahran, who hated each other and were probably vying for leadership over the others.

At first the villagers confined themselves to hurling insults, unwilling perhaps to offer physical violence to armed men. There followed, however, an act of almost unbelievable folly on the part of the senior British officer, Major Pine-Coffin. Seeking, presumably, to defuse the situation but in fact giving the mob precisely the advantage it wanted, he handed over his gun and ordered the other officers to do likewise. To make matters worse, one of the guns, that of Lieutenant Porter, went off, wounding several villagers including a woman. Now in a frenzy of rage and indignation the mob fell upon the officers, raining blows upon them with sticks, hoes and other implements and showering them with stones. However, the attack does not appear to have been inspired entirely by spontaneous fury as at least one of the officers, Porter, claimed to have been robbed, although this may have been simple opportunism.

An attempt was made by the village *ghaffir* (constable) to get the officers back to the horse-drawn cabs in which they had arrived and, although this failed, Captains Bull and Bostock managed to break away and start the six-mile run back to their camp. Bostock, less seriously injured than Bull, swam a canal and eventually staggered into camp to raise the alarm. Bull, however, collapsed into a ditch beside the road where he was eventually found unconscious and died at seven o'clock that evening.

Meanwhile, at Denshawi, the ghaffir had managed to get word to the local authorities who turned up in sufficient force to protect the officers from further violence (Pine-Coffin's arm had already been broken) and escort them from the scene.[1]

That, so far as most people were concerned, was the end of a thoroughly unpleasant but relatively minor incident. It was not even clear if Captain Bull had died of his injuries or of heat stroke. There might be a hanging but more probably a few floggings and terms of imprisonment. In any case, the Turco-Egyptian ruling class cared little for the fate of a few unruly fellahin. But such thoughts were greatly misplaced.

It was not long before a head of steam began to build up – probably fuelled by the English-language press in Egypt and the British correspondents in Cairo of the London newspapers who cried, 'Plot!'[2] Lord Cromer was departing for his annual leave which, in the circumstances, he would have done better to postpone, and the Agency was left in the hands of a diplomat with relatively little Egyptian experience, Charles Findlay. In the absence of the steadying hand of 'el Lord', Findlay, the British judicial and military authorities and, to some extent, the Egyptian Government, heavily influenced by its British Advisers, panicked. Leniency, they believed, would be dangerous, leading to further such incidents, perhaps escalating into a general insurrection against the British Occupation. Examples must be made of the Denshawi fellahin.

Under a General Decree of 1895 offences against the British military committed by Egyptians could, in certain circumstances, be tried by a special tribunal consisting of three British and two Egyptian judges. After a cursory police investigation, fifty-two fellahin were indicted and appeared before the Court within less than a fortnight of the incident.

The President of the Court was a senior judge and former Minister of Foreign Affairs, the Copt Sami Boutros Ghali Pasha (grandfather of the recent Secretary-General of the United Nations). Ironically in the light of future events, his Egyptian colleague was one Fathi Zagloul, brother of the extreme nationalist, Saad Zagloul, whom we shall encounter later. The British were represented by the Acting Judicial Adviser to the Khedive, Mr Hayter, Sir Walter Bond, Vice-President of the Appeal Court and a British Army Judge Advocate, Mr Cuthbert (or, according to some accounts, a Colonel Ludlow).[3]

Captain Lawrence Oates of the Inniskilling Dragoons, later to achieve immortal fame in the Antarctic and a brother officer of Captain Bull, wrote at the time, 'The President is an Armenian and hates the fellahin like poison so I imagine they will get it pretty hot.'[4] While it is true that Boutros Ghali's mother was Armenian there is no evidence that he had any special hatred for the fellahin but Oates' words reflect the general feeling throughout Egypt that little mercy would be shown to the accused and he was right.

The court sat at Shibin el Kum, apparently in the open air, and on 27 June the sentences were handed down. Dervish Zahran, Hassan Mahfouz and two others were to be hanged, two received penal servitude for life, one 15 years, six 7 years, three to one year and 50 lashes and five to 50 lashes. No time was to be wasted on appeals or similar such legal paraphernalia and the sentences were to be carried out on the next day at the scene of the crime. There may have been several reasons for this indecent haste but the most pressing was probably fear on the part of the Anglo-Egyptian authorities of interference from London where questions had already been asked in Parliament.

The sentences were duly carried out on the 28th under the auspices of the Mudir (Governor) of Menufiya Province assisted by Colonel Machell, Adviser at the Ministry of the Interior, and before a large audience of British troops and civilian officials as well as the villagers of Denshawi. Those condemned to be hanged met their deaths calmly, although Hassan Mahfouz loudly denounced those who had given evidence against him (an unnamed woman seems to have the principal

Some of the accused in the notorious Denshawi trial of 1906, four of whom were
hanged for the murder of Captain Bull.

prosecution witness). and the others received their lashes with fortitude.
The fellah is a hardy soul and in those days was not unaccustomed to
the flaying sting of the *kourbash*.[5]

Apparently British officialdom did not expect the violent reaction
which exploded around its ears. The Anglophobe foreign press,
especially that of the French-speaking world, made the most of this
God-sent opportunity to 'bash the British' – one Belgian newspaper
reporting that at least a dozen men had been hanged, all of whom had
been flogged until the blood ran before execution![6] This may have been
inspired by the somewhat theatrical method of carrying out the
sentences by alternating the hangings and floggings, although the condemned men were kept in a tent so as not to witness each others'
punishment.[7]

At home too there were harsh words for the British authorities in
Egypt, the Foreign Secretary, Sir Edward Grey, facing a hostile barrage
from his own Liberal MPs and left-wing commentators such as Bernard
Shaw weighing in with biting sarcasm.[8] Naturally the Government had
sought Cromer's advice as to what, if anything, it should do but alarmed
though he was by this turn of events, he had been against intervention
on the grounds that it would have simply compounded the error by
weakening the authority of the Agency and the British and Egyptian
judges as well as the reasonably compliant Egyptian Government of
Mustapha Fehmy Pasha. Nonetheless, after Cromer's departure in the

following year, under pressure from London and at the behest of Cromer's successor, Sir Eldon Gorst, all the men sentenced to terms of imprisonment were released.'[9]

The Denshawi Incident is now almost forgotten but its memory lingered on for decades, at least for so long as there was a British presence in Egypt. It was the first occasion since 1882 when all shades of Egyptian opinion were united against the Occupation; indeed it was the first opportunity for such unity. Under Cromer's careful management of the relationship between ruler and ruled, few mistakes had been made and the undoubted benefits of British influence were generally recognised, albeit grudgingly. Now, it seemed, the Englishman had proved himself no better than the brutal Turk or Mameluk. Even Judge J. E. Marshall – no bleeding heart liberal he – was horrified, recording in his memoirs: '... to the utter amazement and astonishment of the civilised world, four natives were hanged, others flogged and sentenced to various terms of penal servitude. Bond virtually conducted the proceedings ... The case was conducted with such a want of method that when minutes of the proceedings were called for by Parliament in London, they had to be compiled from reports made by native journalists for their papers.'[10]

Many years later Lord Lloyd wrote of Denshawi: 'However generous and sincere the policy of an alien domination, however numerous its beneficent acts, they weigh but little against one misdirection of justice or one act of oppression ... thus by a single error of judgement a Government may lose its whole reputation for fair dealing however well deserved.'[11]

In some cases these feelings were genuine but to many this was a rolling bandwagon upon which to leap especially at a time when the influence of the nationalist leader, Mustapha Kamel, appeared to be waning and needed revival. However, the effects of Denshawi were chronic rather than acute and the violence of nationalist rhetoric was not matched, in the immediate aftermath, by rioting or civil disorder.

Denshawi raised many questions which have never been, and now never will be, satisfactorily answered. Was there, as the English-language press suggested, a plot – a trap into which Major Pine-Coffin and his officers were drawn?

The inhabitants of Menufiya Province had a reputation for violence and xenophobia and the province was an unruly one (which is probably why British Army patrols were regularly sent through it). Why then did the officers expose themselves to a potentially dangerous situation, escorted by one policeman and armed only with shot-guns which, with almost unbelievable stupidity, they were prepared to hand over to their assailants?

Did they shoot the villagers' tame pigeons and, if so, why? Whatever his shortcomings, the British officer of the day was a sportsman and domestic poultry fluttering around a few feet in the air make poor sport as compared with the wild doves which dart like arrows between the trees.

Did Captain Bull die of his injuries or of sunstroke? The post-mortem found that the cause of death was 'heat apoplexy caused or aggravated by concussion of the brain'.[12]

Incidentally, the behaviour of Captain Bostock, an RAMC doctor, in deserting him seems to have been inexcusable on the face of it but, so far as we know, he was not subjected to any Court of Inquiry or Court Martial. Nor, indeed, was Major Pine-Coffin, an experienced officer with a DSO, for his extraordinarily inept handling of the whole affair. Also, it has been claimed that the British soldiers looking for Bull beat to death a fellah who had been giving succour to the wounded man. In evidence, the sergeant major commanding the search party stated that his patrol had been fired on 'by bandits' at the village of Silsina and returned fire, following which a man had been found dead and others wounded. However, not surprisingly, a Court of Enquiry found no evidence that the patrol was responsible for this.[13]

Above all, why did the Anglo-Egyptian authorities apparently lose their heads and allow a molehill to be turned into a mountain? This was a time of relative peace and tranquillity in Egypt and, for all the fulminations of the English-language press, any evidence that there may been of a plot was purely circumstantial. It is useless to pretend that the judiciary was entirely independent of the executive so it was extra-ordinary that pressure was not exerted upon the judges, especially upon the dominant Bond, to temper justice with mercy – indeed the reverse was probably the case. One hanging and a few floggings would have satisfied nearly everyone but what stuck in Egyptian throats was the ratio of four lives for one.

Captain Bull and the Denshawi fellahin were not the last victims of this tragic incident. By 1910 Sami Boutros Ghali Pasha, President of the fatal tribunal, was Prime Minister of Egypt. At one o'clock in the afternoon of 10 February of that year, he was standing on the pavement outside his office waiting for his carriage to take him to lunch when he was approached by a shop-keeper called Ibrahim Nassif el Wardani and shot dead at point-blank range.[14]

Wardani, who was tried and executed, became a national hero. In the eyes of the masses Boutros Ghali had committed a number of capital crimes. In the first place he was a Christian (for the purposes of mob slogans the Arabic for Christian, Nasrani, rhymed conveniently with Wardani); secondly, he had signed the Sudan Convention of 1899 thus robbing Egypt of what many saw as her birthright; thirdly, he had recently acquiesced to a proposed prolongation of the Suez Canal Company's concession (which was later dropped); but, above all, he was regarded as the principal murderer of the Denshawi 'martyrs'.

CHAPTER 7

After Cromer

L ORD CROMER resigned suddenly and left Egypt in May 1907. He was sixty-six years old and in poor health (although he lived for another ten years). Also perhaps he had been badly shaken by the Denshawi affair and may have felt he was losing his grip. Furthermore, he must have been weary of the lack of appreciation, as he saw it, of his work in Egypt, especially his transformation of the parlous financial situation which he had inherited. For over forty years after his departure the Egyptian pound remained one of the strongest currencies in the world.

He had inspired respect rather than affection, even in the British community, and his departure was a curiously anti-climatic end to his twenty-four year 'reign'. There had been fears of nationalist demonstrations to mark his departure and his route to Cairo railway station was lined with British troops but in the event he left almost unnoticed, '... amid a silence chillier than ice,' wrote Ronald Storrs, a young British official and future Oriental Secretary.[1]

Of the many complaints against him by his critics one of the strongest was that he had neglected education. This may have been true to some extent as he heartily disliked the mainly nationalist middle-class (there was no question at that time of trying to educate the fellahin) and regarded students as cannon fodder for rabble-rousers. But in the year before his departure, he took two significant measures in the field of education one of which was to have enduring political consequences and the other, although largely ceremonial at the time, was to be of considerable value to Egypt and the Middle East as a whole in the future.

The first of these acts was to appoint Saad Zagloul Minister of Education, presumably as a gesture of friendship towards his favourite Prime Minister and Zagloul's father-in-law, Mustapha Fehmy Pasha, little knowing that he was helping the prickliest thorn in the sides of his successors onto the first rung of the ladder to power.[2]

The second was to lay the foundation stone, on 24 May 1906, of a new building in Alexandria which was to house one of the most significant monuments to British influence, Victoria College, and which was to remain a centre of educational excellence until wrecked (like so much else in Egypt) by Nasser in 1956.

The original college had been founded some four years earlier by the British Consul-General in Alexandria, Sir Charles Cookson, and several wealthy merchants of the city, mostly Anglo-Jewish. The school was run, with a mainly British staff, on English public school lines but was non-sectarian and multi-national; thus in 1906 the school roll of 186 pupils was made up of 13 nationalities of whom 80 were Christian, 67 Jewish and 39 Muslim.[3] Bearing in mind the charges of reaction and racism which have been levelled at the British establishment in Egypt, it is hard to conceive of a more progressive and enlightened concept.

The Old Boy list contains names of international renown, including King Feisel of Iraq (assassinated in 1958), the late King Hussein of Jordan, the former King Constantine of Greece, members of leading Sudanese families (including a former Prime Minister), the Saudi business moguls Adnan Khashogi and Hisham Nazir, the actor Omar Sharif, the film producer Yousef Shahin, several senior Egyptian politicians, and numerous leading academics and writers. The *esprit de corps* common to most English public schools is strong amongst its Old Boys who hold regular reunions often in exotic locations.[4]

Throughout its existence the college was generously supported by the British and foreign communities in Egypt, among its benefactors being such prominent Alexandrian families as Peel, Alderson, Finney, Goar, Smouha, Choremi, Matossian, Sursock and Karam.

In 1940 a Cairo branch was opened but never quite achieved the exalted reputation of its parent foundation. Over the years other British educational institutions were spawned: the English School, the English Girls' College, the Scottish School for Boys and the Scottish School for Girls, all of which provided a sound education, not only for the children of British residents who could not afford to send their children home to school, but, as the 1937 *English School Record* put it, 'Christians of all kinds ... as well as Jews and Moslems ... and as far as is known, no complaints have been made [of efforts] to influence religious opinion or to differentiate between children on the grounds of religious belief.'

The English Girls' College was the brainchild of the long-serving British Consul-General in Alexandria, Sir Clifford Heathcote Smith. Built by public subscription at Chatby (a district of Alexandria) it was opened in 1932. About 50–60 per cent of the pupils were British girls from the local community or others whose parents were working in the Sudan, Ethiopia or Libya. The remainder were mostly drawn from cosmopolitan families of all races and nationalities, including, during the war years, the daughters of the Greek Royal Family.

After the 'nationalisation' of all foreign schools in 1956 the English Girls' College managed to maintain its British flavour through the influence of its Headmistress, an Englishwoman married to an Egyptian academic, Mrs Khalafallah, and her successor, a former pupil, Mrs Ennam Diffrawi.

Despite the criticism of Cromer on the subject, education in the public sector during the British era expanded by leaps and bounds. For example, the number of pupils in secondary education rose from only five hundred in 1900 to 9,400 in 1922. During the same period university entrance increased tenfold.[5]

Sandwiched between two imperial giants, Cromer's protégé and successor, Sir Eldon Gorst, remains rather a shadowy and insubstantial figure. He had much Egyptian experience, having been Adviser to the Ministries of Finance and Interior. He spoke fluent Arabic and could read and write the language. Small and by no means imposing, he lacked the physical presence and forceful personality which were the hallmarks of both his predecessor, Cromer, and his successor, Kitchener.

In his memoirs a former British officer of the Egyptian Army, Colonel W. F. Stirling, wrote:

> ... Cromer, whom the natives always called 'the Lord', was indeed lord of all he surveyed. It was magnificent to see him when he drove abroad, his carriage surrounded by the famous running *sayes* [grooms] in their brilliant livery: it was certainly a great psychological error when his successor, Sir Eldon Gorst, acting on instructions from home, suppressed all such splendour and lived like a small city clerk from Peckham. Sir Eldon's habit of riding a bicycle through the streets of Cairo, unattended and wearing a suit of dittos [sic] and an ordinary cloth cap, convinced the Egyptians that the British Empire was no longer what it had been.[6]

A more acerbic critic was Lord Edward Cecil. Under-Secretary (and later Adviser) at the Ministry of Finance, who disliked not only Gorst's liberal policies but also his mode of life. 'His house is full of Greeks and second rate people from home.' Cecil wrote to his wife. '... to be invited to the Agency you must have two qualifications. You must have a pretty wife and a name ending in 'opoulo' or 'ino'. Earlier he had claimed that Gorst's friendship with the Khedive was nothing but a pretence, which was almost certainly untrue, at least on the Khedive's side.[7]

Gorst's term of office, cut short by a premature and painful death from cancer in 1911 at the age of 51, was marked by a somewhat cosmetic relaxation of the British grip and marred by the assassination of Boutros Ghali. But perhaps his most notable achievement was the confidence built up between himself and the Khedive Abbas Hilmi who was hostile to the British Occupation, had been despised by Cromer and was a constant source of irritation to Kitchener.

Their antipathy towards Abbas (and vice versa) had its origin in the famous Frontier Incident of 1894 upon which we have touched earlier.

During an inspection of the Egyptian Army garrisons in Upper Egypt and on the Sudan frontier in that year, the Khedive, apparently influenced by his Under-Secretary of State for War, Mohamed Maher Pasha, had seen fit to criticise everything he saw: the Senior Medical Officer, Graham, was incompetent; drill was poor (the troops were drilled by British NCOs, several of them Guardsmen); negroes (southern Sudanese) should not be commissioned and he falsely accused one of them of being drunk in his presence. Finally, he turned to Kitchener at the end of a parade and remarked, 'To tell you the truth, Kitchener Pasha, I consider it disgraceful for Egypt to be served by such an army!' To which Kitchener replied, 'I beg to tender Your Highness my resignation!' The Khedive appeared surprised and begged him to withdraw which, after a show of resistance, Kitchener eventually did. The incident was reported to Cromer (Wingate, Kitchener's Chief of Intelligence, kept a diary of the tour of inspection and all the Khedive's comments) and the inevitable outcome was that Maher was sacked and the Khedive made to write an open letter to Kitchener expressing his unreserved satisfaction with both the British and the native officers of his army. His humiliation was complete.

The incident is a most curious one as it is difficult to see what either side could have gained from it. Apparently Wingate had been forewarned of what was going to happen, hence the diary. One of Kitchener's biographers suggests that Maher's motives were to force all the British officers out of the Egyptian Army, an extremely ambitious, indeed unreachable, objective, while another concludes that Kitchener overreacted and made a mountain out of a mole-hill, while Cromer was looking for an excuse to cut the Khedive down to size. Whatever was behind it, its effect was to poison relations between the Khedive and Egypt's two most powerful Englishmen, Cromer and Kitchener, permanently and eventually lead to his dethronement in 1914.[8]

If indeed Wingate had been forewarned of the Khedive's and Maher's intention to spark the Frontier Incident, the information may well have come from one of the most remarkable and influential women in Egypt at that time – the Khedive's cousin Princess Nazli (not to be confused with Queen Nazli, the wife of King Fuad). This lady kept a foot firmly in both British and Turco-Egyptian camps, probably inclining towards the former, and little information or political gossip which might be of value to either side escaped her. Field Marshal Lord Grenfell, the former Sirdar and GOC Egypt, wrote of her:

> Among the friends I made in Cairo was the Princess Nazli, a remarkable woman, most intelligent and charming ... In Cairo she succeeded in breaking down the barriers and was a determined champion of female emancipation in Turkey and Egypt.
>
> While she wore a yashmak – a remarkably transparent one – and a feridgi [sic] when she appeared in public, she adopted entirely the life of an educated European lady of rank, received people of any distinction irrespective of nationality, as she spoke most European languages. Her devotion to England was of very great assistance to us in Cairo, where she was greatly respected and a little feared. She was very much attached to Lord and Lady Cromer who were often guests in her palace in Old Cairo. To me she became a great personal friend and some of the pleasantest hours I passed in Cairo were spent in her company. She had a certain amount of influence over the Khedive and Khedivieh and kept her cousin the Khedive posted in the various intrigues of the Palace and politicians. The Khedive Tewfik recognised her great and unmistakable qualities and frequently acted on her advice.
>
> She was a very handsome woman and late in life after I had left Egypt she married a Pasha from Tripoli ... Her first husband had been a Pasha of some distinction who was Turkish ambassador at Paris but he died when she was quite young. She was on very friendly terms with ... most of the officers of distinction connected with the British Army.[9]

But the friendship between Abbas and Gorst was so strong and genuine that the normally selfish and self-indulgent monarch travelled to England to bid a last farewell to Gorst as he lay on his deathbed at Castle Combe.

Of Gorst's ability to attract affection and, in women, even passionate love there is little doubt. His marriage was not a success but he seems to have had numerous affairs of the heart. As for his relations with his colleagues, although the high officials of British Egypt were a quarrelsome lot, one of these, Sir William Garstin, former Adviser to the Ministry of Public Works and one of the driving forces behind the construction of the Assouan Dam, was inspired to write his dying friend a most moving letter of farewell:

> I was so tongue-tied to-day when I saw you and could find no words. It was such a shock to me to see you lying there and to know that we should

not meet again ... you and I have been friends for more than 24 years
and good friends always ... now I feel as if something had been torn up
in my life.

May I tell you what good it did me to see you so calm and brave ...
I just want you to know that I shall never forget you and that I shall
miss you always. You are going now to learn the great secret. I am one
of them who believe that we shall meet again ...

Goodbye my very very dear friend.

W. Garstin' [10]

Perhaps Gorst had been especially supportive of Garstin when, some
years earlier at the time of the campaign to reconquer the Sudan, a
dashing and brilliant young officer of the Rifle Brigade, Major Charles
a'Court, had appeared on the Cairo social landscape *en route* to war and
swept the lovely Mary, Lady Garstin, off her feet.

On his return from the Sudan, to the delicious outrage of Anglo-
Egyptian society, the affair smouldered on (at this stage Garstin seems
to have been complacent) until the military authorities issued an ultimatum. Either a'Court, who was already married, must give up the
liaison or he must resign his commission. The Boer War intervened
and he chose the former course. However, by 1902 the affair had been
resumed; Garstin divorced Mary and a'Court was forced to resign but
his wife would not divorce him.

A'Court added Repington to his name and took up journalism, a
profession at which he was brilliantly, if controversially, successful. As
Military Correspondent of *The Times* in 1905 he wrote the definitive
account of the Russo-Japanese War and during the First World War
exposed the scandalous shell shortage on the Western Front. Unfortunately he was penniless and, although almost entirely dependent on his
earnings as a journalist (he dabbled, not always scrupulously, in art
dealing as well), he clashed frequently with his employers and anta-
gonised the Establishment. Lloyd George was to write of him: '... one
of the most brilliant of our military critics and one who was accorded
the special confidence of the Army leaders at home and was chosen
by them as their special champion in the Press against meddlesome
politicians' – of whom, of course, Lloyd George himself had been the
most meddlesome!

Repington also suffered from *folie de grandeur* and his *Who's Who*
entry gives a smart country house address in Nottinghamshire whereas
he and Mary were in reality living in devoted and penurious sin at
Brighton where he died in 1925.[11]

Garstin died in the same year, he and Mary having shared the tragedy
of losing both their children at early ages, the son being killed in action
in the First World War. Through his work in the Irrigation Department

and at the Ministry of Public Works, where he had been the driving force behind the construction of the Assouan Dam, his contribution to the progress and prosperity of Egyptian agriculture was unrivalled. Cromer wrote, 'It would be difficult to exaggerate the debt of gratitude which the people of Egypt owe to Sir William Garstin,' and even the nationalist press described him as 'the Treasure of Egypt'.[12]

Field Marshal the Earl Kitchener of Khartoum was arguably the most prestigious figure of the first decade or so of the twentieth century. He had smashed the Sudanese Mahdists, faced down the French at Fashoda, crushed the Boers and reduced the Viceroy of India, in the public mind second only to the King in the hierarchy of Empire, to tears. Even the Egyptian nationalists were flattered when they learnt that this mighty paladin had been appointed British Agent and Consul-General in Egypt. Furthermore, he was known to like the Egyptians and to love the country in which he had spent so much of his life. Some old hands, like Judge Marshall, thought Kitchener was easily bamboozled by Egyptian flattery and largesse, which may have been true. On the other hand, he was not without cunning and may well have found it to his advantage to give that impression.

During his brief tenure in office there were few political rumblings and little violence (there was a plot against his life but this was routine in Egypt). Apart from some tinkerings with some minor constitutional matters and, more importantly, moves to alleviate the burdens of debt

The Khedive Abbas Hilmi and Kitchener at the opening of the Esnah Barrage in
1909.

upon the fellahin, his three year sojourn in Egypt was a period of calm and tranquillity before the rushing storm of the First World War swept him and the status quo throughout much of the world away.[13]

He ran Egypt as he had run the Egyptian Army, by relying on a few trusted and devoted subordinates, the principal among these being Lord Edward Cecil whom he promoted to the rank of Adviser to the Minister of Finance and whom he regarded as his 'Prime Minister'.

Lord Edward was something of an enigma. Although he spent most of his rather short working life (he died of TB in 1918 at the age of only 51) in Egypt, he disliked the place, its people and most of his colleagues. As a younger son of the great 3rd Marquess of Salisbury and thus a scion of one of England's leading families, he was not so much a snob but rather a patrician who tended to look down (literally, as he stood 6ft 5ins in his socks) his nose at lesser mortals of whatever nationality. As a subaltern in the Grenadier Guards he had been seconded to the Egyptian Army in 1896 as one of Kitchener's ADCs and had served in that capacity for most of the Sudan campaign. The appointment was a political one as, at that time, neither man liked the other but Kitchener, a very political soldier, wanted direct and unofficial access to Cecil's father, the Prime Minister, while Cecil was eager for operational experience.[14]

Cecil's 1896 diary of the Dongola campaign[15] is highly critical of Kitchener but by 1911 his feelings towards his chief had completely altered – 'you know how much I love him now,' he wrote to his wife in that year.[16] This is an extraordinary, almost embarrassing, admission coming from a normally reserved and cynical English aristocrat of that era, but Kitchener, who mellowed greatly in later life, had a remarkable ability to inspire devotion in his subordinates and personal staff. We find this in his Chief of Staff, Fitzgerald, who drowned with him, and his former ADCs, McMurdo, Maxwell VC and Jimmy Watson, as well as Cecil.

Kitchener's death in 1916 was a severe blow to Cecil and 'ended many dreams of mine for the future' as he had entertained hopes of being appointed, in due course, to succeed Kitchener as British Agent and Consul General in Egypt.

On the personal side it added to the pain which he had suffered when his only son, George, was killed in action in 1914. Indeed, there is something tragic about Lord Edward's final years which is reflected in his letters to his wife Violet. These, though punctuated with his sardonic wit, plead for love and understanding. She had tired of him many years before and her affair, which may or may not have been platonic, with Lord Milner was an open secret. She seldom came to Egypt, did not always answer his letters and was extravagant with money which they did not have, but his devotion to her remained unimpaired to the end, which may have come upon him as a relief.[17]

Another devoted Kitchener disciple was Lieutenant Colonel James (Jimmy) Watson of the 60th Rifles. After service in Burma, Watson joined the Egyptian Army in 1894 and was soon appointed as ADC to the Sirdar in which capacity he served throughout the Sudan campaign of 1896–98, becoming one of an elite band in whom Kitchener had complete confidence (something that Kitchener himself lacked at that time) during that harrowing campaign.[18] Cecil wrote: '... His [K's] office was a sea of papers lying on tables, chairs, window-sills [and] the floor ... He never let anyone touch them except Watson, Bailey [Staff Sergeant, his chief orderly-room clerk, later commissioned – author] ... and a few others in whom he had confidence.'[19]

Oddly enough, during Kitchener's term of office as British Agent in Egypt, Watson was serving as ADC to the Khedive Abbas Hilmi with whom he formed a life-long friendship – rather as Gorst had done. This must have entailed a certain conflict of loyalty, for, as we have seen, no such mutual affection existed between Khedive and Agent.

On the other hand, it may be that Watson's special relationship with both men rendered a difficult, if not impossible, situation tolerable and formed a kind of conduit of communication between Palace and Residency.

When Kitchener was drowned in 1916, Edward Cecil recorded the devastating effect it had on Watson who was serving as Military Secretary to the High Commissioner, MacMahon. 'Jimmy broke down and had to go to bed,' wrote Cecil to his wife. 'He is really awfully seedy now, poor old thing, all his nerve and fight gone.'[20]

Many harsh words have been spoken and written of the man who symbolised, perhaps more than any other, British nineteenth- and early twentieth-century imperialism, but he passed into history mourned not only by the mass of the British people but by faithful friends who knew and understood him.

CHAPTER 8

War and its Aftermath

A T NOON on 3 August 1914 Kitchener boarded the ferry at Dover to return to Egypt after his summer leave. He got no further. As he paced the deck impatiently a telegram was handed to him summoning him back to London and the following day he was appointed Secretary of State for War in which office he was to render his last great service to his country.[1]

If the present generation has any knowledge or 'folk memory' of Kitchener it is thanks to an obscure commercial artist called Alfred Leete who designed and drew the famous recruiting poster – 'Your Country Needs You' – in which Kitchener's pointing finger stirred the patriotism of millions of young men and brought them flocking to the Colours to form the New Army.

He was succeeded in Egypt by a rather pedestrian Indian Civil Servant, Sir Henry McMahon, a stop-gap against Kitchener's early return once the war, scheduled to be 'over by Christmas' (although Kitchener himself had given it three years), had been brought to a victorious conclusion. Of course this was never to be as Kitchener was drowned in June 1916 when HMS *Hampshire*, the cruiser in which he was travelling to Russia, struck a mine and sank off Orkney.

In fact McMahon had little to do as in December 1914 Egypt was made a British Protectorate. Martial Law was declared and most aspects of British authority taken over by the military in the shape of the succession of generals who commanded what became known as the Egyptian Expeditionary Force (EEF). The pro-Turkish Khedive, who happened to be in Constantinople when war broke out, was deposed (a measure which Kitchener had been advocating for some time) and replaced by his more amenable uncle Hussein with the title of Sultan. Unfortunately Hussein, who had co-operated with the British in every way throughout the war, died in 1917 and was succeeded by his brother Fuad, destined to become the first King of modern Egypt.

The Turkish threat to Egypt was lifted in August 1916 by the British

PROCLAMATION

The following proclamation is contained in a special edition of the "Journal Officiel":—

His Britannic Majesty's Secretary of State for Foreign Affairs gives notice that, in view of the state of war arising out of the action of Turkey, Egypt is placed under the Protection of His Majesty and will henceforth constitute a British Protectorate.

The Suzerainty of Turkey over Egypt is thus terminated, and His Majesty's Government will adopt all measures necessary for the defence of Egypt, and protect its inhabitants and interests.

Cairo, December 18, 1914.

PROCLAMATION

PROCLAMATION.

A supplement of the *Journal Officiel* was published to-day containing the following proclamation :

His Britanic Majesty's Secretary of State for Foreign Affairs gives notice that, in view of the action of His Highness Abbas Hilmi Pasha, lately Khedive of Egypt, who has adhered to the King's enemies, His Majesty's Government have seen fit to depose him from the Khediviate, and that high dignity has been offered, with the title of Sultan of Egypt, to His Highness Prince Hussein Kamel Pasha, eldest living Prince of the family of Mohammed Ali, and has been accepted by Him.

Cairo, December 19, 1914.

THE SULTAN OF EGYPT.

G.C.B. CONFERRED UPON HIS SERENE HIGHNESS.

London, Saturday.
The King has conferred on Sultan of Egypt the Grand Cross of the Bath on his accession to the Sultanate. Reuter.

victory at the Battle of Romani about twenty miles to the east of the Suez Canal but as the war progressed, often unfavourably for the Allies, and shortages of manpower and material developed, the Egyptians, who had been promised a neutral role provided they behaved themselves (which they did), found their young men being pressed into service in a Labour Corps and their animals requisitioned for military transport. Hundreds of thousands of men (turnover was rapid as the term of service was three to six months) were conscripted, often by corrupt methods implemented for profit by village *omdahs*. The Camel Transport Corps alone required no fewer than 70,000 camels for its task of supplying the British and Imperial forces in the Sinai and Palestine campaigns.

Under its intrepid commander, Colonel Charles Whittingham, a former Grenadier Guards sergeant with an unrivalled knowledge of camel management acquired as an officer of the Sudan's paramilitary Anti-Slavery Department, this Corps played a vital part in supplying the EEF in Allenby's campaigns, perhaps the last major military operations to be sustained almost entirely by animal transport. Most of its

British officers of the Egyptian Labour Corps at Kantara in 1916.

officers were British nationals resident in Egypt with some knowledge of Arabic and commissioned 'for the duration' while the drivers were fellahin, theoretically volunteers, on six-monthly contracts.[2]

In his books *The Transit of Egypt* and *Egypt and the Army*, Lieutenant Colonel P. G. Elgood, a soldier and administrator of long experience in Egypt, has amply exposed the heavy hand of military government and the evils and iniquities of the system of conscription (known as 'compulsory volunteering') and requisition, which, together with inflation and inflamed by nationalist rhetoric, were the root causes of the anti-British violence which erupted soon after the war. At the same time there was much talk, particularly on the part of President Wilson of the USA during the Versailles negotiations, of 'independence' for small nations.

At the end of his Preface to *The Transit of Egypt*, Elgood wrote: 'And lastly I venture to add that my affection for Egypt is second only to my love for Great Britain.' He died in 1941 but his widow, Bonte, a doctor, outlived him by many years. Her sentiments were the same, indeed, she might even have put it the other way round, so it is a sad irony that at the time of the Suez crisis in 1956 she was arrested by Nasser's Gestapo (el Mabahiz), flung into a dungeon with prostitutes and other female malefactors and unceremoniously deported.

Major C. S. Jarvis, however, who served in the EEF during the war and, as we have seen, later joined the Frontiers Administration, took a rather different view. He pointed out that many sections of Egyptian society benefited handsomely from the war. The hundreds of thousands of British and Imperial troops who poured into or transited through Egypt for the Gallipoli. Salonika and Palestine campaigns, spent as lavishly as their pay and allowances permitted and the purchase locally of their requirements of food, fodder and other supplies enriched many traders and merchants. Jarvis has one camel contractor explaining apologetically. 'They brought me one day to Ismailieh and demanded from me thousands of camels at £35 per head and next day another general at Suez ordered me to buy every camel captured from the Turks at £10 per head. I bought the camels one day at Suez and sold them the next day at Ismailieh with a £25 profit. Wallahi, I am a friend of the Ingleez and did not wish for more than £20 profit but they insisted. What could I do?' [3]

Means and methods of transport may change but echoes of the easy pickings to be gleaned from the British military in the Middle East reverberate down the years.

In 1997 the Household Cavalry Regiment took part in Exercise Bright Star in the Western Desert (an indication, incidentally, of the excellent relations obtaining between the Lion and the Sphinx nowadays) involving a multi-national force designed to protect Egypt from an unspecified but neighbouring aggressor. 'It was great fun working with the Egyptians,' wrote the CO of the Household Cavalry, 'but it did take them and us a little time to understand each other's modus operandi. An example of this concerned the contract we let for transport. On our final recce in July we had turned down a bid to provide this tendered by a firm of contractors not unconnected to Egyptian Military Intelligence. We found a cheaper and better firm and returned to England smugly thinking we had been rather clever. It was not to be. When the advance party arrived at Cairo Military Airport it was met by a senior officer from Military Intelligence who smilingly informed us that, very regrettably, this new firm we had found did not meet military security requirements. If we wished to leave the airport we would have to sign a new contract with the Military Intelligence contractors and at a greatly inflated price!' [4]

Probably it is fair to say that both Elgood and Jarvis were right up to a point and that the principal beneficiaries of British military needs (and/or extravagances) were the commercial middle-classes, many of them foreign, rather than the fellahin. Thus, as is so often the case, the heaviest burden had fallen upon those least able to bear it.

Nor was British popularity improved by the behaviour of its war-time soldiery, especially the large Australian contingent of which Lord Edward Cecil wrote, 'The Australians are wonderful fighters but unattractive in other ways ... They must be very like Nelson's sailors. They are hopelessly insubordinate, drink like fish and have a strong criminal tendency – but they are men.'[5]

The pre-war Army of Occupation had been small and, although occasionally boisterous, well, indeed sternly, disciplined. Not so the vast hoard of newcomers, the stories of whose antics, often brutal and violent, are legion but few worth repeating. It is hard, for example, to share C. S. Jarvis's apparent amusement at an Australian soldier knocking down an Egyptian servant for the crime of being a Moslem on Christmas Day.[6]

Most people, especially those whose involvement in a war is involuntary, like to be on the winning side and news of Allied setbacks at Gallipoli and in France (both theatres in which Egyptian labourers were forced to serve) did little to enhance British prestige. The attitude of most Egyptians to the protagonists in both World Wars was probably one of 'A plague on both your houses!' as borne out by a conversation overheard on a railway station in 1918 by Lawrence Grafftey-Smith. One Egyptian asked another who was the better, the English or the Germans to which the reply was, '*El etnain awlad kelab!*' – 'They are both the sons of dogs!'[7] However, Lord Edward Cecil claimed, probably with some truth, that 'No one, however silly, wants to change us for the Turks.'[8]

Be that as it may, although the British won the war perhaps they did not seem as invincible as they had been before it started and the prospect of rising up against them in 1919 not quite as daunting as it might have been in 1909.

At the end of 1916 General Sir Reginald Wingate, Sirdar of the Egyptian Army and Governor-General of the Sudan, replaced Sir Henry McMahon as High Commissioner in Egypt and few men were better qualified for the job. He had been closely involved with Egypt since first he joined the Egyptian Army in 1882. As Kitchener's Director of Intelligence he had played an important role in the re-conquest of the Sudan and, as we have seen in an earlier chapter, skilfully dealt with a potentially explosive situation within a few days of his arrival in Khartoum as Governor-General in 1900. Thereafter he continued to guide the Sudan into the twentieth century with a sure and steady hand for the next sixteen years.

He spoke fluent Arabic and was acquainted with all the leading royal, political and administrative personalities of Egypt. He was a man who believed in a subtle mixture of firmness and conciliation and his advice to the British Government soon after the Armistice that they should receive the nationalist leader Saad Zaghloul, as part of a delegation to London to discuss Egyptian independence, was sound, although it was to bring an end to his career.

Wingate has been ill served by posterity and today the name is associated in most people's minds only with the eccentric Chindit commander of the Second World War (a cousin). Of his two biographies one is an uncritical work of hagiography by his son while the other damns him with faint praise – if, indeed, any praise can be found in its lifeless pages. It is couched in terms of scantily veiled hostility and refuses to admit of any action on his part which was not motivated by self-interest and/or financial necessity. At a time when British politics and diplomacy were still largely the prerogative of the upper classes, Wingate was handicapped by his *petit bourgeois* origin. His father, a Lowland Scot in the textile business, having spawned a family of eleven children, died in early middle age leaving Reginald and his siblings to be brought up in genteel poverty. A short, tubby man, feelings of social insecurity manifested themselves in a rigid adherence to convention in which he was encouraged by his wife, Although, on the whole, he was popular with his staff to whom he was known as the Master, grandees like Lord Edward Cecil liked to bait the Wingates by, for example, upsetting dinner-party protocol at the Residency. On one occasion, Lord Edward, instead of escorting a lady of exalted rank into dinner as instructed, gave his noble arm to the pretty young wife of a railway official to the alarm and confusion of the assembled company, most notably the host and hostess.[9]

Similarly it may be conjectured that Lord Curzon, that 'very superior person' at the Foreign Office, would not have treated Wingate in such a cavalier manner when he was recalled to London 'for consultations' in January 1919 by refusing to see him for a fortnight had he regarded him as a social equal.

However, by the time Wingate was summoned, the Government may well have already decided to dismiss him for what it saw as his weakness in dealing with Egyptian nationalism, which, having kept him dangling for months, it did in a particularly shabby manner, even to the extent of trying to cheat him out of part of his salary.[10]

After recovering from the initial shock and bitterness of his dismissal, Wingate seems to have accepted his lot philosophically. In December 1924, having already embarked upon a successful business career, he wrote to his old chief Field Marshal Lord Grenfell:

> Since my severance with Egypt and the Sudan some five years ago, no communications have passed between any of the Government Offices and myself. I think there is nothing unusual in this and I gather it is the

invariable custom of HMG to avoid reference to previous holders of high office abroad on the grounds that it may add to the difficulties of 'the man on the spot'. I remember writing to Cromer from Khartoum a few months before his death, saying how thankful I was he was at hand in London to explain to HMG the intricacies of the Sudan situation and the reasons for my advance into Darfur. To my great surprise he wrote 'It is now eight years since I landed in England from Egypt and during the whole of that time I have never been consulted by HMG on Egyptian or Sudan affairs!'

Wingate goes on to say:

> I am pestered with requests for information articles, books etc on Egypt and the Sudan by pressmen, magazine and book publishers etc. etc. – but I tell them all that I will not be interviewed nor shall I be induced to make a public statement at present.
>
> I wish to do nothing to hamper a Government which is composed of good and loyal men doing their utmost to serve their country – and for me at such a juncture to begin a campaign of 'I told you so' – and 'Why didn't you listen to the man on the spot who had had 35 years experience at his back' – would be a disservice and an unpatriotic act.[11]

While Wingate kicked his heels in Britain Field Marshal Viscount Allenby was appointed Special High Commissioner to Egypt, an appointment which was confirmed in October 1919 thus officially bringing Wingate's pro-consulship and, indeed, his public career, to an end.

Of all the British pro-consuls appointed to Egypt perhaps, on the face of it, the least suitable was Allenby.

He was one of the few generals on either side to emerge from the Great War with his reputation in credit. Although he had been no more (or less) successful on the Western Front than the other Army Commanders, he had had the good fortune to be appointed to command the British and Imperial forces in the Palestine and Syrian campaigns of 1917–18. The circumstances and the terrain allowed for relatively open and fluid operations which suited his skills as a cavalry tactician and he was well served by some able subordinates. Thus he was able to defeat the demoralised and outnumbered Turks with (by First World War standards) a small 'butcher's bill', earning the gratitude of the Prime Minister. Lloyd George, and his Coalition Government. Therefore, once confidence in Wingate had been lost, Lloyd George turned to his favourite general to keep the lid on the Egyptian cauldron while he and many of his senior cabinet colleagues were preoccupied with the Versailles Treaty negotiations.

Unfortunately it was to prove that Allenby lacked the subtlety and experience of civilian administration and the diplomacy to cope with the twists and turns of Egyptian political manoeuvring.[12] 'The Egyptian loves bargaining,' wrote his successor, Lord Lloyd, 'he approaches it with the glint of confidence in his eyes, watches his opponent with rapt attention and. like the natural poker player, has an uncanny instinct in detecting from the slightest movement or expression the innermost thoughts of his adversary.' Allenby was ill-equipped to cope with this national characteristic. However, like most senior British officials of his generation, he held a Joker in his hand. So dominant and successful had the British been as a world power for the best part of a century up to 1914, that it was widely believed, especially in what we now know as the Third World, that 'behind every guileless and even stupid British exterior there lurks an unfathomable cunning'.[13]

A generation earlier the great Nubar Pasha had seen the British character from a slightly different but equally disconcerting perspective. Loosely translated from the French, he is reputed to have remarked, 'The Englishman is naive; but just when you think you've fooled him. he turns round and gives you a terrific kick in the backside!'[14] These fears sometimes prevented an opponent, wary of a Machiavellian trap, from exploiting a diplomatic, political or even military weakness. To some extent this may account for Saad Zaghloul's failure to take affirmative and co-operative advantage of Allenby's goodwill.

Alexander Keown-Boyd, who met Allenby first in Jerusalem in 1918 and was later to become his Oriental Secretary at the Cairo Residency, did not 'think him to be a genius or even a man of outstanding brain power but he is quick, prompt, very much alive and very energetic.'[15] This was not enough and his failure either to control or come to terms with Zagloul, who, in turn, was to lose control over some of his extremist followers, led to tragedy and, in effect, an end to the careers of both men.

Allenby is perhaps best remembered for his ferocious temper and explosions of, usually short-lived, rage over trivialities, which earned him the nickname, the Bull. For example, he would not tolerate military abbreviations and on one occasion in Palestine two RAF pilots were wheeled in to be congratulated for their excellent reconnaissance work. When asked to which major unit they belonged the senior of the two replied, '5 Cav Div, sir,' whereupon Allenby's face assumed a purple hue and he bellowed, '5 Cav Div! 5 Cav Div! There is no such formation – if you mean the Fifth Cavalry Division, bloody well say so! Get out!' When one of his staff, accustomed to this kind of thing, pointed out that the men had been brought in to be congratulated and perhaps recommended for decorations, he had them recalled and carried on a pleasant and friendly conversation with them for some minutes.[16]

Nor was his first encounter with the Cairo Residency staff auspicious. 'On the evening of his arrival on 25 March 1919,' wrote Lawrence Grafftey-Smith, 'John Cecil took in some papers for him to sign. Something displeased Allenby and Cecil was all but blasted out of the room. He stood his ground. "I don't like your tone, sir," he said. "This is a Foreign Office Mission, not a camp ..." A very great man apologised and his relations with his staff were instantly courteous and soon affectionate.' [17]

He also possessed a somewhat sardonic sense of humour. One day, it seems, he was carrying out a dismounted inspection of a cavalry regiment which had once been under his command. He stopped in front of a particularly old soldier but no spark of recognition passed between Field Marshal and Trooper. Turning to the colonel, he enquired, 'Tell me, do all your men wear socks?' Falling headlong into the trap the colonel replied, 'Why yes, of course they do, sir!' 'Then tell this man to take one of his boots off,' ordered Allenby. Needless to say the removal of the boot revealed a gnarled, grubby and sockless foot and the Great Man passed on without a word. Afterwards in the Mess the colonel rather nervously enquired, 'How on earth did you know that man wasn't wearing socks, sir?' 'Hah! Caught you out there, didn't I! The fellow was my batman when I was commanding the Regiment and he never wore socks – at least I guessed he didn't because he never pinched any of mine!' [18]

There was in him, however, an unexpectedly liberal streak, which tended to take allies and opponents alike by surprise. Within (and sometimes outside) the parameters set by his masters in London he genuinely tried to accommodate Egyptian patriotic aspirations and towards the end of his life, perhaps scenting the renewed horror of global war, he became the improbable advocate of world government and an international police force.[19]

But perhaps his most marked characteristic was his tenacity and firmness of purpose and, for better or for worse, it was Allenby, in the teeth of opposition from both the Egyptian political establishment and a strong group (led by Churchill) within the British Cabinet, who forced through the unilateral Declaration of Egyptian Independence in 1922.

In Wingate's absence and before Allenby's arrival, alarmed by Zagloul's Anglophobic rantings, the senior British official in Egypt, Sir Milne Cheetham, had him and several of his supporters deported to Malta. Whether the combustion which followed was spontaneous or planned it is hard to say but it was certainly sparked by the deportation and no such level of violence had been seen in Egypt since Orabi's coup of thirty-seven years before.

CHAPTER 9

Revolution

THE SO CALLED EGYPTIAN REVOLUTION of 1919 was short and bloody. The revolutionaries, uncoordinated and without strategic or even tactical leadership, chose an unpropitious time to revolt in that there were still tens of thousands of British and Imperial troops in the country. Nevertheless, the martial law authorities seem to have been taken by surprise and it was several days before they were able to organise effectively the means of its suppression. During that time a number of appalling outrages were perpetrated by frenzied mobs and gangs of hooligans.

With the deportation of Zaghloul and others to Malta on 8 March 1919, the students took to the streets of Cairo and Alexandria, waving banners calling for independence and the return of their hero and displaying photographs of the Denshawi 'martyrs'. They were soon joined by a rabble bent on pillage and looting rather than political demonstration. Strikes were called and the trouble spread rapidly to the provinces, involving the usually passive fellahin and even the Bedouin of the desert. It was in Upper and Middle Egypt that the situation was at its most dangerous for Europeans as there were fewer troops in that area than in the Delta.

Paradoxically, one of the calmest areas was the province of Menufiya, scene of the notorious Denshawi incident thirteen years earlier. According to Colonel Elgood, 'Major A. Wise, a cool and resolute inspector of the interior at one end and the Reverend W. W. Cash at the other, kept a semblance of tranquillity through the length and breadth of a province notorious for lawlessness.' [1]

The role of Mr Cash is unclear but Wise Bey was a well-known and popular figure in the Sudan and Egypt for over half a century. Of Anglo-Irish stock, he was commissioned in the Connaught Rangers, passing out of Sandhurst in the same year as Winston Churchill and with better marks! After the Boer War, in which he was severely wounded, he joined the Egyptian Army in 1904 and served, principally

Allenby and Zaghloul in conversation.

with the Camel Corps, in various parts of the Sudan until 1913, taking part in operations against disaffected tribes in the Nuba Mountains and Sennar Province. On one occasion he suffered the embarrassment of having to charge one of his men with spitting at the famous Slatin Pasha.[2] When asked why he had done this, the culprit replied that he could not respect a man who had changed his religion to save his skin. Once Slatin had departed Wise quietly dropped the charge.

During the First World War he served under Colonel Clayton in the Arab Bureau and joined the Egyptian Civil Service in 1918. By 1922, when his post was 'Egyptianised', he had risen to the rank of Inspector-General of the Provincial Police. On retirement from public service, for many years he was Secretary to the Egyptian Association of British Manufacturers but in 1956 he and his wife, in common with most British citizens, were expelled from Egypt with one suitcase, leaving behind the accumulated possessions of a lifetime. He died in 1973 aged ninety-eight.[3]

On 17 March General Bulfin, a tough, no-nonsense Irishman, was brought from his command in Syria to take charge of a deteriorating situation. The most useful military unit at his disposal was an Anzac mounted division out of which he quickly formed mobile columns to deal with the worst trouble spots.

Egyptian State Railways, which was under direct British Management (until 1924 the General Manager was an officer of the Royal Engineers), and its passengers were particular targets of the mob. There were two hundred incidents of line wrecking and over sixty stations were destroyed or damaged.

On the morning of 18 March 1919 two British officers, Major Cecil Jarvis DSO MC [4] and Lieutenant Frank Willby, and five NCOs boarded the train at Luxor to return to Cairo from leave. For reasons unexplained they were unarmed (later even civilians were issued with revolvers) – perhaps the victims of some fatuous local Standing Order or War Office regulation governing the carrying and use of weapons which have cost the lives of so many British soldiers over the years, not least in Northern Ireland in more recent times.

At Assiut they were joined by a British official of the Prison Service, Alexander Pope Bey and his Egyptian *mamour* (assistant), Rifaat Hafiz Effendi. The trouble started two stations later at Benni Korra when a train coming from the north discharged a horde of ruffians who swarmed all over the train carrying Pope and the soldiers, shouting, 'Where are the English?' The exact sequence of events is unclear but, by one means or another, Hafiz and an Egyptian railway employee managed to get all the British into one 1st class carriage, closed the doors and shutters and urged Pope to disguise himself as a woman, or at least to wear a *tarboosh* (fez), which he refused to do. Then Hafiz, evidently a man of great courage and loyalty, stood at the door and tried to persuade the mob that there was only his wife in the compartment. When this failed, he shouted to them that Pope was not an Englishman but a Syrian. This too had no effect and he was knocked out of the way while Pope was dragged out onto the platform and beaten to death.

Meanwhile the soldiers defended themselves desperately with bottles and pieces of luggage; some seem to have managed to escape from the compartment but by the time the train reached Dairut all had been hunted down and killed or mortally wounded and their bodies hideously mutilated before being thrown naked into the brake-van. A witness recorded seeing one of the victim's legs being cut off and the drinking of the blood of another. A dying man's mouth was stuffed with earth.

Further up the line there was a curious and rather moving incident. At Mellawi the body of one of the soldiers was dragged from the train and subjected to nameless horrors and humiliations but a prostitute called Hanem Aaref pressed forward and tried to protect him and wipe the blood from his face until she was beaten and driven off by the mob.

When, in due course, news of her courage and compassion reached the investigators of the murders she was found to be in prison for some minor offence. She was released and a collection was made for her at the Turf Club, raising the princely sum of £E92.50. A missionary lady, Sister Margaret, was deputed to bring her to Cairo and discover what she wanted done with the money. Taken to the Muski (bazaar) she eventually chose gold bracelets. Sister Margaret explains why.

> I suggested she might like a gold necklace for the sake of variety, but she explained to me it would not do. If you have a dispute with your friends the first thing they do is to clutch at your neck: they might break the necklace and they might also strangle you, whereas heavy gold fetters on your arm make it a formidable fighting weapon!

One of the bracelets was engraved: 'To Hanem Aaref. A gift of the English in recognition of her compassion towards a dying British soldier on the 18th of March 1919.'

The story has a happy ending. Two years later the good Sister learnt that Hanem had abandoned the oldest profession in the world and was married.[5]

It is a bitter irony that these soldiers, who had survived the bloodiest war in history, and, at least in the case of Major Jarvis, had served with highly decorated distinction, should have perished so miserably at the hands of a civilian mob.

On the day of their deaths they were buried in the Greek Cemetery at Minieh but later disinterred and laid to rest, appropriately, in the Cairo War Memorial Cemetery.

But theirs were not the only deaths on a train during these violent times. At Beni Suef station another train was attacked and a railway workshop inspector by the name of Smith butchered. More fortunate were Dick Graves of the Ministry of the Interior and an unnamed American woman tourist (for whom Graves had developed a strong dislike) who were travelling in another part of the train. 'Graves and the lady climbed out onto the track and were hustled by a heroic little ticket-collector into a stores shed and there locked in,' wrote Lawrence Grafftey-Smith. '... The ticket-collector swore the oath of divorce that the shed was empty and the key long lost: but the mob thrust their blades through the woodwork, just on chance, and those inside had some bad moments.'[6]

At Assiut the British and other foreign residents took refuge in a bank where they were besieged by armed attackers but gallantly defended by a small detachment of Punjabi infantry. Holding out for several days and running out of ammunition they were relieved by one of Bulfin's columns on 25 March.

On 2 April an editorial in *The Times* complained of censorship of the news from Egypt and it was not until the 3rd that the first report of the atrocities on the train from Luxor appeared in its columns followed by a fuller account on the 7th.

Much, of course, was made of British casualties but little was heard of the unfortunate Greek, Armenian and other, usually Christian or Jewish, minorities who, as shopkeepers, small traders and sometimes moneylenders, were so often the easy and defenceless targets of the mob. Accurate figures are not to be found but probably hundreds were killed and injured or their livelihoods destroyed when their premises were sacked, There is a certain ironic truth in Roly's cruel cartoon of the Greek grocer 'who died for England's sake'.[7]

" *Greek grocers who die for England's sake* "

Many members of the lower middle-class minorities, Christian and Jewish, were targets for the mob during the 1919 Revolution.

Allenby did not arrive until 25 March by which time Bulfin had brought the situation more or less under control. Under Martial Law he had plenary powers and it was rumoured that he was about to confiscate the bank balances of certain wealthy Wafdists – a sobering prospect even for the most fervent supporter of independence. Better to remain rich under the British yoke than suffer poverty for the sake of freedom, they reasoned. Furthermore, they were mostly landowners and a Peasants' Revolt, which smacked of Bolshevism, was not really what they had in mind.[8] Perhaps the word was put out that Zaghloul and the other exiles would soon be released and, what with one thing and another, the time had come for law and order to return to the land. At the same time, Sultan (later King) Fuad issued a proclamation appealing to everyone to maintain calm and 'follow his customary occupation'.[9]

This was just as well for the British who had problems of their own. Most of the troops in Egypt were conscripts or wartime volunteers and anxious for home and demobilisation. Some pre-war trade unionists even refused to take over the jobs of Egyptian strikers in essential services so the sooner they were no longer needed the better.[10]

A number of explanations for the 1919 Revolution were offered and were probably most accurately summed up by Anonymous writing to *The Times* of 12 April. He suggested that the principal causes were:

1. The removal of General Maxwell (see below), who knew and understood Egypt and her people, as GOC in 1915.
2. Recruitment for the Egyptian Labour Corps.
3. Failure to provision the army from home and thereby forcing up the price of local products.
4. The folly of deporting Zaghloul – a blunder which neither Cromer nor Kitchener would have made.

Also through the medium of *The Times* these thoughts were supported by Coles Pasha, the former Director-General of Prisons. He too drew attention to the discontent caused by high prices and recruitment to the Labour Corps, adding, 'Years ago the late Lord Cromer found it was safer to have Zaghloul in the Ministry rather than leading the Opposition and possibly none of these troubles would have occurred had Zaghloul been given a portfolio early in the War.'[11]

Retribution came swiftly in the form of special tribunals (shades of Denshawi) set up under martial law but supervised by British civilian judges. 2,304 cases were heard resulting in 1,613 convictions and 102 death sentences of which 47 were carried out.[12] One of those executed was a student, a ringleader in the brutal train murders, recently returned to Egypt from Wye Agricultural College in England. By his last morning's post he received the prize as Wye's most promising student of his year![13]

Inevitably accusations of an excess of zeal were levelled at the security forces who, as everywhere else and in every period of history, were expected to bring murderous and destructive mobs under control without hurting anyone. They were damned if they reacted too mildly and damned if their measures were too harsh, but, on the whole, both the British military and the Egyptian police, under British officers, behaved with reasonable restraint and few of the charges against them were substantiated.

Lloyd George's Coalition Government, deeply involved in complicated international negotiations at Versailles, beset with post-war problems at home and faced with unrest in India and Ireland as well as Egypt, had been caught unawares by the upheavals there. Bulfin's stern measures could deal with the problem in the short term but beyond that ministers had no solutions and little time to think up any. They resorted, therefore, to that time-honoured and durable device – a committee of enquiry, which has the dual advantage of postponing the need for immediate decisions while being seen to be sensibly examining what those decisions might be. Ministers knew that they wished to retain their grip on Egypt but desired to know how best to do this without resorting to direct rule or annexation. Thus was born the Milner Mission.

Alfred, Lord Milner was the Colonial Secretary with no party affiliations and a strong belief in Britain's imperial mission. As High Commissioner in South Africa from 1897 to 1905 he championed the cause of the Transvaal Uitlanders (non-Boers) and has passed into history as the 'provocateur' of the Second Boer War. It was in South Africa that he met and fell in love with Violet Cecil (née Maxse) whom he married after Lord Edward's death. He had some Egyptian experience having served as Under-Secretary of Finance under Cromer, who held him in the highest regard, in the 1890s, as had two other members of his six-man Mission, General Sir John Maxwell and Sir Rennell Rodd.[14]

Maxwell had served for many years in the Egyptian Army, had commanded a brigade in Kitchener's Nile campaign of 1896–98 and, as GOC Egyptian Expeditionary Force 1914–15, had been, to all intents and purposes, military governor of Egypt during that period. In 1916 he had had to deal with the Easter Uprising in Ireland.[15] Rodd, for his part, had served under Cromer at the Cairo Agency as a young diplomat, had led the Rodd Mission to the Emperor Menelik of Abyssinia in 1897 and had been British Ambassador to Italy throughout the First World War.[16]

The other members were a distinguished lawyer, Sir Cecil Hurst, a leading liberal journalist, J. A. Spender, and a Labour MP, General Sir Owen Thomas.

Despite its heavyweight composition the Mission, which arrived in Egypt after many delays in December 1919, suffered from the disadvantage of a boycott by almost all Egyptians of any importance or standing. Zaghloul, who had been released from exile at Allenby's insistence, had installed himself in Paris with his acolytes (who, it seems, passed their idle hours boosting the fortunes of night-club hostesses) whence, out of reach of British authority, he dominated the Egyptian political scene.[17] For reasons which are far from clear Zaghloul had set his face against any co-operation with the Mission and, such was his influence over the population as a whole and the fear which his links with terrorism inspired, few dared gainsay him. However, through the good offices of the moderate Egyptian statesman, Adly Yeghen Pasha, he did hold meetings with members of the Mission in London during the summer of 1920 after their return from Egypt but these were inconclusive.

By the end of 1920 the Mission had completed its business as best it could and produced its report. This report was to form the basis of the 1922 Declaration of Independence forced through by Allenby in the February of that year in the teeth of opposition, not only from Zaghloul, who, being presented with a yard demanded a mile, but also from a divided British cabinet.

Subject to certain 'Reserve Points' martial law was to be lifted, the Protectorate terminated and Egypt was to achieve 'Independence'. Of course the reserve points and the degree of independence from British authority were the bones of contention. These were:

1. Security of communications of the British Empire in Egypt.
2. The defence of Egypt against all foreign aggression.
3. The protection of foreign interests in Egypt and the protection of minorities.
4. The Sudan.

The first two points involved the continued British military occupation of Egypt, the third British control over the Ministries of Justice and Interior and the fourth confirmed British determination that Egypt should have virtually no say in the administration of the Sudan.[18]

Early in 1920 Alexander Keown-Boyd, Oriental Secretary at the Residency and a former member of the Sudan Political Service, had been despatched to Khartoum to consult with the Governor-General, Sir Lee Stack, and prepare recommendations on the future of the Sudan for the Milner Mission. In essence his report, when submitted in March 1920, recommended that the Egyptian (as opposed to Sudanese) units of the Egyptian Army serving in the Sudan should return to Egypt and two battalions be disbanded; that all Egyptian officers should be withdrawn from Sudanese units and that a Sudanese Army should be formed under British and Sudanese officers.

As far as Egyptian civilian personnel were concerned Keown-Boyd's report recommended the replacement of Egyptian *mamours* with Sudanese; prohibition on the employment of any further 'Egyptian personnel in permanent posts'; expansion and enlargement of the Sudanese educational system to enable this policy to be carried out over a period.[19]

For obvious reasons these recommendations were not spelt out in discussion with the Egyptians nor, indeed, were Egyptian units removed from the Sudan until after the assassination of Sir Lee Stack in Cairo in 1924, which led to Allenby's punitive demands upon the Egyptian Government of which this withdrawal was one of the most important elements.

Thus, over a period of years, the Sudan was entirely 'de-Egyptianised', much to the satisfaction of the British and Sudanese but to the fury and frustration of almost all shades of Egyptian opinion, which clung doggedly but futilely to the belief that the Sudan was theirs and that they should rule it.

A year later Keown-Boyd addressed himself to the problem of implementing, or rather maintaining, the other three 'Reserve Points'. He knew, and it was a point of view which he held until the end of his life, that the presence of the British Army in Egypt, especially the Cairo and Alexandria garrisons, was the most visible, provocative and detested element of the British occupation. As an alternative to that presence, in a briefing to Allenby dated 21 October 1921, he urged 'everything possible should be done to strengthen Adly [Yeghen Pasha] and his class [the Turco-Egyptian aristocracy] and to weaken Zaghloul and his followers.' This achieved, then regular British troops might be replaced by a kind of gendarmerie, 2,000 strong and equipped with machine-guns, to be based in Cairo and Alexandria but with sufficient mobility to enable this force to be deployed wherever necessary throughout the country.[20]

It is perhaps fortunate that this recommendation did not find favour with the British Government as any such militia would have inevitably attracted to itself the semi-mythological opprobrium that is associated, in Irish nationalist folklore, with the Black and Tans.

Nevertheless, Keown-Boyd's influence upon Allenby was strong and his views on matters of internal security were, at that time, rather more hawkish than those of his chief. Nor did this influence diminish when he was transferred from the Residency to the Egyptian Government in 1922, briefly, as Director-General at the Ministry of Foreign Affairs and finally, for many years, as Director-General of the European Department of the Ministry of the Interior. This last appointment gave him practical, if not theoretical, control over the police and an unofficial network of sources of intelligence and information. One Egyptian historian has been quoted as giving the opinion that, during this period, 'Keown-Boyd virtually ruled Egypt through the police'.[21]

CHAPTER 10

Assassination

A SSASSINATION, in other words murder for political motives, has
played a significant and occasionally decisive role in world history.
Paradoxically, however, the consequences for good or evil of an assassination are often disproportionate, one way or the other, to the importance
of the victim.

For example, the assassination of President Kennedy, perhaps the
most sensational and controversial of modern times, has barely, so far
as we can judge, altered the course of history. On the other hand, the
murder of a relative nonentity, the Archduke Franz Ferdinand of
Austria, in 1914 was perhaps the most significant single act of violence
of the twentieth century. In a few seconds a nineteen-year-old Serbian
student, Gavrilo Princip, sparked a chain of events which led to the
two most devastating wars in history; the fall of three great European
dynasties; the re-drawing, twice in a generation, of the map of Europe
dividing the Continent into two separate ideological and economic
blocks.

To it also can be attributed indirectly the premature dissolution of
the British, French, Belgian, Dutch, Portuguese and Italian empires,
which has led to conflict, famine, disease and misery on an unprecedented
scale.

In the case of Egypt throughout her history assassination has been
almost commonplace. Some Egyptologists believe that Tutankhamoun
was murdered, so this phenomenon covers the widest spectrum of
personalities over a vast span of time – kings, presidents, prime ministers,
soldiers, policemen, civil servants, diplomats, foreign residents, tourists
and passers-by have all, at one time or another, met their deaths by the
assassin's bomb, bullet or dagger. In Egypt there is always someone
more extreme than the extremist: for example two of the British era's
leading sponsors of terrorism, Ahmed Maher and Nokrashi, themselves
perished at the hands of terrorists.

As far as the British were concerned the majority of such murders

were concentrated between the years 1919 and 1924. A police report,[1] compiled in 1946 and probably incomplete, lists thirty-four
assassination attempts on British subjects during those years of which
twelve were successful, most of the victims being chosen at random.
The successes included the murder of Warrant Officer Steel of the
Indian Army, which, about three years later, was to lead to the conviction
of the principal murder gang.[2]

The last and most prominent British victim of the period was Major
General (or, to give him his Egyptian rank, El Ferik) Sir Lee Stack
Pasha, Sirdar of the Egyptian Army and Governor General of the
Sudan, who was attacked by terrorists in Cairo on 19 November 1924
and died of his wounds on the following day – a sensational case with
far reaching consequences which will be examined in detail later.

Of course most murders in Egypt – about a thousand a year in the
1920s – had nothing to do with politics. Usually they resulted from
domestic disputes or feuds between families and were principally a
rural phenomenon.

In 1917 a New Zealander, Professor (later Sir) Sydney Smith, was
appointed Principal Medico-Legal Expert to the Egyptian Ministry of

El Ferik Sir Lee
Stack, the last
Sirdar of the
Egyptian Army, who
was assassinated in
Cairo in November
1924.

Justice and was attached to the Parquet or criminal investigation branch. He was to play an important, perhaps conclusive, part in the Stack case.[3]

The Egyptian criminal law (complicated by the Capitulations – see Appendix C) followed the French system based on the Code Napoleon. Thus, at least in theory, the Parquet supervised the police in the investigation of crime and was responsible for the interrogation of suspects and witnesses. However, the lines of demarcation between the two departments were rather blurred, frequently leading to controversy and misunderstanding.

Not only was Professor Smith a forensic expert but also he had acquired a good working knowledge of ballistics and possessed remarkable powers of deduction. Nor was he a man to hide his light under a bushel and one suspects that from to time he must have given cause for considerable irritation to his colleagues in the Parquet and the police.

Be that as it may, by 1923 he had been involved in hundreds of murder cases, many of a macabre and gruesome nature, but his name first came to prominence during the investigation into the murder of a rich Alexandrian called Tewfik Karam: a 'society' murder which, unlike most sordid village killings, excited the imagination of the educated classes. This case is recounted here, not simply for its own sake, but to illustrate the importance of Smith's forensic work in the solving of crime in Egypt, both political and otherwise.

As no *procès verbal* or other official account of this case is to be found, the reader should bear in mind that the following narrative relies principally on the memoirs of Professor Smith, written thirty-five years after the event and no doubt lacking some details and inaccurate in others. Other participants, had they cared to record their versions, might have given us a different point of view.

On the morning of 15 January 1923 Karam was found dead on the floor of his bedroom by his wife, Linda. He had been beaten about the head with an iron bar, which was found at the scene, and shot through the head with a revolver, which was not. There were signs of a struggle and the keys to his safe, which he usually kept under his pillow at night, were lying in the middle of the bed.

According to Smith the other occupants of the house were Tewfik's brother and sister-in-law (who are simply mentioned but play no role in his account) and a maid called Katina. Surviving acquaintances of the Karam family believe that Tewfik and Linda's two young children and probably a nanny must have been in the house at the time of the murder but they are not mentioned by Smith. Linda was much younger than Tewfik and was known to have a lover, who had been at a party in the house that same night.

The investigating officers found a hole in an outside door, which would have enabled an intruder to draw back the bolts and enter the house. Also the bell and telephone wires had been cut but as some fragments which came from the hole in the door were found on the outside and as the bell wires were rather inaccessible, requiring, in the opinion of the police and Parquet, a knowledge of their whereabouts, the detectives deduced that this was an inside job. Nor was anything of value missing, adding weight to this theory, and, inevitably, suspicion fell on Linda Karam.

Meanwhile Professor Smith's department had carried out a post mortem on the body and had examined the iron bar with which Karam had been attacked, concluding that it was a burglar's jemmy. It seems curious that the police did not come to the same conclusion, unless they believed the weapon had been obtained specifically for this crime by Linda, her lover and/or whoever had committed the murder on her behalf.

On visiting the house Smith decided that the hole in the door, contrary to the police theory, had been made from the outside (he does not say why). Furthermore, he found 'professional touches' to the way in which the wires had been cut and in the absence of fingerprints in the relevant places. Not an inside job, he told the doubtless exasperated officers of the police and Parquet, and proceeded to reconstruct the crime for them.

'Two professional burglars,' he explained patiently, 'broke in by drilling through the door. Somehow they had obtained an intimate knowledge of the house and they cut the telephone and bell connections. Then they went to an antechamber and tried to open the safe. Unable to do this they went to Karam's bedroom and tried to abstract the key from under his pillow. He woke, jumped up and tried to ring for help. One of the burglars struck him three or four times with the jemmy in an attempt to stun him. He managed to jump out of bed, entangling himself in the mosquito net and probably yelled for help. At that moment ... the other burglar shot him from the side at close range. Alarmed by the noise both burglars ran away.'

The police objected. Why did nobody hear the shot? Linda Karam and her maid claimed to have been woken at three or four in the morning by what sounded like a window-shutter banging in the wind and gone to sleep again. The police did not believe them (the maid was suspected of being privy to the plot) but Smith managed to prove, apparently to everyone's satisfaction, that a shot could sound like a banging window and his theory was accepted.

Now Linda Karam offered a £E2,000 reward for information leading to the arrest of the murderers and the advertisement was seen by a

French tart called Henriette who went to the police. It is not clear what excited her suspicions but she told them that her pimp, a German, had a friend, also German, known as Ferid Merkel, alias Fritz Doelitzsch, who shared a room with a third German, Klaus Chefer, alias Hermann Klauss. By the time Henriette had gathered enough incriminating information about these men to give good cause to the police to search their room they had disappeared. However, the contents of the room revealed that the men, merchant seamen by legitimate trade, were also professional burglars. Above all, Smith's forensic tests linked some fragments of wood and other debris found on a pair of gloves and in the pockets of their clothes to the Karams' door.

Meanwhile Klauss had signed on a ship and sailed for India whence he was eventually extradited – but not before the wrong man whose name happened to be Klausen had been brought to Egypt and then, no doubt apologetically, returned to India!

At about the same time Doelitzsch had sailed for Germany but his ship had called at Trieste where he was arrested and brought back to Egypt.

Under the terms of the Capitulations the trial was conducted in Cairo by German judges under German law. Smith's reconstruction of the crime was re-enacted in court and both men confessed to being implicated but blamed each other for the fatal shot. The prosecution demanded the death penalty on the grounds of premeditation. This could not be proven, nor was it certain who had fired (it was probably Klauss) and they were condemned to penal servitude for life.

While it is undeniable that Klauss and Doelitzsch were the actual perpetrators, Alexandrian society never accepted the verdict at its face value and to this day there are those who believe that the two Germans were hired hit men. Certainly there are many unanswered questions, for example, how did they acquire their knowledge of the geography of the house and why should they have assumed, without prior briefing, that Karam kept his keys under his pillow? On the other hand, it is unlikely that two such ruffians would have gone to prison for life without implicating their paymaster – or paymistress.[4]

In 1915 a young terrorist called Mohamed Neguib el Helbawi threw a bomb at the Sultan Hussein. It failed to explode and the Sultan was uninjured but Helbawi and an accomplice, Mohamed Shams el Din, were arrested, tried and sentenced to death. Another suspect in the case was one Mahmud Enayat but he died before being arrested. The sentences were commuted to life imprisonment and the pair toiled in the sweltering quarries of Tura Prison until 1924 when they were released under an amnesty.

The Special Branch of the Egyptian Police (known as the Zapt) knew that Helbawi, Shams el Din and the late Enayat were 'foot-soldiers' in a gang which had originated with the assassination in 1910 of the then Prime Minister, Sami Boutros Ghali, but which, in common with many other terrorist organisations before and since, went under a number of different names.

At its core was a lawyer by the name of Shafik Mansur who was closely connected with a number of Wafdist (followers of Saad Zaghloul) politicians, the most senior of whom were Ahmed Maher (a son of the Maher of the Frontier Incident), the Minister of Education, and Mahmoud Fehmy el Nokrashi, an Under Secretary in the Ministry of the Interior. Although the police were convinced that this gang had carried out most of the political murders since 1919, including those of two anti-Saadists, Ismail Zuhdi and Abdel Ragib Pasha, hard evidence was difficult to come by and their investigations were often trammelled by strategically placed Wafdist politicians and sympathisers in the civil service.

There were, however, a number of dedicated Egyptian civil servants and police officers who saw it as their duty to track down and bring to justice the perpetrators of political crime, just as they would ordinary criminals, regardless of their motives or political consequences. Among such men were Hassan Rifaat, Director-General of Public Security, and Yuzbashi (Captain) Selim Zaki of the Special Branch, the latter being a man not only of considerable shrewdness but of great courage. He himself had been the target of terrorist attack more than once. In December 1919 he had been travelling in a car with a leading politician. Youssef Wahba Pasha, when a medical student called Irian Youssef threw two bombs at them in Sharia Suliman Pasha, one of the main streets of Cairo.

The bombs either failed to explode or did little damage but, in any case, Zaki sprang from the car, pursued the bomber and arrested and disarmed him single-handed. The terrorist was eventually sentenced to ten years' penal servitude.

Zaki had kept in touch with Helbawi and came to realise that his resentment was directed, not at the authorities who had sent him to the quarries, but at the political puppet-masters who had persuaded him to attempt the assassination. Zaki must also have recognised in the ex-convict a strong mercenary streak and considerable courage and intelligence to go with it. Above all his former co-conspirators would have no reason to distrust him so long as he and his handlers behaved with the utmost discretion. In other words, Helbawi possessed all the necessary characteristics of the ideal police informer.

All this Zaki discussed with his superior officers, Kaimakam Douglas

Baker and the Assistant Commandant Cairo City Police, Kaimakam Alexander Gordon Ingram. Ingram was a Canadian Scot who had served in the British Army in the Boer War and had joined the Egyptian Police as a Constable in 1903. He spoke fluent colloquial Arabic and being of dark complexion would sometimes disguise himself, with varying degrees of success, as an Egyptian.

Presumably with the approval of the relevant British officials of the Ministry of Interior and Parquet, it was agreed that Helbawi, in return for infiltrating himself back into the terrorist underworld, would receive a retainer of £E30 per month, a princely sum for a penniless ex-convict.

This arrangement had been in place for some months, miraculously without reaching Wahfdist ears but also without tangible result, when El Ferik Sir Lee Stack Pasha was shot and mortally wounded on 19 November 1924.[5]

Lee Oliver Fitzmaurice Stack, the son of a colonial police officer, was born in 1868 and commissioned in the Border Regiment in 1889. In 1898 he was appointed to the staff of the international force which occupied Crete.

In the following year he joined the Egyptian Army on the usual two-year renewable contract and was to remain in the Egyptian service for the rest of his career – indeed, for the rest of his life.

His only active command was that of the Shambe Field Force, a punitive expedition against a section of the Dinka tribe in the Bahr el Ghazal Province of the Sudan in 1902 (see Appendix E). Members of this tribe had murdered a British District Inspector, Bimbashi Scott-Barbour, and a number of his men. Stack carried out his mission with a balance of ruthlessness and restraint which impressed the Governor-General, Wingate, and he was marked for promotion.

In 1913 he was appointed Civil Secretary, in effect chief executive, of the Sudan Government and when Wingate was transferred to Egypt at the end of 1916 he stepped into his shoes as Acting Sirdar of the Egyptian Army and Governor-General of the Sudan, which appointment was confirmed three years later.[6]

He was an able administrator and, by all accounts, a charming and popular man with many friends in all the various national communities of Egypt and the Sudan. However, at the same time he symbolised British control over both the Egyptian Army and that coveted prize of Egyptian nationalism, the Sudan.

At about one o'clock in the afternoon of 19 November a hired Cadillac driven by Fred March, a former Australian soldier, arrived at the War Office in Cairo to take Stack and his ADC, Bimbashi Patrick Campbell of the Black Watch and Egyptian Army, to lunch at the Sirdaria (the Sirdar's house). Twenty minutes later they ran into a traffic jam on the corner of Sharia Kasr el Aini at a point where the terrorists had anticipated that the car would be brought to a standstill and were mingling with the lunchtime crowds. There were six in the gang, which consisted of two younger brothers of the late Mahmud Enayat, the students Abdel Fatteh and Abdel Hamid; Mahmoud Rashid, a clerk; Rageb Hassan of the Telephone Administration; and two railway work-shop artisans, Ibrahim Musa and Ali Mohamed Ibrahim. Campbell takes up the story:

> No sooner had the motor car turned the corner than the first shots were fired. The occupants of the car being unarmed the only chance was to get away with the greatest possible speed. As soon as the first shots were fired March without a moment's hesitation changed down into second speed and at the same time called back to me saying, 'I'm hit'. To avoid being brought to a standstill by the carts and people immediately in front which would have been fatal, March swerved sharply to the left, displaying in a moment of intense excitement marked skill in driving his car through a mass of traffic. The car was an eight-cylinder Cadillac and considerable pressure was required to put out the clutch to change gear and the steering is not light. During the time the above manoeuvres were being carried out March was continuously shot at and in spite of the fact that he was wounded in the leg and arm, displayed the greatest courage and resource.

A bomb was also thrown which, although it hit the car, did not explode. Two policemen were wounded, Shawish (Sergeant) Abdel Maguid, as he got off a tram and Nafar (Private) Mohamed Abdel Gawad of the Cairo Guard Company who, it was thought, had attempted to arrest one of the gunmen. Two Englishmen on a motorcycle, Messrs Long and Wade, both officials at the Ministry of Public Works, were fired on but managed to take the number, 688, of a waiting taxi in which some of the terrorists made their escape and reported it to a British constable. The taxi was found within hours and the driver, a Berberi from Wadi Halfa called Mahmud Saleh, arrested. This led, briefly, to the suspicion that the assailants might have been dissident Sudanese, a theory soon discarded, presumably as a result of descriptions provided by the taxi-driver.[7]

March kept his head and drove at full speed to the Residency where Lord and Lady Allenby were entertaining the visiting former Prime Minister, Herbert Asquith, to lunch. Stack, who was the most seriously wounded, was carried into the High Commissioner's office. There seems to have been some, perhaps unnecessary, delay in getting him to the Anglo-American Hospital. a few minutes drive away on Gezira Island.

At any rate, he was still at the Residency when Saad Zaghloul, the Prime Minister, arrived to express his shock and dismay. There was some suggestion that he should be taken in to see Stack but there were objections on the grounds that it would offend Lady Stack who was already with her husband. Allenby, pointing to Campbell and March who were still in the hall, growled to Zaghloul, 'This is your doing!' to which the latter was heard to mutter in French, 'It's the end for me!'[8]

Two of Stack's three wounds were superficial but the third, in the abdomen, fatal. Dr Frank Madden of the Anglo-American and Colonel Benjamin Biggar, PMO of the Egyptian Army, struggled desperately to save his life, but, although for a while he seemed to rally, he died at 11.45 p.m. the following night. Professor Sydney Smith, who carried out the post mortem, certified that there had never been any chance of his recovery, especially as the bullets, which he had extracted from the body, were dum-dums.[9]

Campbell, who had been hit on the right side of his chest, and March, in the arm and leg, both recovered after a spell in hospital. Campbell, who had been wounded twice in the First World War, retired from the army shortly afterwards but returned to serve in Egypt again in the Second. He died in South Africa in 1970.[10] Of March we will be hearing more later.

Allenby, although no stranger to violence and sudden death – he had lost his only son in the war and had seen thousands die under his command – was personally affronted by this outrage. Not only had Stack been a friend but he had ranked second only to Allenby himself in the Anglo-Egyptian hierarchy. Here was a mortal insult to Great Britain and a savage blow to her prestige. It is hard to say whether he believed that Zaghioul was directly involved but he knew that some of the more extreme elements of his party and government were. Perhaps naively, being neither a diplomat nor a politician, he had expected some gratitude from the Egyptian political establishment as he had wrought mightily on its behalf in the face of its own internecine quarrels, a suspicious King Fuad and a hesitant and divided British cabinet.

Punishment must be swift and condign.

Stack was buried in the Old Cairo Protestant Cemetery on 22 November with great pomp and circumstance. His coffin was borne on a gun carriage escorted by cavalry along streets lined with British troops of the Cairo garrison. A 17-gun salute was fired and he was carried to his grave on the shoulders of British Warrant Officers of the Egyptian Army. For a while Allenby stood at the graveside in sad and silent

contemplation before returning to the Residency where his staff were
putting the finishing touches to the demands he intended to impose
upon Zagloul.

These were:

1. Apology for the crime.

2. Prosecute enquiry into the crime and bring to justice the criminals whoever
   they are.

3. Forbid and vigorously suppress all popular political demonstrations.

The funeral procession of El Ferik Sir Lee Stack Pasha; the Prime Minister Saad
Zaghloul Pasha leading the Egyptian mourners (extreme right).

4. Pay a fine of £500,000 to the British Government

5. Order within 24 hours the withdrawal from the Sudan of all Egyptian officers and all purely Egyptian (as opposed to Sudanese) units.

6. Increase the area at Gezira (Sudan) to be irrigated from 300,000 *fedans* (acres) to an unlimited figure as need may arise,

7. Withdraw all opposition to the wishes of the British Government concerning the protection of foreign interests in Egypt.[11]

Allenby did not wait for Foreign Office approval of these demands but, driving to the Prime Minister's office informally dressed but escorted by an entire regiment of cavalry, the 16th/5th Lancers, presented them personally to Saad Zaghloul, reading out to him the English version – Zaghloul probably understood English but would not speak it – and leaving him a French translation. The cavalry, of course, symbolised power and the casual dress (casual in those days went no further than a ordinary business suit as opposed to top hat and tails) contempt. We do not know what effect it had on Zaghloul but apparently it upset King George V, a stickler for protocol, when he was told.[12]

More alarming for the Foreign Secretary, Sir Austen Chamberlain, were the demands themselves, some of which he regarded as extravagant and others unnecessary, especially as Allenby was also suggesting taking hostages against further anti-British outrages and had ordered the seizure of the Alexandria Tobacco Customs, Egypt's largest single source of internal revenue, by the British Naval authorities there as collateral for the indemnity. Had the Bull broken loose and was he rampaging out of control in Egypt's china shop? As he had already shown by his almost unilateral declaration of Egypt's 'Independence' in 1922, he was no lackey of Whitehall and, when his blood was up, was capable of unauthorised extremes in either direction. It was felt that he had had many of these demands in mind for some time and had simply been waiting his opportunity to make them.

The steadying hand of professional diplomacy was seen to be needed and Nevile Henderson, kicking his heels in England between posts, was despatched to Egypt with the authoritative title of Minister Plenipotentiary. Nothing could have been better calculated to infuriate the High Commissioner who tendered his resignation, which was refused.[13]

Meanwhile telegrams crackled between the Cairo Residency and the Foreign Office. Was the demand for an indemnity dignified? Perhaps not but it was the sort of thing the Egyptians understood. Well, perhaps it should be bigger, say, one million pounds? Or smaller, say, £250,000? All right, stick to £500,000.

You can't possibly take hostages – you might have to shoot them, which would be un-British and, by the way, for goodness sake give them their Customs back. As for the Sudan water you can't expect the Egyptians to sign a blank cheque. Why not set up a Commission? When in doubt always set up a commission. And so on.

In the end only the apology – and there was a good deal of argument with both King Fuad and Zaghloul as to its form – and the indemnity were forthcoming. Of the £500,000, £40,000 was paid as compensation to Lady Stack. £5,000 to March and £3,000 to Campbell. The balance went to Sudanese medical charities. The British Treasury got its cut too, pocketing the interest which accrued between receipt of the money from the Egyptian Government and its distribution![14] Zaghloul, the victim of his own extremists, resigned, never to return to office, although he continued to play an influential role in Egyptian politics until his death in 1927.

As to the investigation into the crime, to which we will come in the next chapter, this was at first hampered by certain Egyptian officials and politicians but later pursued with vigour and at least partial success.

The Egyptian troops in the Sudan were removed, more or less by force, under the plan mooted in Keown-Boyd's report to the Milner Commission in 1920. The Egyptians themselves put up little resistance but under their influence, disturbances broke out among the Sudanese troops, the most serious of which occurred in Khartoum when some officers and men of the 11th Battalion seized the Medical Department building, killing one British and two Syrian doctors and an RAMC sergeant in the process. British troops, Argylls and Leicesters, were brought in but repeated attempts to storm the building were thrown back by stubborn Sudanese resistance. Two British officers and five men were killed and ten wounded and a field gun had to be brought up to pulverise the building and its occupants.[15] There was no further trouble and in January 1925 the Sudan Defence Force, under British officers and entirely independent of the Egyptian Army, was formed. This fine little force was to serve the Sudan well for the next thirty years, defending the country against Italian invasion in 1940 and playing a distinguished role in conquering the Italian colonies of Eritrea and Ethiopia in the following year.

But in one respect the assassination of Stack had achieved its objective. He was the last Sirdar and his rank and title were abolished. The Egyptian Army was to be supervised rather than commanded by a British Inspector-General, Major-General Sir Charlton Spinks,[16] who had been serving with the Egyptian Army since 1902. He was in fact little more than the head of a training mission and remained in that role until such a mission was officially designated in 1936. A British civilian was, henceforth, to be Governor-General of the Sudan.

Sir Nevile Henderson, who, as the last British ambassador to Berlin before the Second World War, will be always associated with Neville Chamberlain's (Austen's brother) 'appeasement' policy, wrote his memoirs in 1942 while, as he put it, 'under sentence of death' from cancer. He died in 1943.

When he arrived at Alexandria in December 1924 he found that the authorities were taking no chances. He wrote:

> As we anchored a long way out from the quayside, a large picket-boat with about thirty Egyptian policemen led by Ingram Bey dashed alongside ... There was a fleet of motor cars waiting and I got into one with Ingram ... and policemen into the rest and off we went through the town to the station with motor horns blowing full blast all the time ... Two compartments had been reserved for me and at the door of each stood a British detective in civil clothes both holding revolvers in their hands ... I had not anticipated anything quite so sensational as this but I suppose that Keown-Boyd, the Director of Public Security, feared lest the murderers of the Sirdar might repeat their coup on me ...
>
> Throughout my three years or so in Egypt I always had an RAF gunman [sic] attached to my person and living in my house ... I made only half-hearted protests against it as the gunman was a very useful addition to my household and looked after and drove my car.

His first long interview with Allenby, on the night of his arrival, was stormy, both men (or, at least, by his own account, Henderson) struggling to keep their tempers but 'at midnight Lord Allenby suddenly looked at the clock and said, "Good Heavens, it's twelve o'clock. You must be tired after your journey. Come along with me and I will show you to your room." I have always remembered that abrupt change from an angry and resentful man to a charming and courteous host.'

Henderson stayed in Egypt for three years, by his own admission with little to do. With the arrest of the terrorists and their sponsors and the two trials which followed, Egypt entered a period of relative calm and after Allenby's departure in June 1925, the experienced Residency staff was well able to cope with day-to-day affairs. Henderson went duck-shooting and visited the Sudan.[17]

Allenby was not a man to justify his decisions or actions and he has left no account of his stewardship in Egypt or, indeed, of any other period of his career. But several biographies have done him justice.[18] He died in 1936 and has passed into history as one who, for all his shortcomings, always strove to do his best by his country in war and peace and, in the case of Egypt, played no small part in her journey towards independence.

The assassination of Stack and the resignation of Zaghloul had a curious archaeological side effect.

In 1901, following a serious motor accident (one of the first perhaps) and in delicate health, George Edward Stanhope Molyneux Herbert, the 5th Earl of Carnarvon, had been advised to winter regularly in Egypt. Much preferring to be at home at Highclere with his horses and dogs, after several winters of boredom the Earl sought Cromer's advice as to how he might pass the idle hours in the Land of the Pharaohs. 'Why not try your hand at Egyptology?' suggested Cromer. 'You might find it amusing and I'll introduce you to just the man to do all the hard work.'

Howard Carter, the son of a Norfolk artist, had come to Egypt in 1891 as a draughtsman to the Archaeological Society of Egypt and by 1903 had been appointed Inspector-in-Chief of Archaeology for Lower Egypt, but had resigned 'owing to an incident with foreigners'. This apparently involved a row with some drunken French tourists who had insulted his workers at a site where excavation was in progress. Required to apologise – probably something Carter never did in his life – he refused and resigned.

An accomplished water-colourist, he was painting full time when introduced to Carnarvon by Cromer in 1907 and, encouraged by the Director of the Egyptian Antiquities Service, the Frenchman Gaston Maspero, the two men came to a working agreement, which was to endure for the next sixteen years. Roughly speaking, Carnarvon was to provide the money and to handle such matters as dealings with the Egyptian Government, from whom he had obtained a concession to excavate in the Valley of the Kings, and public relations, while Carter was to do the digging.

As is well known their great triumph came in 1922–23 with the discovery of the tomb of Tutankhamoun, perhaps the most sensational archaeological find of the twentieth century and one which excited enormous public interest throughout the world.

But after Hubris comes Nemesis.

Carnarvon had negotiated an exclusivity deal with the London *Times* under which he was to receive £5,000 down and 75 per cent of the royalties on the sale of the story to other newspapers. This outraged *The Times*' competitors, many of whom embarked upon a campaign of vilification against Carnarvon. Worse still, the Earl and Carter began to quarrel over the way in which all the various problems should be handled. Furthermore, it was rumoured that Carter and Carnarvon's daughter, the Lady Evelyn Herbert, had developed a 'tendresse'. A suitable business partner Carter might be but his lower middle-class origins excluded him as a son-in-law. Be that as it may, after one

Lord Carnarvon (right) and his daughter Lady Evelyn Herbert being met at Luxor Station by Howard Carter (left) and the Provincial Governor, November 1922.

particularly stormy exchange, Carter ordered his patron from his house and, as it turned out, the two men had little time left to patch up their relationship.

Soon after the opening of the tomb in February 1923 Carnarvon was bitten by a mosquito on the cheek. The bite became infected and his temperature rose sharply. Lady Evelyn, his constant companion, ordered him to bed in the hotel at Assouan. He seemed to recover slightly but relapsed and on 14 March he was removed to the Continental-Savoy Hotel in Cairo where he died of pneumonia at 1.45 a.m. on 5 April 1923, aged fifty-seven. His wife, the exotic Almina, had characteristically flown out from England in a tiny Puss Moth aircraft and his son, the Viscount Porchester ('Porchie'), a cavalry subaltern, had arrived hotfoot from India to be at his bedside.[19]

His demise was surrounded by the wildest rumours that he was the victim of the 'Curse of the Pharoah'. It seems that strange events did occur at the moment of his death. An electric power failure plunged Cairo into darkness (not a unique phenomenon) and, at the same time, thousands of miles away at Highclere, his elderly terrier bitch, Susie, sprang from her basket, howled, foamed at the mouth and expired.[20]

Curse or no curse, the surviving partner was faced with a sea of troubles. With Carnarvon's powerful influence and high connections with both the British and the Egyptian authorities removed, Carter, stubborn, opinionated and quarrelsome, was temperamentally unsuited to dealing with Zaghloul's Wafdist government, Pierre Lacau, the French Director of the Antiquities Service, or the Press. The Wafd regarded the whole affair as a political issue in which Egyptians had been forced into the background while all the credit for the discovery went to the British. No doubt they were encouraged in this opinion by Lacau, following the French tradition of impeding and hampering all British activity in Egypt. They also suspected that the British intended to spirit much of the tomb's priceless contents out of the country.

A particular thorn in Carter's side was Morcos Hanna Bey, the Minister of Public Works, recently released from gaol where he had been serving a sentence for incitement to rebellion against the previous government. Originally he had been sentenced to death but this had been commuted to seven years of which he served only a few months before being released when Zaghloul came to power.

Although financially stretched to the limit, Almina[21] had taken on her husband's concession but this was revoked when Carter suspended work on the official opening of the sarcophagus after an absurd row with Hanna over the presence of the wives of the excavation team at the event. Refusing to compromise, Carter left for a lecture tour of the United States. Hanna may have set a trap for Carter but when it sprang he was caught in it himself as without the expertise and unique knowledge of the tomb and its contents possessed by Carter and his team, no progress could be made with the sorting, labelling, cataloguing and packing of the various treasures and artifacts for transportation to Cairo.

However, after a lengthy legal wrangle, fate was to intervene in November 1924 with the murder of the Sirdar and the fall of the Zaghloul government. Its more amenable successor renewed Almina's concession. Carter's great work was completed eight years later in 1932 but his health had suffered severely and he died in London in March 1939 aged sixty-four, unhonoured by either the British or Egyptian governments. He remained a bachelor; romantics may wish to believe through love of the charming and vivacious Lady Evelyn.[22] Soon after her father's death Evelyn married a baronet, Sir Brograve Beauchamp, who, among his other distinctions, was godfather to the present author.

CHAPTER II

Detective Story

THE TWO MOST PROMINENT British officials involved in the Stack Case were men of very different kidney. Thomas Russell Pasha, a cousin of the Duke of Bedford, had joined the Egyptian Civil Service in 1902 and had been appointed Commandant of the Cairo City Police in 1918. He was a man of great physical courage and fine physique and, despite limited intelligence, was a highly accomplished self-publicist who became the most famous policeman of the British 'Imperial' era. If he is remembered today it is for his efforts to suppress the Egyptian drug traffic, efforts which, through no fault of his, were ultimately as futile as all such attempts have been all over the world.[1]

But the public image which he managed to create for himself of the cool, steady, iron-nerved police officer seems to have been highly misleading. For example, in 1936 the British Ambassador Sir Miles Lampson (later Lord Killearn), recorded '... an almost hysterical and panicky letter from Russell Pasha saying that he could not be held responsible for any trouble at King Fuad's funeral to-morrow – typical and fatuous letter. However, such is RP (Russell Pasha). The man is a bundle of nerves and on top of that is a first-class advertiser ...'.

On other occasions Lampson describes Russell as 'the jumpiest man I know' and 'a curious fish'. When the new King Farouk returned to Egypt after his father's death Lampson received one of 'Russell Pasha's typical letters ... saying that he must disclaim any responsibility for any disorders on Farouk's arrival this morning ... I am coming to regard Russell as one of our major post (1936) treaty problems.'[2]

In complete contrast to Russell, and frequently the target of his jealous enmity, was Alexander Keown-Boyd, a son of the Ulster squirearchy whose family's fortunes had been brought low through an uncle's reckless gambling. He had shone at Oxford, both as an Arabic scholar and as an oar, and had been selected for the Sudan Political Service in 1907.

Sir Reginald Wingate, on his appointment to Egypt as High Commissioner at the end of 1916, had brought Keown-Boyd with him

Senior British and Egyptian police officers at Abdin Palace in 1931. Those
identifiable are: front row, fourth from left Jarvis Bey; 5th from left Baker Pasha; 6th
from left Russell Pasha. Far right: Henn Bey. Doorway left, Lucas Bey.

from Khartoum as his Private Secretary. As Oriental Secretary to
Allenby, Keown-Boyd played a role not dissimilar to that of Lord
Edward Cecil under Kitchener, exciting the comment from Russell that
he was 'a residency pet' and 'one of the two or three people who run
Allenby'.[3] No doubt there was a good deal of truth in these remarks.

Later, when K-B (as he was widely known) was appointed Director-
General of the European Department of the Ministry of the Interior,
Russell complained that '... from the first he [K-B] arrogated to himself
not only the powers of DGPS [Director-General of Public Security]
but of an Adviser.'[4] What Russell meant was that this gave him control
over the police and therefore over Russell, which was also true. Especially
galling to him was that he was older than K-B and had been in Egypt
for very much longer.

Adding to the discord between the two men was the intense dislike
their wives felt for each other. Both women were powerful, not to say
overbearing personalities and we may be sure that the younger and
prettier Joan Keown-Boyd never allowed Dorothea Russell ('... a clever
and entertaining woman but by God she's spiky ...' – Lampson)[5] to
forget their husbands' respective positions in the Anglo-Egyptian hierarchy.

Fortunately for all concerned K-B and Hassan Rifaat, the Director-
General of the Ministry of the Interior, were firm friends and remained

so all their lives. Rifaat, who had been trained by the Tsarist secret police before the First World War, has been described by Grafftey-Smith as 'the implacable enemy of Wafdist extremism and the alter ego of Keown-Boyd'. Through Rifaat's network of spies and informers K-B was able to keep the Residency appraised of political undercurrents, manoeuvrings and potential threats to British interests in Egypt.[6]

Rifaat was a great survivor, both in the political and physical sense, remaining in Public Security for many years and was, to a large extent, responsible for the internal tranquillity which, against the odds, obtained in Egypt throughout the Second World War. Even Russell paid tribute to him in his memoirs, which were largely dedicated to blowing his own trumpet, while avoiding any mention of K-B with whom, *force majeur*, he was obliged to work closely for fourteen years.[7]

Curiously, although he remarks upon the importance of the Stack case in these memoirs, Russell deals with it only briefly, perhaps because in a more detailed account of the case too much credit would have to be given to others. However, it is to him that we owe much of our knowledge of it as his papers contain a good deal of information on the subject.

Russell remained as Commandant of the Cairo City Police until 1946. a quite remarkable total of twenty-eight years in that difficult, and for an Englishman, invidious position. Whatever his shortcomings may have been, there is no doubt that he was trusted by his men, both British and Egyptian, as well as by the majority of Egyptian politicians.

K-B retired from government service under the terms of the 1936

Alexander Ingram Bey of the Egyptian Police was the most famous detective of the British era and led the hunt for the murderers of the Sirdar in 1924.

Anglo-Egyptian Treaty to become a successful businessman. He, Russell and Rifaat all received knighthoods and died within a year of each other in 1954–55.

On the day of Stack's death in a dispatch to the Foreign Office Allenby wrote '... it is not possible or desirable for the existing British Public Security officials to control the course of the enquiry ... I think there-fore the whole responsibility should be placed on Egyptian shoulders and, on my instructions, the Director-General [Keown-Boyd] has written to me asking on his behalf and that of the Commandant of Police [Russell] to be absolved from responsibility ...'.[8] This 'absolu-tion' apparently also covered the British Chief-Inspector of the Parquet, G. H. Hughes. As the detectives and Parquet personnel investigating the case, together with the uniformed officers and Haggana (Frontier Camel Corps) who made the arrests, worked entirely under the direction of the officials named in Allenby's dispatch (which was also quoted in *The Times*) plus Hassan Rifaat, this can only have been a deliberate smokescreen. What its purpose was one can only guess – perhaps to protect the personal security of the men concerned or perhaps to put pressure on Egyptian officials who may have been inclined to drag their feet. It is worth recalling, for example, that the suspect Mahmoud Fehmy el Nokrashi was Under-Secretary at the Ministry of the Interior! It is not surprising, therefore, to find officials of that Ministry sup-pressing evidence, as seems to have been the case with an eyewitness account of the murder provided by the Italian Consul.[9]

The eye-witness was a rare bird in Egypt, particularly where political crimes were concerned. The Egyptian has a built-in suspicion of the Hukuma (Government) and especially of the police. Unless there is something in it for him, he will not willingly come forward and get involved. Furthermore, as Russell put it in a report to the Residency, 'Political murderers have openly and tacitly been regarded as national heroes and, as such, have had general sympathy and the best brains and ample funds to assist them.'[10]

The early stages of the investigation were handled by the CID Chief, Kaimakam Douglas Baker Bey, as Ingram was on leave. On the night of 19 November (the day of the attack on the Sirdar) the Egyptian detective Yuzbashi Selim Zaki met the informer Helbawi. This was probably a stormy meeting as the police were furious that he had not forewarned them of the attack. According to Russell, Helbawi told Zaki that he had not heard of the murder plans in advance but 'was much upset at having failed in his promise and was determined to justify himself by getting the facts.'

Secret meetings in sleazy and inconspicuous locations were held regularly over the next few days between the two men and it may well have been at one of these that the shrewd Helbawi, who probably did know of the intended assassination and, indeed, those who were behind it and had carried it out, decided to turn the situation to his further advantage and demand the enormous 'bounty' of £E10,000 in return for the arrest and conviction of the assassins.[11]

We do not know if this is how such a colossal (the salary of a senior British official was about £E1,500 p.a.) reward came to be negotiated but it seems improbable that the authorities would have had such a sum in mind from the outset or that they would have authorised a relatively junior officer like Zaki to make such an unsolicited offer. Be that as it may, this was the agreed figure, apparently without much bargaining.

In January 1925 Ingram was recalled from leave and replaced Baker, something of a plodder, in charge of the case. Russell's explanation for this is that Ingram 'had expert knowledge of the old murder cases'[12] but he was also generally regarded as the best detective in the country.

Meanwhile, Helbawi's handling of his handlers as well as his quarry was brilliant. As time passed with little progress the police became suspicious that he might be playing a double game. So on the night of 4 January he arranged for Abdel Fattah Enayat, one of the late Mahmud's brothers and a known terrorist, to come to his room in what Russell describes as a 'rat' hotel. There they discussed the murder of the Sirdar and an old case in which a terrorist had blown himself up while practising bomb throwing in the desert. By arrangement with Helbawi, Zaki's assistant, Mulazim Awal (Lieutenant) Ahmed Hamdi, was installed in the next room and could overhear the conversation confirming that the two men were completely in each other's confidence and that Helbawi was keeping to his side of the bargain.

By the last week of January Helbawi had 'ascertained' (Russell's word) from Abdel Fattah the names of the other assassins and conspirators, information which he may well have possessed prior to the murder but which it would have profited him nothing to reveal before the £E10,000 bounty had been agreed. Of course he had to allow himself a realistic amount of time in which make these 'discoveries'.

The culprits known, evidence was now required so the police and Helbawi worked out a plan. On 28 January two of the organisers of the murder, the lawyer Shafik Mansour, a kind of terrorist Fagin who had been involved in the assassination of the Prime Minister Boutros Ghali as far back as 1910, and a government clerk called Mahmoud Ismail, who had been fingered by Helbawi, were arrested. It was then leaked to the press that the latter (who actually gave himself up) had confessed

Dr Shafik Mansour, a leading member of the terrorist gang which assassinated the Sirdar. He was sentenced to death and executed.

to the Minister of the Interior, Ismail Sidky Pasha, implicating the other assassins and this appeared in a special midday edition of at least one newspaper.

When the news broke Helbawi dashed with a copy of the paper featuring the story to Abdel Fattah Enayat, who had been selected as the weakest and most easily influenced member of the gang. Helbawi persuaded him that the game was up and that he and his younger brother Abdel Hamid, also a gang member, must escape to Tripoli via Alexandria. First, however, Shafik Mansour must be consulted but on arrival at his house the brothers were horrified to see a policeman at his door. Slipping quietly away they reached their own house and, finding it unguarded, collected their clothes before going to the house of the 'armourer' of the gang, Mahmoud Rashid, and removing four of the pistols which had been used in the murder of the Sirdar (and others).[13]

We do not know what Rashid's reaction was to this or even if he was in the house at the time but presumably Helbawi had persuaded them that they should not undertake the dangerous desert journey unarmed as it was a vital part of the police plan that when eventually apprehended they should have the murder weapons in their possession.

They then repaired to Helbawi's 'rat' hotel room to wait for the 6.40 p.m. train to Alexandria, little knowing that Detective Zaki was conveniently installed in the next room. Somehow Helbawi managed to let Zaki know that all was going according to plan and when they left the hotel for the station they were followed – probably by street urchins, frequently used by the Cairo police for such work. Thinking the suspects were escaping, one of the 'followers' dashed into a chemist's shop and telephoned Ingram, shouting down the line, 'Come quickly and bring the handcuffs; they're escaping!' Ingram tried to reassure him all was well, but, thinking this stupid Inglizi had not understood, the boy took a taxi to Ingram's office where, after further expostulations, he was persuaded that their 'escape' was intended.

On arrival in Alexandria Helbawi took the Enayats to a hotel, which he had chosen in advance, knowing that Detective Hamdi would be on watch from one opposite. Once there and reading a second leaked newspaper report that they had been arrested in Cairo, another police ruse intended to panic them into instant flight which, on this occasion, seems to have back-fired, the Enayats were so paralysed with fear that they refused to leave the hotel for the station. This was awkward for the police and Helbawi as the plan entailed the fugitives being arrested in a frontier district where they would not come under the jurisdiction of the Parquet, many of whose officials were distrusted by the police.

Helbawi, who managed to keep in contact with Hamdi, urged that they be arrested in Alexandria. When told of this Ingram and Zaki flew there by plane, in itself a dramatic move in those days, to take charge and consult with Helbawi. Finally, Helbawi at his most persuasive accompanied the armed Enayats onto the train on the morning of Saturday 31 January, shadowed by two Bedouin police agents in their compartment and Selim Zaki in another.

Meanwhile, a Light Car Patrol of the Frontier Districts Administration under Kaimakam (later Sir) Talbot Chetwynd Bey and Bimbashi Fairman had left Cairo on 25 January and were waiting at Burg el Arab on the coast some miles to the west of Alexandria. Their role was to board the train at El Hammam, two stations down the line from Burg el Arab, with their Sudanese Camel Corps troopers and arrest the fugitives but, realising that it was market day there and that their quarry might be lost in a crowd of hundreds of Bedouin, Chetwynd mounted the engine at the station before El Hammam and stopped the train opposite a spot where his men lay in ambush.

In a trice the Sudanese had stormed the Enayats' compartment, probably identified by a signal from the Bedouin agents, and seized the bewildered and unresisting fugitives and the indignant Helbawi and tied them up. Chetwynd photographed the arrested men but, in a nearly disastrous oversight, the weapons were either forgotten or overlooked. However, they were eventually found when, according to one version, a basket of fruit under the seat where the Enayats had been sitting was kicked over and the guns and ammunition spilt out! [14]

The initial interrogation of the prisoners took place at Burg el Arab, but they denied everything beyond the fact they had attempted to escape to avoid arrest. Abdel Fattah feigned madness by chewing Epsom Salts 'to produce the necessary flow of lunatic saliva'!

They were then removed to the Frontier Administration Depot near Cairo. Here they were kept in separate cells and Abdel Fattah was confronted with Helbawi who admitted he was working with the police and advised his 'friend' to do the same. Abdel Fattah, realising the hopeless situation he was in and probably promised leniency or even a pardon (although Russell denies this), made the first of at least two confessions.

Over the next few days the remaining members of the murder gang were arrested: the 'armourer' Mahmoud Rashid, the two railway artisans Ibrahim Musa and Ali Mohamed Ibrahim and the telephone engineer Rageb Hassan. Shafik Mansour and Mahmoud Ismail were, of course, already in custody.[15]

Under interrogation by Ingram, Hassan Rifaat, Keown-Boyd and probably Hughes representing the Parquet, confessions were extracted from most of the suspects, no doubt by sheer persistence sweetened by the usual promises of leniency. Ingram in particular seems to have reached a curious kind of rapport with the prisoners. Grafftey-Smith, Assistant Oriental Secretary at the Residency at the time, recalled, 'Ingram's influence over criminals had something of a psychiatrist's "identification". Night after night one or other of the prisoners would ask that he should come and talk to them and bits of the jigsaw were then fitted into place.'[16] They were talking themselves to the gallows.

But in the case of Shafik Mansour, Professor Sydney Smith played an important role.

Smith's account of the case was written some thirty-five years after the event and contains some errors of fact, but there is no reason to doubt his version of the work in which he was directly involved, mostly of a forensic and ballistic nature. However, to Mansour he seems to have been something of a Father Confessor. The lawyer feigned madness and made speeches to himself so the prison authorities asked Smith to examine him. Apparently he feared that he would be flogged and that King Fuad had ordered his execution. Smith assured him that such things could not happen without a trial, arranged for him to be transferred to more comfortable quarters and even to be taken for drives around Cairo. This seems to have had the required effect as, in due course, he was to make the fullest and most damaging confession – according to Smith, entirely voluntarily.

Confessions are all very well but are often regarded with suspicion by judges, while defence lawyers almost invariably question their validity and/or encourage their clients to withdraw them. Corroborative evidence was therefore vital. The police already had the murder weapons and Smith was able to prove that the bullet which killed Stack had been fired from one of these, a Colt .32, and that the dum-dum ammunition with which it was loaded when found matched that bullet. It also matched bullets which had been used in previous assassinations, including that of Warrant Officer Steel in 1922.

Furthermore, in his confession, Shafik Mansour revealed the whereabouts of a hidden wooden receptacle built into a door in Mahmoud Rachid's house where the weapons had been stored. This bore certain scratches which matched exactly with the sights of the Colt pistol.

Rachid's toolbox was also found containing saws, vices and files. As some of these tools bore traces of metallic particles identical with filings from the seized bullets it was a fair assumption, if not conclusive proof, that they had been used to cut the tips of the bullets to make dum-dums.[17]

The accused were brought to trial on 11 May 1925 before three judges, Ahmed Erfan Pasha (President), Judge J. F. Kershaw, and Mohamed Mazhar Bey.[18] Grafftey-Smith recorded his impressions of some of the defendants. 'To me the most sinister was Sheikh Ibrahim [Ibrahim Musa] ... a devout member of one of the more fanatical Sufi sects. Tidy, respectable and impassive, he brought to murder the conviction of answered prayer. Two very young men, the brothers Enayat ... drugged by the flattery and authority of another prisoner, Shafik Mansour, a pince nez'd Wafdist lawyer who had been a candidate for the office of Director General of Public Security ... There was brash young Ismail Effendi [Mahmoud Ismail] and he, like Sheikh Ibrahim, behaved as if indifferent to the legal proceedings ...'[19]

Although most of the confessions were withdrawn they could not be unsaid and no doubt weighed heavily with the judges (there was no jury). But Smith's evidence was the most conclusive and he recalls his final examination by the Procurator-General (Prosecuting Counsel), Taha Nur Pasha.

Rachid's door with the hidden receptacle, his tools and the murder weapons and ammunition were exhibited in court.

The exchange, which followed, was dramatic.

'Were any of these pistols used in this case?' asked the PG.

'The Colt has a fault in its barrel which makes a special groove on any bullet fired through it,' replied Smith, 'The bullets taken from the Sirdar and from Captain Campbell have this special groove ... I declare definitely that they were both fired from this Colt.'[20]

The Court was adjourned on 1 June and reconvened on the 7th for the passing of sentences. All (except the taxi-driver, the Sudanese Mahmoud Hassan Saleh, who was given two years penal servitude) were sentenced to death for murder or, in the cases of Shafik Mansour and Mahmoud Ismail, complicity and incitement to murder. The sentences were in respect only of the murder of the Sirdar and it was never established precisely how many of the political killings since 1919 had been perpetrated by this gang but it was no coincidence that such assassinations ended with the arrest, trial and execution of these men.

The death sentence upon the elder and most vociferous Enayat, Abdel Fattah, was commuted to life imprisonment on the recommendation of George Hughes, the Chief Inspector of the Parquet. Apart from his early and decisive cooperation with the police, Abdel Fattah was needed as a witness in the subsequent trial of the Wafdist politicians accused of sponsoring the assassination. This was supported by Nevile Henderson, the Acting High Commissioner (Allenby had left) who also asked that clemency be shown to Ali Ibrahim and Ragheb Hassan on the grounds that they were only 'ignorant and foolish workmen'.[21] This was not granted.

The executions were carried out between 7 and 11 a.m. on 23 August. The last words and demeanour of the condemned men were recorded in detail. With the exceptions of Shafik Mansour and Ragheb Hassan they went calmly and with dignity to their deaths. Ibrahim Musa was concerned about his debts (320 piastres and one pound respectively); some money, which was owed him and what should be done with it. But the most significant remarks were made by Abdel Hamid Enayat, the first to be hanged. '... I have served my country,' he said. 'Ever since my youth I went on murdering ... and I murdered about thirty-five men ... After my confession in the Sirdar's case, Ingram Bey swore to me by his Honour, by the Honour of his Country, by the Honour of King George V and by the Honour of the Government that a Royal Pardon will be given for me if I confessed in the other cases.'

On the prison record sheet this last sentence is in brackets and below is written by hand, 'Left out of copies to Ministry in case it gets into the Press'.[22]

Early in the investigation about forty people had been arrested on the recommendation of Russell and Keown-Boyd, including a number of leading Wafdist politicians, but all had been released for lack of evidence. Now, following the successful outcome of the trial of Shafik Mansour & Co., a number of these were re-arrested and eventually charged with incitement to murder. They included Ahmed Maher and Mahmoud Nokrashi, both future Prime Ministers. But Hughes and Keown-Boyd were never very optimistic that convictions would be obtained, except against a known terrorist, Mohamed Fehmy Ali, who had already confessed to complicity in the Sirdar murder, as most of the evidence against the others was based on the confession of Shafik Mansour and lacked corroboration.[23]

Nor was the British War Office very co-operative, refusing leave to

Captain Campbell, who had apparently left Egypt by then, to give evidence at the trial. Keown-Boyd was obliged to write to an official at the High Commission: 'Cannot the War Office give him three weeks leave to attend the trial of the murderers of a British General?' Eventually Whitehall gave in but then quibbled about who was to pay his fare![24]

The trial took place in May 1926 and in the event the pessimists were to be proved right as only Ali was convicted and hanged, while all the others were acquitted by a majority verdict of two Egyptian judges to one British, Judge Kershaw.

Despite the previously expressed reservations of Hughes and Keown-Boyd as to the value of the evidence, there was a strong suspicion in some quarters that the Egyptian judges had been blackmailed or terrorised into reaching their decision and so incensed was Kershaw by this verdict that he resigned and forewent his pension. His son, Sir Anthony, confirms this view, writing, 'The two Egyptian judges were intimidated. They told my father that they would acquit. One of them came to our house the night before the verdict and wept, saying, "You are an Englishman, we are Egyptians," meaning I suppose, "we live here and so do our families".'[25]

In an unprecedented move, Judge Kershaw wrote a long report to the High Commissioner which ended: 'for these reasons I have no shadow of doubt that Mahmoud Osman Mustafa, El Hag Ahmed Gedallah, Ahmed Maher and Hassan Kamel el Shishini were wrongly acquitted ... such as to amount to a miscarriage of justice and I regret that I must persist in resigning my position as Conseiller à la Cour.'

To the Minister of Justice he wrote:

> In my view the judgement in the cases of Mahmoud Osman Mustafa, El Hag Ahmed Gedallah, Ahmed Maher and Hassan Kamel el Shishini is so greatly against the weight of evidence as to amount to a grave miscarriage of justice.
>
> So serious in my opinion is this miscarriage of justice and so grave the dangers that might result from the verdict that I considered it my duty to disregard on this occasion the principle that the secrets of deliberation must not be revealed and consequently, after pronouncing the judgement, I proceeded at once to the residency and informed His Excellency the High Commissioner in his capacity as protector of foreigners in Egypt.
>
> Before doing so I had realised that this technical breach of my duty entailed my placing my resignation in your hands. I also felt that it would not be right for me to do so until the judgement had been prepared and had been signed ... There is now therefore no impediment to my sending you my resignation ...[26]

Although this step on his part seems to have been rather extreme and perhaps misguided, as the resignation of an experienced British judge could have given nothing but satisfaction to the opponents of the Occupation, there is no doubt that the British authorities were convinced of the guilt of all the accused, including Nokrashi, although Kershaw did not include him among those who had been 'wrongly acquitted'.

The High Commissioner, Lord Lloyd, rounded off the subject with a letter to the Prime Minister, Adly Pasha, reiterating the reasons for Kershaw's resignation and, after praising the work of the police and Parquet, concluded:

> ... I must point out to your Excellency that the effect of this judgement must be to endanger the safety of foreigners in Egypt, for which His Majesty's Government retained responsibility at the time of the proclamation of Egyptian independence and upon which they based their demands made and accepted after the murder of Sir Lee Stack.
>
> In these circumstances His Majesty's Government must reserve complete liberty to take such steps as the future may show to be necessary for the discharge of the duty thus incumbent upon them.[27]

For several years, in its regular intelligence reports to the Foreign Office (probably prepared by Keown-Boyd), the Residency pulled no punches in its comments on Nokrashi and Maher. Of Nokrashi:

> He has been a suspect of murder from the first. He was interrogated on a murder charge in 1922 and arrested in May 1923 but released for lack of evidence ... as Under-Secretary of State for the Interior ... he turned that Ministry into a hot-bed of intrigue ... and made co-operation by British officials impossible. After the Sirdar's murder he interfered at every possible moment with the course of the enquiry ... He was arrested on 27 November in connexion with the Sirdar's murder but released for lack of evidence ... He was arrested again in May 1925 on a charge of complicity in the whole murder campaign and acquitted in May 1926.

Of Maher:

> This is a tainted family and Ahmed is by far the worst of them ... There is no doubt of his close connexion with the murder campaign. He was arrested after the murders of Hassan Abdel Razak and Zohdi in 1922 but nothing was proved ... Shafik Mansour, who was hanged for the Sirdar's murder, was in Ahmed Maher's office near the scene of the crime while it was being committed ... Clever and quite unscrupulous, he stands for all that is undisciplined and extremist in Egyptian political life ...[28]

Ironically, both these men, as Prime Ministers, were themselves assassinated in the 1940s.

One serious embarrassment for both British and Egyptians emerged from these trials. This was a possible link, through the King's Chef de Cabinet and right-hand man, Hassan Nashaat Pasha, between the Palace and the terrorists. At the first trial it emerged that one of the accused, Mahmoud Ismail, was a protégé of Nashaat and at the second Ismail's brother, in evidence, denounced Nashaat as an accessory and demanded that he too should stand trial. Furthermore, there was a curious incident in which Nashaat had apparently lied to Hassan Rifaat about some ammunition which had been taken from his drawer.

As Grafftey-Smith puts it, '... To have established such a link would have been political dynamite', and the matter seems to have been quietly dropped. However, before long the King had been persuaded by the Residency to sack Nashaat and have him posted as Ambassador to Spain. Later he was to represent his country in Berlin and, throughout the Second World War, in London, where he married a beautiful English girl.

It is impossible now to say with any certainty whether any such link existed. The probability is that Nashaat, as the King's confidant, felt it his duty to maintain some tenuous connection with the underground world of terrorism, if only for the protection, both physical and political, of his royal master. A more cynical view is that the Palace would have welcomed any action which would damage Zaghloul and bring him down.

Let us now glance at what fate had in store for some of the leading protagonists in this drama.

Helbawi pocketed his Thirty Pieces of Silver, in the form of £E10,000, and disappeared into the footnotes of history. It was rumoured that he had been given a South American passport and a new name. As the archetypal Judas, for all his courage and ingenuity, it is difficult to regard him with anything but distaste.

Of Enayat the Elder, who is thought to have been released from prison in about 1945, we will hear a little more in the next chapter, as we will of Stack's chauffeur, Fred March.

Ingram was promoted to Commandant of Police in Alexandria where, in 1929, he died of typhoid at the age of only forty-five. His *Times* obituary read, in part, 'It was entirely due to his perspicacity, experience and patience that the murder gang implicated in the assassination of Sir Lee Stack was run to earth and convicted.' [29]

The use of the word 'entirely' here is an exaggeration, Selim Zaki's role being at least as important as that of Ingram, if not more so.

Tragically, one of Ingram's young sons died of the same disease in the same year.

So far as is known Ingram left no papers, at least none which throw any fresh light upon the Sirdar case or, indeed, upon any of his numerous other investigations. Were they to exist, they would make fascinating reading. However, quite recently an unidentified collection of photographs found in a Toronto apartment building were proved by the finder, Mrs Peg Forbes, after many months of detective work worthy of the great sleuth himself, to be those of Ingram and his family. One of these photos is reproduced in this book.

His able assistant, Selim Zaki, rose to the rank of Lewa (Major-General), carrying with it the title of Pasha, on succeeding Russell as Commandant of the Cairo City Police in 1946. It is to be hoped that the worthy Hamdi also prospered in his career.

Professor Sydney Smith left Egypt in 1927 and as Regius Professor of Forensic Medicine at Edinburgh University was professionally involved in many notorious murder cases over the next thirty years, often finding himself at odds with another famous pathologist, Sir Bernard Spilsbury, for whom he has some harsh words in his memoirs. Before leaving Egypt he was awarded the Order of the Nile and was knighted in 1949. He died, much respected, in 1969.[30]

Finally, we come to the police constable, Nafar Mohamed Abdel Gawad, who had so gallantly tried to prevent the escape of the assassins and had been so richly rewarded for his courage. A delegation led by no less a personage than the High Commissioner, His Excellency Field Marshal Viscount Allenby, had waited upon Mohamed in his hospital bed. With these ringing words – 'You have performed a distinguished action and you have been wounded in bravely pursuing, unarmed, the murderers of the Governor-General of the Sudan and Sirdar of the Egyptian Army. In token of the appreciation of His Majesty's Government and the Government of the Sudan, I present you with one thousand pounds. Your Commandant will see that you make the best possible use of it' – ten one hundred-pound notes were handed to the dumbfounded constable (whose salary was probably a pound a month).

Unfortunately his Commandant did no such thing. Poor Mohamed resigned from the police, invested unwisely and was soon asking for a job at the Residency. One was available, it appears, at £E3 per month but we do not know if he took it.[31]

But that is not quite the end of his story. Professor Smith had examined the wounded hero in the hospital and found that he had been shot in the bottom – 'winged in flight by a stray shot' as Smith put it. No doubt chuckling to himself he showed some photographs of the wound to Lord Allenby. Upon examining these, H.E. adjured Smith to silence, 'I think this is a matter we should keep to ourselves, Sydney Smith!'[32]

These trials brought to a temporary end the series of political murders which had begun in 1919, although reporting to the High Commissioner in May and June 1926 after the acquittals in the second trial, Keown-Boyd was by no means sure that they would.

'It is the opinion of Ingram Bey,' he wrote, '... that it is in Berlin that we must watch most carefully as the hatching place of further political crime in Egypt ...', then, referring to an attempt to assassinate Zaghloul, '... only one point stands out clearly and that is that his assailant was taught to use a pistol in a Berlin club ... Ingram describes the Berlin students as red-hot extremists, who do not care a jot for Zaghloul and believe only in opposition to the English ... the British authorities [in Germany] should give us any assistance they can in obtaining information as to any student clubs, subversive organisations and dangerous individuals in Berlin. Some funds could of course be provided for the purpose.'

Bearing in mind that Germany had been the principal enemy in the recent war and the state of near anarchy which obtained there at the time, there may have been an element of paranoia in all this. However, presumably steps along the lines suggested by K-B were taken in Berlin as about a month later he reports, 'I am informed by an agent that Abdel Hamid Bey Said is working the Berlin students through Mansur Rifaat to whom he sends instructions and money.' We must assume that these two men were suspected terrorists or sponsors of terrorism.

Elsewhere Soviet connections with Egyptian terrorism are suggested through a sinister and shadowy Afghan called Abdel Kira, but fortunately nothing seems to have come of all this, perhaps for the reasons set out by K-B in another report.

Such elements of hope as I see are the following:

1. The deterrent effect of the execution, and miserable end after confession and implication of other persons, of Shafik Mansour, who was personally known to every dangerous Egyptian of standing.

2. The element of suspicion caused by the knowledge that a man (Helbawi) whom above all they had every reason to trust became a paid Police Agent.

3. The removal of the Enayats and members of the gang who might have done further recruiting.

4. The fact that the execution of assassins or would-be assassins has always been followed by a period of calm.

5. The character of Maher, Shishini and Biali (acquitted in the second Stack trial) is such that their recent tribulations will deter them from dangerous activities in the future.

On the other hand

The character of Nokrashi is unlike that of Maher and the others; he is so strong and whole-minded that he will certainly take to political murder again should he judge it to be in the interest of Egypt or his party. [33]

K-B, for the rest of his life in Egypt, was never without an armed bodyguard, the best remembered of these sturdy fellows being Detective Shinawi, a cheerful, smiling man for whom no service was too much trouble or regarded as outside his terms of reference

It is an irony that, in the next series of political assassinations, which broke out in the 1940s, one of the victims should have been Nokrashi himself. However, K-B must have had a certain admiration for the man. At the time of the murder, long retired from his security role, he was on holiday in Upper Egypt and was heard to express genuine regret at the violent demise of his erstwhile adversary.

CHAPTER 12

A Distinguished Australian

IN HIS CORRESPONDENCE with the Foreign Secretary, Austen Chamberlain, on the subject of compensation for the surviving victims of the attack on the Sirdar, Campbell and March, Lord Allenby wrote:

> March is a professional taxi-cab driver here. He was engaged temporarily by the late Sirdar, He is married, is dependent on what he earns and his ambition is to retire to his home as soon as possible. His temporary incapacity is proving a hardship to his wife.

Two addresses are given, one in Cairo and one in Sydney.

Incidentally, it is a mark of Allenby's fair-mindedness that although his Head of Chancery, Arthur Wiggin, had originally recommended £2,500 and the MBE for March and £3,000 for Campbell, Allenby insisted on £5,000 and an Empire Gallantry Medal (later replaced by the George Cross) for March, an Australian ex-horse trooper, while accepting £3,000 for Campbell, a well-connected officer of a famous Highland regiment, the Black Watch.[1]

That said, it is amusing to note that most of the information in Allenby's letter to Chamberlain, which, no doubt, he supplied in good faith and was based on March's word, was probably false. It is unlikely, though not impossible, that there was a wife at that time; the Sydney address was, perhaps, his mother's and he had no intention of returning to Australia – at any rate, having received the very considerable sum for those days of £5,000, March remained in Cairo.

At the time of the murder in 1924 March was thirty-three years old, although quite often for convenience sake, his date of birth was adjustable, and had already led a varied and adventurous life – although perhaps not quite as varied and adventurous as he would have his listeners believe.

Unfortunately, it is difficult to discriminate between the reality of Fred March's life, what he invented for himself and what was invented for him by others. So we will not try very hard and will allow probability to speak for itself, bearing in mind Fred's undoubted courage, toughness and resilience.[2]

Born into a poor family in New South Wales in 1891 (sometimes he preferred 1881) he stowed away on a ship from Sydney to San Francisco while still in his teens. Drifting across the continent, eventually he found work in the Cadillac plant in Detroit where he developed the mechanical and driving skills from which he was to make his living in years to come.

In about 1913 Fred returned to Australia where he was employed as a chauffeur with a car-hire firm. With the outbreak of war, he made his way to England where he enlisted in the Royal Naval Division among whose officers were included such literary and military luminaries as Rupert Brooke, Compton Mackenzie, A.P. Herbert and Bernard Freyberg. The Division fought as infantry at Antwerp and in the Dardanelles and it was at Gallipoli, after helping Freyberg to win the DSO (later, on the Western Front, he was awarded the Victoria Cross – without Fred's assistance) that he was buried alive by a Turkish shell. Miraculously he survived to be invalided home to Australia where, on recovery, he enlisted in the Australian Imperial Forces.

Certainly military records prove that he did enlist in September 1915, giving his profession as chauffeur, and that he sailed for Egypt in the following month as a trooper with the 7th Light Horse. Unquestionably he served in the Palestine campaign and probably by the time he was demobilised in 1919 he had reached the rank of sergeant. But little else of his proclaimed military career can be authenticated. Was he with the RND? Did he serve with Lawrence of Arabia? Was he a pilot with the Royal Flying Corps? Was he mentioned in despatches for deeds of valour at the Battle of Beersheba? There is no record of any of this, nor of the awards of the White Eagle of Serbia, the Médaille Militaire or the Croix de Guerre, worn so proudly with those medals to which he was genuinely entitled (now unfortunately lost. Only his miniatures survive at the Canberra War Memorial Museum).

After the war Fred may (or may not) have been employed for a time as a driver by the New Zealand brothers Nairn who provided cross-desert transport to and from Jerusalem, Damascus and Baghdad. It is a matter of fact that many of their drivers were British and Empire ex-servicemen. It may also be true that he tried to join the Egyptian Police, which, again, employed some former NCOs of the British and Imperial forces.

What we do know for certain is that he was driving the Sirdar on 19 November 1924 and that it was through no fault of his that his employer did not survive – indeed, if anybody gave him a chance to live it was Fred.

With the compensation money he may have bought a garage cum

car-hire business of his own in Cairo. Fred's management skills were probably limited and it is not known how long this business survived – long enough, at any rate, for him to enjoy his membership of the Cairo Motor Cycle and Light Car Club, his penchant for motor-cycle trialing, booze and night-clubs before the cash ran out, probably in about 1927.

Of the next twenty years or so his biographer's researches reveal little or nothing. The likelihood is that he worked for various oil companies throughout the Middle East on road construction as a foreman or chargehand fitter. His claim to have served with the Royal Engineers in the Second World War is another which cannot be substantiated. Nor is it certain when he arrived in the Sudan, where he found the employment which was to occupy him for the rest of his working life, namely as a digger (appropriately enough) of *hafirs* or water storage catchments in remote parts of the Sudan under contract to the Ministry of Agriculture.

For ten months of the year, usually under conditions of considerable hardship in great heat and with only his Sudanese labourers as company, he would toil at this demanding but reasonably well-rewarded work. It was not surprising, therefore, that on his return to the fleshpots of Khartoum, such as they were, he would indulge himself in wine, women and song: that is to say, whisky, an Italian lady by the name of Ilona and the Gordon Cabaret (where he probably found Ilona).

For all his experience of the rough and tumble of life, Fred was naive and trusting and Ilona found little difficulty in relieving him of his hard-earned cash which, it appears, he had entrusted to her to invest in Italian property for his retirement. By now Fred was well into his sixties and the brutally hard life of *hafir* digging beyond him. He was a popular man and the local Greek and Italian contractors would help him out with the odd earth-moving job, but without pension or savings he slipped deeper and deeper into poverty.

However, in 1967 he took the sensible step of marrying a lady of mixed Italian-Eritrean blood who had been housekeeper to the family of one of Fred's contractor friends. At the same time ultimately suc-cessful efforts were made by the British community in Khartoum and the Australian Embassy in Cairo to get him a pension, which, considering that he had left his native land over half a century before never to return, was a remarkable victory over bureaucracy.

Thus was Fred permitted to end his life in modest comfort. In 1957 he had been awarded the MBE (first suggested, it will be recalled, in 1924!) for his not inconsiderable services to Sudanese agriculture, and in the year of his death, 1977, as a George Cross holder, he received the Queen's Jubilee Medal.

He died in the October of that year, reportedly aged ninety-six while in fact he was ten years younger, and was buried in the Christian Cemetery at Khartoum, mourned by his widow Teresa, his old dog Paddy, and many friends. About a year later, at the insistence of the Australian Returned Services League, he was re-interred in the nearby Commonwealth War Graves Commission Cemetery.

In fairness to Fred's memory it must be said that friends remember him as a shy, almost retiring man who would recount his stories with no hint of boastfulness – and they believed them.[3] One would like to think, lack of official records notwithstanding, that they were all true.

Not unreasonably, his headstone bears the epitaph 'A Distinguished Australian'.

Author's Postscript

One day in the mid-1960s I was in my office in Khartoum when my clerk announced, with a slight curl of his lip, that 'an old Egyptian' wanted to see me about advertising. In happier days for the tobacco

The grave in the Khartoum War Cemetery of Fred March, whose courage and driving skill might have saved the life of the Sirdar, Sir Lee Slack.

industry, few such opportunities were refused without due consideration and I told the clerk to show him in.

There entered a small, shabbily dressed man in his sixties. 'You are Mr Kinboyd?' he asked. I agreed that I was. 'I knew your father, Sir Kinboyd. He was a great man in Egypt.' I was accustomed to this opening gambit, which always led up to a touch, but again I agreed.

'I am a journalist and I am writing my memoirs. Printing and publication are expensive and on every other page there will be advertising. You will advertise your cigarettes on many pages,' he announced, naming a hefty price per page.

But I was ready for this one. 'My advertising budget set by London,' I informed him with regret, 'is already overspent so, unfortunately. I must decline your attractive offer, but here's ten pounds towards your expenses!'

Of course this was what he had come for, there being no book and no advertising, so without further ado he murmured his thanks and left for the office of his next victim.

Vaguely curious, I asked a Sudanese friend who this man might be, mentioning the name he had given. My friend laughed. 'Journalist! He's no more a journalist than I am. I don't know how he lives but he is the only survivor of the murderers of Sir Lee Stack who was Governor-General of the Sudan in the British time. And I'll tell you something else. If you go to the bar of the Grand Hotel at lunchtime you will see him at one end and Stack's driver, March, at the other!'

Forty years before these two men had stared into each other's eyes as one had pumped bullets into the other. Now they never so much as exchanged a glance.

CHAPTER 13

The Last Pro-Consuls

ALLENBY'S SUCCESSOR, George Lloyd, could not have been a greater contrast to his predecessor. If Allenby can be described in political terms he was, in 1980s parlance, a Tory 'wet', while Lloyd was very much to the right of the Conservative party and a strong believer in Britain's Imperial Mission.

A dapper Welshman, his reputation as a no-nonsense Governor of Bombay who had locked up Gandhi, alarmed Egyptian nationalists and King Fuad alike and delighted the Turf Club. Writing in 1927, Judge Marshall declared, 'The appointment of Lord Lloyd of Dolobran to succeed Lord Allenby in 1925 was one of the few instances of sanity which have been displayed by the British Government in its relations with Egypt during recent years.' [1]

Were the days of Cromer about to return? But the wags in the Cairo cafés, as ever, made light of it: 'I know Lloyd George but who is this George Lloyd?' asks Mohamed. 'It's the same man,' replies Ahmed, 'but he's coming arse-first!' [2]

India had imbued in him a love of pomp and circumstance which, he believed, impressed 'Orientals'. However, even his most fervent supporters in the Turf Club became irritated when they were confronted with closed streets and traffic jams allowing the High Commissioner's Rolls, accompanied by numerous motor-cycle outriders, to sweep past unimpeded. Even his departure from the Residency for his early morning ride was a ceremonial occasion, marked by a fanfare of bugles, stentorian commands from the sergeant of the guard, the crash of Lee-Enfields coming to the Present and the stamp of ammunition boots. A particular victim of this disturbance was the American Minister, a late and light sleeper who lived opposite the Residency. On at least one occasion Uncle Sam's representative was seen at his bedroom window shaking his fist at the great Pro-consul as he passed. [3]

Lloyd had been opposed to the 1922 Declaration of Independence and came to Egypt determined to crack the whip. One of his first moves was to persuade the King to remove Nashaat Pasha, still under suspicion over the Stack affair, from the Palace. This, at least, pleased the Wafdists, as Nashaat had been a leading participant in their unending four-cornered struggle with the Palace, the Residency and their political adversaries.[4]

But by 1926 the shadows were already beginning to creep towards the flag upon which the sun must never set. Up to 1914 the unique nature of Britain's virtually unchallenged occupation of Egypt symbolised her self-confidence in her status as *primus inter pares* of the Great Powers. For a variety of reasons which are quite outside the scope of this book, both self-confidence and status had begun to fade by 1919 and gradually were replaced by the querulous self-doubt which, punctuated by brief and temporary Indian summers, characterised the nation and her leaders for three-quarters of the twentieth century.

George Lloyd was a man after his time. He wanted to rule Egypt as he had ruled Bombay, thus not only pitting himself implacably against the Egyptian political establishment, however divided, but also against the Foreign Office at home which had already adopted a policy of appeasement in its dealings with Egypt. A determination in a High Commissioner or Ambassador to put British interests first, as he may see them on the ground, has always excited the animosity of Foreign Office mandarins and it was his successes rather than his failures that stiffened their resolve to bring him down. For example, in what was known as the Army Crisis in 1927, by the use of gunboat (or rather battleship) diplomacy, Lloyd forced the Egyptian Government to abandon plans for an expansion of its army and the abolition of the post of (British) Inspector-General. Indeed, Lloyd even strengthened the British position by insisting on the appointment of a Deputy Inspector-General. This kind of thing was not at all what the Permanent Under-Secretary at the Foreign Office, Sir William Tyrrell, an elderly alcoholic, and his successor, Sir Ronald Lindsay, had in mind. With a change of government from Conservative to Labour in 1929, these two arch-intriguers struck. Like Wingate before him, Lloyd was lured to London, where, with some show of reluctance, the new Foreign Secretary, Arthur Henderson, forced his resignation.[5]

However, before we allow him to depart the Egyptian scene, we must note that it was during his tenure of office that Saad Zagloul, so long the hero of Egyptian nationalism and the Hammer of the British, died on 23 August 1927.

His last word, echoing that of a much greater man, was '*Intaha*'. 'It is finished', we are told.[6] But the murder of Stack had ended his ministerial career nearly three years earlier, although, as President of the Chamber of Deputies, his political influence remained potent.

Both as a man and a politician he remains something of an enigma. He did not hate the British in the way that, for example, Abbas Hilmi II or, later, Nasser did. Gerald Delaney, the 'neutral' Irishman who represented Reuter's in Egypt for many years and regularly acted as a kind of unofficial liaison officer between British officials and Egyptian politicians, noticed that on his writing table were two signed photographs, one of his father-in-law, the anglophile statesman Mustafa Fehmy Pasha, and the other of his original patron, Lord Cromer. More surprising was Delaney's belief that, after the First World War, Zaghloul would have accepted for Egypt Dominion status within the British Empire. So far as we know, no such offer was ever made by the one side nor suggested by the other; nor did any British minister or pro-consul ever come to a meeting of minds with Zaghloul and nor did Zaghloul ever make any effort to bring that about, thus the extent of his contribution towards eventual Egyptian independence is a matter for debate. His powerful personality and magnetism as an orator were stronger elements in his character than political acumen or administrative ability.

On a lighter note, the explanation he gave Delaney for the bad blood between King Fuad and himself is amusing, if rather less than the whole truth. 'He never liked me since the days I took money off him when we played poker together in the Club. He felt that it was not befitting the dignity of a Prince to be bluffed and he never forgave me!'[7]

He was a notable gambler who was reputed to have cleaned out an entire British Officers' Mess at Suez on his way into exile. Perhaps he gambled too much in politics as well and bluffed himself into believing in his own infallibility.

Be that as it may, Grafftey-Smith remembered following his funeral procession and feeling 'a respect and sense of regret not less sincere than the clamour of the mourners in the streets.'[8]

Lord Lloyd's treatment by the British Government was not much different to that meted out to both Wingate and Allenby. Only 'Untouchables' like Cromer and Kitchener escaped the consequences of the vicious intrigue, in-fighting, policy changes and prevarication of Whitehall and Westminster. Egypt was something of a poison chalice but Lloyd drank deep of its deadly contents and survived as a public servant, ending his political career as Colonial Secretary in Churchill's wartime cabinet. He had neglected his health and overworked for many years and died on 4 February 1941 aged only sixty-one.[9]

His title is now as extinct as the Empire he served with such loyalty and enthusiasm. But for all his devotion to that cause he did not lose his sense of proportion. In the introductory chapter to his great book *Egypt since Cromer* he wrote of the British Occupation, 'Set in its true perspective in the unending history of the Nile Delta, it becomes a moment so fleeting that only the longest record would find a place for it.'[10]

After Lloyd Whitehall plumped for 'a safe pair of hands' which it found attached to the urbane figure of a career diplomat and 12th baronet, Sir Percy Loraine. Sir Percy, who happened to be an old friend of Lloyd, had no previous Egyptian experience, although he was married to the daughter of the flamboyant Eddie Montagu-Stuart-Wortley, one of the would-be rescuers of General Gordon, but had served as Minister to Persia from 1921 to 1926.[11]

A keen racing man, Loraine cut a popular figure with all sections of Egyptian society, identifying with Court circles and the Turco-Egyptian aristocracy, while the up and coming Egyptian political class, as exemplified by Zaghloul's successor Mustafa Nahas, were pleased to find that he confined his interference in local affairs to those matters which pertained strictly to British interests and the 'Reserved Points'. Indeed, it may be said that Loraine's sojourn in Egypt passed almost unnoticed, as though he were a kind of caretaker holding the fort between the departure of his uncompromising predecessor and his overpowering successor, Sir Miles Lampson who replaced him in 1933.

But not so Loraine's later career. As Ambassador to Turkey he was to become the personal friend and confidant of the great reformer, Kamal Ataturk. According to legend, on his deathbed, Kamal offered Loraine the presidency of Turkey, an offer wisely but no doubt diplomatically declined.

The outbreak of the Second World War found him as Ambassador to Italy but all his skills could not keep Mussolini from joining the losing side.

In Egypt he had struck up a special friendship with Alexander Keown-Boyd whose finger on the political pulse of the country and foreknowledge of potential security dangers were invaluable to all the latter-day pro-consuls. But it was probably their mutual interest in horse racing which cemented their relationship and it was Loraine who, on K-B's death in 1954, provided *The Times* with a supplementary obituary of his friend. In this he wrote:

He had an interesting kind of resilience. He knew about the grim things of life and about the hard things of life; but there was a bubbling well of gaiety in the man that kept him in balance and was a great asset to his companions ...

He needed these qualities for the work he did in Egypt, where for twenty years his natural understanding of the Oriental mind proved to be of the greatest value. He had a facility for interpreting and reconciling the interests of the British and Egyptian Governments and this gift helped him greatly in the discharge of his complicated responsibilities ...

Among the Egyptians themselves he had a vast acquaintance and quantities of friends. Not a few of them will, I believe, regret his loss and honour his memory.[12]

On his retirement from the Diplomatic Service Loraine was to become a familiar and respected figure on the English bloodstock and racing scene, advising the government on policy and methods of operation of the National Stud as well as winning several Classics.

He died in 1961.[13]

Arriving in the twilight of British power in Egypt. Sir Miles Wedderburn Lampson was able, thanks largely to the Second World War and Egypt's geographical importance in that conflict, to turn the clock back for a while.

With the signing of the 1936 Treaty of Alliance[14] 'between His Majesty, in respect of the United Kingdom, and His Majesty the King of Egypt' signed in London on 26 August by the Foreign Secretary Anthony Eden and the Prime Minister of Egypt, Mustafa Nahas Pasha, Egypt achieved almost total independence – but almost is the key word.

The Capitulations were abolished in the following year and the Mixed Courts (which lingered on until 1949) fell virtually into disuse; the post of British Inspector-General of the Egyptian Army was abolished and the remaining British officers on contract to that army were replaced by a Military Mission.

British troops were to withdraw from Cairo and Alexandria to the Suez Canal Zone once the necessary accommodations and infrastructure had been prepared for them and their presence there was to be reviewed after twenty years.

In the light of the outbreak of war only three years after the signing of the Treaty, Article 7 was crucial. It read:

Should ... either of the High Contracting Parties become engaged in war, the other High Contracting Party will ... immediately come to his aid in the capacity of an ally.

The aid of His Majesty the King of Egypt in the event of war ... will consist in furnishing His Majesty the King and Emperor on Egyptian territory ... all the facilities and assistance in his power, including the use of his ports, aerodromes, and means of communication. It will accordingly be for the Egyptian Government to take all the administrative and legislative measures, including the establishment of martial law and an effective censorship, necessary to render these facilities and assistance effective.

It was this clause, somewhat broadly interpreted, which enabled the British to re-assume control of Egypt, except for purely domestic affairs, from 1939 to 1945, with a veneer of legality.

On the civilian side, by 1937 the number of British officials had shrunk from a peak of about 1,500 to 576, many of whom were lecturers, schoolmasters and technicians on short-term contracts.[15] Among those who taught English at Cairo University for a while were the verbaliser Malcolm Muggeridge and, very briefly, the poet Robert Graves. Muggeridge, a Soviet apologist at the time, also reported for the *Manchester Guardian* and fell foul of the authorities for filling his students' heads with Karl Marx instead of William Shakespeare. At the end of three years his contract was not renewed (he may even have been deported before it had expired).

The last of the British 'Advisers', of course no longer known by that hated name, were now to go. Redundancy payments and pensions were reasonable if not generous – Keown-Boyd, for example, received a lump sum of £5,500 and a pension of £1,000 a year[16] (he was also knighted – one of the few men to be dubbed by King Edward VIII). It is worthy of note that the payment of these pensions by successive Egyptian Governments, albeit greatly reduced in value over the years by inflation, was never interrupted, even by Nasser. Was this a bureaucratic oversight or tacit recognition of the services these people had rendered to Egypt over the decades, unacknowledged in any other way, except in private conversation?

Some British police officers found senior appointments in Britain; two, W.F. Henn and Walter Lucas, as Chief Constables of Gloucestershire and Monmouthshire respectively. Others, perhaps surprisingly, for example Russell and Baker as Commandants in Cairo and Alexandria, remained until 1946.[17] While this was undoubtedly of benefit to the British authorities during the war, it probably also suited the Egyptian political establishment who could rely upon these men not to back a particular party or political faction, although their incorruptibility must have been, on occasion, an irritant.

The career of Miralai Walter Lucas Bey in the Egyptian Police was particularly distinguished. A completely fearless man who had won a DSO in the First World War, he was renowned for his skill and daring

in bringing rioting mobs under control. However, these duties had left
their mark. In the middle of his forehead was a deep dent. In later
years, when asked by admiring children how he had sustained this
injury, he would reply, 'Chap threw a stone at me – knocked me out
cold – saved by my man Hanafi [his police orderly] – picked me up like
a baby and carried me away at the double – good man, Hanafi!'[18]

By the 1950s almost all the British civil servants had departed but
some remained on as consultants to their former ministries – for example,
Dr H.E. Hurst, who had arrived in Egypt in 1906 retired as Director-
General of the Physical Department of the Ministry of Public Works
in 1946, having served under twenty-five different ministers. His knowledge of the Nile and the usage of its waters was unrivalled and he
remained for many years as a consultant to the ministry. His last visit
to Egypt was in 1968 at the age of eighty-eight.[19]

King Fuad died in 1936 and was succeeded by his only son. Farouk.

Though financially dishonest and by nature authoritarian, Fuad was
a better ruler than most of his dynasty and certainly than his son. His
Italian upbringing and his inability to speak Arabic fluently did not
endear him to his people, although the only attempt upon his life
had been made by a former brother-in-law, Prince Ahmed Seifeddin,
incensed by the divorce of his sister, Princess Shevekiar. Whether this

Foreign judges and other officials at the funeral of King Fuad in 1936. Full-face to
the camera (bareheaded) is Sir Alexander Keown-Boyd.

divorce was a wise move on Fuad's part, quite apart from unknowingly endangering his life, is open to doubt as his second wife. Queen Nazli had a reputation as nymphomaniac who, it was said, provided her astonishingly complacent husband with the longest horns in Egypt.

It appears that one day in 1898, long before his accession to the throne, Fuad was taking his ease in the Silent Room of the Khedivial Club when the outraged Seifeddin approached him and opened fire with a revolver. One bullet pierced the royal throat, the wound causing a permanent defect in his speech, taking the form of a high-pitched bark which occasionally and unexpectedly interrupted his conversation, a phenomenon deeply disconcerting to any unwary interlocutor.

The would-be assassin was arrested, not by the police, but by Private Crosbie of the Northumberland Fusiliers who happened to be passing the steps leading up to the entrance of the club as Seifeddin was descending them.[20]

At Seifeddin's trial, although warned by the presiding judge of the exalted rank of both victim and accused, Crosbie, when asked to recount the circumstances of the arrest, allegedly replied as follows: 'Hearing sounds of gunfire from the Club. I proceeded to investigate. I saw the nigger standing at the top of the marble steps. I closed with him and overpowered him.'[21] Bearing in mind that Seifeddin was probably as white, if not whiter, than a sunburnt British soldier, this public-spirited Geordie must have been a firm believer in the old, but today probably criminal, adage that 'Blacks begin at Calais'!

Seifeddin was sentenced to the dreaded quarries at Tura for seven years but was soon certified insane and transferred to a private lunatic asylum at Ticehurst in Sussex. Here he languished for thirty years until one day, accompanied by two male nurses, he decided to abscond which he did by bus to Folkestone and ferry to Boulogne. Reaching Istanbul he joined his sister, by then on her fifth husband, to the embarrassment of Fuad who had been administering his ex-brother-in-law's enormous estates in Egypt and pocketing the proceeds![22]

Farouk, young, handsome, charming and fluent in Arabic, got off to a good start with his people, but he and Lampson, now, following signature of the 1936 Treaty, Britain's first Ambassador to Egypt, never reached any kind of rapport. This was almost certainly the fault of the older man, but whether a closer and friendlier relationship between them would have altered the course of Egyptian, or British, history it is impossible to say.

CHAPTER 14

Uneasy Allies

GREAT BRITAIN'S POSITION in Egypt during the Second World War was less clear-cut than it had been during the First when the country had been declared a British Protectorate. However, as we have seen in the previous chapter, both countries had obligations towards each other under the 1936 Treaty. Although Egypt was not, until 1945, a belligerent, she was, in a sense, an ally in that all her resources and infrastructure were at the disposal of the British. For their part the British were committed to defend Egypt against foreign invasion, which the vital strategic importance of the Suez Canal made it imperative for them to do anyway. In effect, for the duration of the war, Egypt was to return to the status quo ante.

In 1940, when Italy joined Germany and was threatening Egypt's frontier with Libya (an Italian colony), the two leading British personalities were the Ambassador, the massive – in every sense of the word – Sir Miles Lampson and the Commander-in-Chief Middle East, General Sir Archibald (later Field Marshal the Earl) Wavell, a calm, taciturn protégé of Allenby upon whose staff he had served in the First World War and the author of two books on the Bull.

A cultivated and erudite Wykehamist, Wavell wrote clearly and fluently but in speech was laconic to the point of total silence even when something needed to be said. His Chief of Staff of those days, General Sir Arthur Smith, used to tell the story of Wavell's first, and perhaps only, meeting with de Gaulle, which took place in Wavell's office in Cairo. The Frenchman had no English and Wavell's French was halting. The 'conversation' went thus:

Wavell to de Gaulle: '*Enchanté, mon General!*'

De Gaulle to Wavell: '*Enchanté, mon General!*'

A lengthy silence.

Wavell to Smith: 'Arthur, why don't you take the General to the map-room and show him the set-up?'

Smith removes de Gaulle to map-room and returns with him a few minutes later.

De Gaulle to Wavell: '*Très interessant, mon General.*'

Wavell to de Gaulle: '*Bon.*'

A further silence finally broken by de Gaulle: '*Alors, mon General, au revoir et merci.*'

Wavell: '*Merci à vous, mon General, et à bientôt.*'

When Smith returns having accompanied de Gaulle to his car, Wavell remarks: 'I like that fellow, Arthur, he doesn't talk too much!' [1]

This kind of thing was anathema to Churchill who thrived on argument and discussion and ruthlessly bullied Wavell at long range but with early successes against the Italians in the desert and Ethiopia with extremely limited resources and manpower, Wavell proved his worth as an area commander. However, following the arrival of Rommel and his Afrika Korps early in 1941 and the failure of the doomed campaign to save Greece, Wavell was replaced by Auckinleck with whom he exchanged as C in C India, eventually to be appointed Viceroy.

Characteristically and like his mentor, Allenby, Wavell saw no need for explanation or justification for any of his decisions and went silently to his grave in 1950.

Lampson was the last of his kind, a big man representing a great power and a huge empire. On balance, in the years of the Desert War from 1940 to 1943, he was the right man in the right place at the right time. He brooked no nonsense from the Egyptians or anyone else. But some people saw him in a different light. To Joan Keown-Boyd, never one to understate her case, writing to her mother in England early in the war he was '... this useless Ambassador who does nothing and is just like a sponge ... They must move him. He has been utterly futile and allows these people here to do exactly as they wish.' [2] Needless to say, this was not a view shared by the Egyptians although they too would have liked him removed for precisely the opposite reason.

Although inclined to bulldoze his way through problems, he was not without wisdom and built a remarkable relationship with that most shrewd of all Egyptian politicians, Nahas Pasha, leader of the Wafd, whose wife, the famous Zenab el Waqil, was reputedly even more cunning than he. As a result this theoretically dyed-in-the-wool anti-British party remained loyal to the Allied cause throughout the war.

Taking stock at an early stage, Nahas probably came to two conclusions. Firstly that the Germans and their poodles the Italians were nastier and, in the long run, more difficult to dislodge should they ever conquer Egypt, than the British ... better the devil etc. Secondly, he may have calculated that the British were more likely to end up on the winning side anyway, particularly if the Americans came into the war, and nailed his flag to their mast accordingly.

Lampson's support for Nahas, and vice versa, came to a head and was tested in February 1942 in what became known as the Abdin Incident.

For a diplomat, the British Ambassador was, in some ways, a rough man and his roughness was exposed in his handling of King Farouk whom he despised and made no secret of it. Their relationship was not dissimilar to that between Kitchener and Abbas Hilmi. There is no evidence that Farouk ever directly supported the Axis cause, although his Italian connections, inherited from his father, were strong and his personal staff included several Italians of dubious background and reputation; but with the outbreak of the Second World War, as opposed to the First, the British were given no excuse to exchange one Egyptian monarch for another. Nonetheless, Lampson (and others) would have liked to see Farouk's anglophile uncle, Prince Mohamed Ali, on the throne.

Farouk for his part enjoyed irritating Lampson in minor ways, for example, drawing attention to the lineage of the Ambassador's young wife (they had married in 1934 after the death of his first wife), Jacqueline, the daughter of an Italian surgeon with a practice in Harley Street called Sir Aldo Castellani. This, perhaps understandably, Farouk was wont to do when complaints were made about his own Italian staff who were, in fact, little more than pimps.

However, in February 1942 Lampson's opportunity to get rid of Farouk presented itself over the relatively minor issue of the closing of the Vichy French Legation in Cairo. This the British had been urging for some time and eventually prevailed upon the government of Sirry Pasha to do it. Farouk, who had not been consulted, was enraged and forced first the Foreign Minister and then Sirry himself to resign. His intention was to bring back to power the former anti-British Prime Minister, Ali Maher (the brother of Ahmed who had been tried and acquitted of the Stack murder in 1926), whom he had dismissed at Lampson's insistence in 1940.

Lampson was having none of this and decided that, come what may, a Wafdist government under Nahas must be installed. After some days of futile negotiation, on 4 February an ultimatum was drawn up by the Defence Committee under the Minister of State for the Middle East, Oliver Lyttelton (later Lord Chandos). Farouk must either appoint Nahas or face the consequences – in other words, abdication – the ultimatum to expire at 6 p.m.

The British military commanders, including General Stone, GOC British Troops in Egypt, were nervous about this. The crisis had already

Ahmed Hassanein Pasha, explorer and right-hand man to King Farouk who saved the King's throne during the Abdin Incident of 1942.

sparked off demonstrations so what if the whole Egyptian people rallied behind their King? Troops would have to be withdrawn from the desert to deal with the situation to the benefit of the Germans who were less than a hundred miles from Alexandria. But Lampson, supported by Lyttelton, a man not easily influenced or persuaded, had his way.

Abdin Palace was surrounded by British troops and a platoon of officer cadets (NCOs training for commissions) ordered to stand by at the gates. There are varying accounts of what followed and the exact sequence of events and who precisely was involved are uncertain but the ultimatum expired unanswered at 6 p.m. Last-minute consultations between Lyttelton and Lampson decided that, even so, Farouk's agreement to a Nahas government when personally confronted by Lampson should be accepted and that he should be allowed to remain on the throne.[3]

Accompanied by a reluctant Stone and two armed ADCs Lampson arrived at the palace gates at about 9 p.m. It seems that Farouk had given orders that no resistance was to be shown but the gates were locked. According to one account the padlocks were shot off by a British officer[4] but another has an armoured car being driven straight at the gates and smashing them open.[5] However that may be, Lampson and his companions entered the palace and marched up the stairs to Farouk's office where the King was waiting with his Chamberlain, Ahmed Hassanein Pasha, an intrepid desert explorer[6] of Bedouin origin and reputedly the lover of Nazli the Queen Mother, and a bodyguard or two. According to Farouk's alleged version of events, recounted later to a friend, one of these, the Sudanese Nejumi (see Chapter 5) '... unable to restrain himself at the sight of drawn revolvers on the part of the British, drew his own gun. A trigger-happy British colonel shot him in the hand before he could use it.'[7] This is almost certainly a flight of fancy as few British officers were or are capable of such Wyatt Earp-style gunplay, particularly with that notoriously inaccurate weapon, the service revolver. However, Stone's ADC, Captain Harold Morrison of the Scots Guards, told a brother officer that when he noticed one of the bodyguards, presumably Nejumi, fiddling with his holster he tapped his own significantly and the moment passed.[8]

Farouk, according to his own account, remained calm and simply said to Lampson, 'You want Nahas? Have him!'[9] but other versions have him prevaricating and preparing to sign the article of abdication before being urgently pressed by Hassanein in whispered Arabic to agree the British terms and save his throne.[10] Whatever the truth, Nahas was appointed that very night and Farouk survived for another ten years.

Egyptian disapproval of this ruthless exercise of power was almost universal but there were three schools of British thought as to its wisdom and efficacy. The first, which included Stone and a number of Old Hands such as Russell and Keown-Boyd, believed it to have been unnecessary in that either the problem could have been resolved by persistent negotiation or a satisfactory compromise reached without an ultimatum and the direct threat of violence, as such matters had usually been in the past. The second felt that Lampson and Lyttelton had got it about right and the third, which may have included Lampson himself, that an opportunity to depose Farouk and replace him with his uncle Prince Mohamed Ali had been missed. A certain weight is added to this last school of thought in the light of events which were to unfold ten years later.

However, at least one British historian has taken the opposite view and recorded his belief that the Abdin Incident was to bring about the Revolution of 1952, the downfall of the monarchy, and the end for the Wafd and the British position in Egypt.[11] Of course this opinion, like most historical judgements, was formed with the benefit of hindsight and, taking into account the circumstances of the time, it is hard to fault the decision taken by 'the men on the spot', which, incidentally, had the support of the British Government.

Despite the recent entry into the war of the United States the tide had not yet turned in Allied favour. The Japanese were rampaging, virtually unchecked, through South-East Asia; the Germans had penetrated deep into Russia and, most dangerous of all to the British in Egypt, Rommel's formidable Afrika Korps threatened the Suez Canal and, ultimately, the whole of the Middle East. Priority had to be given to the establishment of a stable, pro-Allied Egyptian government while longer-term considerations and Egyptian sensitivities could not and should not have been taken into account.

Finally, however, it must be said that had the relationship between the British pro-consul and 'that boy', as Lampson was wont to call Farouk, been of a more friendly nature the crisis might never have arisen in the first place.

Readers of such enjoyable books as *Cairo in the War* by Artemis Cooper and Lady Ranfurly's *To War with Whitaker* will have come, quite rightly, to the conclusion that Egypt must have been by far the most comfortable of the 'front-line' states of the Second World War. Of shortages there were few; hotels, bars, restaurants and clubs flourished; lavish parties and balls were given in private houses. Even for the troops fighting in the desert and enduring its hardships, there was always the prospect of leave in the fleshpots of Cairo or Alex, with their welcoming civilian populations and the virtually open house hospitality (at least for officers) of the British and other Allied, including the Egyptian and especially Coptic, upper class communities.

Even for Other Ranks leave facilities were first-class. Many British ladies opened and ran clubs where a soldier would be confronted with a huge menu, which, if recently arrived from Britain, included dishes he had not seen or tasted for years – if ever. Joan Keown-Boyd recalled being asked by one of the waiters to find out what a particularly miserable-looking customer at her Corner Club in Cairo wanted. Apparently the man had refused all the culinary delights which the menu offered and had mumbled something incomprehensible to the waiter. 'What can we do for you, sergeant?' asked Joan. 'Well, mam,' was the reply, 'you can tell 'im to bring me a bit o' burnt toast with a scrape o' marg on it and a cuppa tea slopped in the saucer – I'm 'omesick!'

In March 1941 six thousand men used one such club in one day [12] and people from all walks of life rallied to the cause and worked to keep them running. The hostel accommodation at the Corner Club was managed by Bill Leonard who had arrived in Egypt in the 1890s as a trooper in the 21st Lancers and had taken part, with Winston Churchill, in the famous charge at the Battle of Omdurman. Later he had transferred to the Military Police and, on retirement, joined the British firm of Egyptian Markets. He married locally and never left Egypt where he died at a great age in 1959.

Another (temporary) helper at the Corner Club was Joyce Britten-Jones, the mistress of King George of Greece. The pair had escaped to Egypt when Greece fell to the Germans. Joan Keown-Boyd, usually censorious of such irregular liaisons, was 'very fond' of her and had her to stay while she looked for a flat.

Many of the men were quite capable of diverting themselves in the numerous and relatively inexpensive cinemas, bars and bordellos, but official entertainment was laid on notwithstanding. ENSA (Entertainments National Service Association) parties toured the war zones and included well-known stars of stage, screen and opera. But the efforts of some well meaning members of the British community to 'do their bit' for the troops were not always appreciated. One lady of high standing in Alexandrian society sought to exercise her talents as a singer for their benefit and went bravely ahead with her repertoire despite suffering from a nasty cold. 'Sorry, boys,' she exclaimed between songs, 'but I'm a little hoarse!' – a fatal excuse to an audience of Cockney riflemen. 'No yer not,' came the instant response from the back of the hall, 'yer a fat old cow!'

At the same time, the private sector catered for a broad range of sexual taste, sometimes leading to misunderstanding.

The story, doubtless apocryphal, used to be told of the British officer who had lost his luggage at Alexandria harbour and was waiting impatiently for the Harbour Master's office to open. He is approached by a pimp.

'Sair, you like my leetle sister? She pink like Lady Allenby!' (Lady Allenby had left Egypt nearly twenty years earlier but her pinkness apparently lingered on.)

'To Hell with your little sister – I want ...!'

'Okay, sair, maybe you like my leetle brother, he ...!'

'Damn your little brother – I want the Harbour Master!'

'Sair, I get you the Harbour Master – but Harbour Master he vary expensive!'

Many of the British civilians, marooned in Egypt for the duration of the war, were themselves homesick, especially those who were to be separated from their children for nearly five years. Transport for civilians, except on very official business, to and from the United Kingdom was virtually unobtainable and, although some left for the Sudan, East or South Africa in moments of panic, most endured five or six sweltering summers, the luckiest managing the occasional holiday in Palestine.

Their letters home reflected their feelings of frustration and, especially in the early years of the war, anxiety.

Once again the least popular of the visiting soldiery, not only with the Egyptians but also the Provost Marshal's department, were the Australians and New Zealanders. It should be remembered that until very recently these fine Dominions were not exciting places to live, with notoriously draconian licensing laws. As Noel Coward once famously remarked, he couldn't say what New Zealand was like because when he was there it was closed. The result of this was that these fit, tough but unsophisticated young men when faced with almost unlimited opportunities for getting into trouble, often did.

The 76,000 New Zealanders who passed through Digla Camp near the smart suburb of Maadi had a mixed relationship with their civilian neighbours, most of whom did their best to welcome them, but some were less than enchanted by their presence and '... were afraid to venture out after dark ... as the soldiers, returning from drinking bouts in Cairo, awoke Maadiites by singing lewd songs and engaging in drunken brawls.' One of these fights led to the death of a soldier who was knifed by another and in 1943 a householder was murdered by a Maori intruder who hit him over the head with a flowerpot. That said, the New Zealanders' reputation, as aggressive infantry was second to none. Of the 76,000, 29,000 were killed, wounded or missing and one of their number, Captain Charles Upham of the 20th Battalion (Canterbury Regiment), was the only double VC of the war.[13]

As had been the case in the First World War, when somebody counted a hundred and seventeen generals in Cairo, GHQ was immensely fecund and spawned numerous offspring while little empires sprang up and expanded in accordance with Parkinson's Law, all with their (sometimes deliberately) incomprehensible acronyms.

Administrative Officers, Training Officers, Ordnance Officers, Intelligence and Counter-Intelligence Officers, Signals Officers. Weapons Officers, Military Police Officers, Welfare Officers, Medical Officers, Veterinary Officers, Transport Officers, all attended by platoons of batmen, clerks, drivers, motorcyclists, orderlies, ATS, WAAFS, WRNS, WVS and locally employed civilian cooks, waiters and bottle-washers, proliferated. No doubt many of these were necessary but they sometimes seemed to outnumber the front-line troops to whom they were known collectively as the Gaberdine Swine.

Additionally, and far more usefully to both the war effort and the Egyptian economy, thousands of local artisans and labourers were employed in workshops, depots, docks and storage facilities at high wages. However, in the Second World War Egypt was not declared a Protectorate, thus, fortunately for all concerned, the British were in no position to introduce any form of conscription, a measure which had caused such resentment in the First World War and which, as we have seen, was a contributory factor to the rebellion of 1919.

Although prices rose, the war was a time of prosperity for many Egyptians and foreigners of all classes – the only exceptions being the (very large) Italian and (rather small) German communities, most of whom were interned and their assets sequestrated.

The highest ranking and most mysterious of the 'Parkinsonian' officers mentioned above was the colossal Field Marshal Lord (Henry Maitland 'Jumbo') Wilson. GCB, GBE, CB, DSO. In *Who's Who* his wartime appointments are listed resoundingly as follows:

General Officer C-in-C, Egypt, 1939

Military Governor and GOC-in-C ,Cyrenaica, 1941

GOC-in-C British Troops in Greece, 1941

GOC British Forces in Palestine and Transjordan, 1941

C-in-C Allied Forces in Syria, 1941

GOC 9th Army, 1941

C-in-C Persia-Iraq Command, 1942–43

C-in-C Middle East, 1943

Supreme Allied Commander Mediterranean Theatre, 1944

Promoted to Field Marshal, 1944

Head of British Staff Mission in Washington, 1945–47

Despite these high-sounding titles, the most careful study of the history of the Second World War in the Mediterranean and Middle East fails to reveal what this officer actually did which was of any significance. The only achievement for which he is now remembered was the employment as his Personal Assistant of the beautiful, efficient, and incredibly determined Countess of Ranfurly whom everybody else was trying to send home.[14]

Vast as he was of stature and girth, he seems to have glided through the war either unobserved or under the special protection of the Prime Minister. However, he did have his enemies, in particular the acerbic Major-General Sir Louis Spears, who had been Churchill's personal representative to the French Government before the fall of France and later Head of the British Mission to Syria and the Lebanon.

In his book *Fulfilment of a Mission*, Spears wrote of Wilson:

During my trip to Jerusalem I had met General Wilson ... He was an enormous, bald man, active for his size, unexpectedly so, like an outsize child's balloon rising into space at the lightest touch. He had the good fortune to resemble a benevolent owl, which ever since the days of Pallas Athene has conjured up the concept of wisdom ... His nose like a beak was bracketed with dewlaps. Pouches, like billiard table pockets, seemed designed to catch his perfectly round eyes should they fall out. Feathers alone were missing. But his personal characteristics were not a reliable guide to his character, and I personally never located the benevolence his wide paunch seemed to proclaim ...

Spears continues,

> For Winston Churchill, although no great classical scholar, Jumbo Wilson's evocation of Minerva was powerful enough to cast a veil over that General's shortcomings, and in fact it led to his being classified as one of the infallible demigods, with the result that by the end of the war he had floated like a Montgolfier balloon levitated by hot air alone and propelled by a strong breeze from 10 Downing Street, until finally and surprisingly he landed on high Olympus as a Field Marshal.

But Jumbo travelled light. On transfer from his Italian HQ to Washington his baggage list ran into only eight columns on Hermione Ranfurly's typewriter. Nor was he concerned with his personal comfort, taking with him to the USA only ten domestic staff, consisting of one colour-sergeant, two sergeants, a corporal, a lance-corporal, a rifleman ('personal waiter'!) two Sudanese valets and two Indo-Chinese house-boys. But the faithful Hermione had to be dumped when the realisation dawned on Lady Jumbo that, protocologically, a countess would take

The cartoonist Jon's Two Types heading for Cairo on leave, *c*.1942. (*By kind permission of Mrs Sylvia Philpin Jones*)

preference over the wife of a mere knight at grand Washington dinner parties.[15] In 1946 Jumbo was elevated to the peerage as a baron but even that would not have been enough to reverse the position.

But Spears' judgement was harsh. One military commentator has concluded, 'Although he [Wilson] is unlikely to be remembered in history as one of the great wartime field commanders, he deserves to be remembered, like Eisenhower, as a leader who moved nations to work together in a common cause.'[16]

The opening shots of the North African campaign were probably fired by 4th Troop 'A' Squadron of the 11th Hussars (Prince Albert's Own) on the Libyan frontier during the night of 11 June 1940.[17] On 16 May 1943 Hermione Ranfurly recorded in her diary, 'Last week all Axis forces in Tunisia surrendered. The struggle for North Africa is ended.'

The Desert campaign of 1940–43 was the longest and, arguably, the least unpleasant of the Second World War. Fatal casualties were relatively light, few civilians were involved, and, at least for the Allies, comfort and relaxation was not all that far behind their front lines.

There was also a kind of informality about the desert war, as illustrated by the cartoonist Jon and his flamboyantly dressed Two Types, which did not exist elsewhere; and perhaps the last traces of chivalry between combatants.

Sometimes in some inexplicable way even personal messages would get through to individuals on the battlefield. Just before he was severely wounded, one young officer of the 60th Rifles was passed a message

11th Hussars marching through Cairo.

by a puzzled wireless operator, which read: 'When in east wear tummy band stop your father always did stop love mother.' [18]

Few atrocities were committed by either side and prisoners were usually treated with reasonable consideration – although, curiously enough, it was less disagreeable to be captured by the Germans than the Italians. Also the desert was relatively clean and, despite the shortage of water, men did not suffer the appalling hardships of the Burmese jungle and certainly there were no horrors to compare with the savagery of the Russian front.

The provision of food and other resources of many kinds for the Allied forces in North Africa were, to a large extent, the responsibility of an organisation known as the Middle East Supply Centre based in Cairo. Set up in the early days of the war by General Wavell under the Chairmanship of Sir Alexander Keown-Boyd (who, on retirement from Egyptian government service in 1937, had been appointed Managing-Director of the textile firm of Beida Dyers), its task was to maximise and coordinate the production and transportation of supplies from all those parts of the Middle East and North and East Africa under Allied control, thus to reduce the volume of tonnage required for 'long-sea' shipment from Britain, the Dominions and the United States. In this endeavour the Centre was highly successful and its Chairman and executives lost little time in exploiting new sources of supply as they became available.

For example, 1941 saw the conquest of the Italian colonies of Eritrea and Ethiopia by British, Sudanese, South African and Ethiopian 'Patriot' forces and the Emperor Haile Selassie restored to his throne. The infrastructure and such industries as these countries possessed, having been almost entirely Italian owned and run, were in a state of collapse and of little value to the war effort in that condition, but the prospects for foreign investment were bright. Keown-Boyd immediately flew to Addis Ababa and, with pledges of capital from Egypt's wealthy Coptic (religiously akin to Ethiopian Christians) and Jewish communities in his pocket, arranged with the Emperor to set up various joint-venture companies in the fields of transport, manufacture and coastal shipping with Ethiopian, Egyptian and British participation, but without the need for any public financial input. The encouragement of wheat growing, its collection and transportation to Egypt was of special importance. [19]

Italian managers, technicians and artisans, having little or no desire to return to their homeland even if they could, were only too ready and able to return to work and with a plentiful supply of relatively cheap local labour, most of these enterprises thrived. Some, despite the upheavals of revolution and civil war, survive to this day.

The campaign in the desert, although dismissed by some military historians as a side-show, nonetheless immortalised the names of the most famous commanders on either side, Montgomery and Rommel. These two men, totally different in character and style, shall always be numbered among the great captains.

Although by the summer of 1943 any direct threat from the Axis to Egypt had receded, the country remained a British dominated centre of Allied command. The Germans still occupied the Balkans and Greece and most Allied operations in support of the various groups of partisans, often keener to fight each other than the Germans, were mounted from Egypt.

In November 1943 the Cairo summit conference was held at Mena House attended by Churchill, Roosevelt and the Chinese leader Chiang Kai-Shek, the last accompanied by Churchill's special representative to China, General Carton de Wiart VC, who had been brought up in Egypt and who had already enjoyed – and the word is used advisedly – an amazingly adventurous war in Poland, Norway, in a plane crash in the Mediterranean and on the run from an Italian POW camp.

Mena House is a luxury hotel, now greatly enlarged, built around the turn of the century in the shadow of the Pyramids of Giza. Here in the pleasant Egyptian autumn there gathered an immense host entirely devoted to the comfort, security and well being of these great panjandrums. Hermione Ranfurly's diary records, 'Mr. Churchill will stay at the Caseys'[20] villa, Mr Roosevelt and Generalissimo and Madame Chang Kai-Shek will have two villas near by and so will the Chiefs of Staff. Many houses along the Mena road are being requisitioned for the enormous staffs that are coming. A wire fence has been put up round the conference zone and precautions against land and air attack have been taken ... Food and furnishing arrangements are vast.' It was even rumoured that an anti-aircraft gun had been installed on top of one of the Pyramids!

Churchill was irritated to see some soldiers not wearing the Africa Star, in the design of which he had taken a personal interest. 'Now all the ribbon in existence is being made up and any desert soldier who sees Churchill will wear it but will have to return it at the gate on departure for others to wear.'

Later that year the swash-buckling American General Patton arrived in Cairo desirous of seeing the sights. Hermione Ranfurly was instructed to find him an expert guide, which she did in the shape of a learned professor of Muslim art, almost certainly the eccentric and irascible

King Farouk and Sir Miles Lampson (Lord Killearn) watching a polo match at
Gezira, *c.* 1938.

Professor Creswell, notorious for lashing out with his walking stick at
any Cairene who happened to get in his way.

When he told Patton they would start with the mosques, the dis-
appointed General roared, 'No, no, no, I don't want to see any of your
goddam mosques ... I guess we'd better go see the Sphinx.' The
Professor, who had neither interest in nor knowledge of Pharaonic
Egypt, farted loudly, turned on his heel and departed. An ADC bought
a guidebook and did the job himself, apparently to the General's
satisfaction.[21]

In October 1944, with Egypt no longer in danger from the Axis, Farouk
was able to dismiss Nahas, apparently without protest from Lord
Killearn (who had been elevated to the peerage in the previous year)
and replace him with Ahmed Maher, the former terrorist suspect and
brother of Ali.

This would have been an opportune moment for Killearn to depart
the scene and the process of healing the wounds, some perhaps necessarily inflicted upon the Egyptian monarch, to begin. However, this did
not happen for another two years when the man whom we may regard
as The Last Pro-Consul was replaced by a rather self-effacing Scottish
bachelor, Sir Ronald Campbell, and by then it was too late.

CHAPTER 15

Happy Days Are Here Again

F OR VISITORS from post-war Britain, in the grip of such political
puritans as Clement Attlee and Stafford Cripps, Egypt seemed a
paradise. Bustling Cairo, the superb beaches of Alexandria, the towering
pyramids, the glittering Nile, the wonders of Upper Egypt; all this
without ration books, sweet coupons, 'red' petrol, freezing winters
without coal and a bossy wartime bureaucracy now strengthened and
reinforced by peacetime doctrinaire socialism.

For the twenty-three-year-old Edward O'Farrell, recently released
from three years in the German PoW camp, Stalag Luft 3, and now
to join his uncle's business in Egypt, it was almost too good to be true.
He writes:

> At the end of 1945 I went to Cairo and fell in love with Egypt and the
> Middle East. I remember parts of the flight in a DC3, owned by BOAC
> but operated by a seconded RAF crew. We left Hurn, near Bournemouth,
> and flew to an airfield near Marseilles and then landed, late in the evening
> at Malta ... When we arrived we were taken off to the Officers' Mess
> where a dance was in progress ... Despite the terrible gaps and loss of
> life it was good to have survived; wives and husbands were re-united and
> somehow the girls had found attractive dresses for themselves. Moreover
> there was food and wine aplenty ...
>
> But we did not stay long [and] in the morning we reached Cairo and,
> looking down. I saw the Pyramids and the Sphinx, as I had always
> imagined them, the desert and the Nile and the sprawling city bestride it.[1]

But all was not as it seemed on the surface.

In 1928 a schoolmaster called Hassan el Banna had founded a funda-
mentalist (as it would be called today) Islamic movement, el Ahwan el
Musslemin or Moslem Brotherhood. During the war it had been carefully watched by the police and military security, aware of its anti-British,
pro-Axis and anti-Wafdist line and once or twice Banna had been taken
into custody. As a result there had been few terrorist outrages, apart

from the apparently politically motivated but unsolved murders of two British servicemen at Maadi at the end of 1944. But, when on 24 February 1945 the Prime Minister, Ahmed Maher, announced Egypt's declaration of war on Germany in response to a Yalta Conference decision that only Allies could join the United Nations, he was assassinated. The killer, one Mahmoud Mohamed Issawi Awadalla, was a member of a pro-German terrorist group, Young Egypt or Misr el Fatat, but the murder had probably been organised by the Ahwan. Awadalla was sentenced to death and hanged but it was the beginning of a new burst of assassinations, not dissimilar to those of 1919–24 with the difference that most of the victims were carefully selected Egyptians. After the murder of another Prime Minister, Nokrashi Pasha, in 1948, the Government lost patience and Banna was himself killed, probably by the secret police.[2]

The only important British casualty of this period in Egypt was the Minister of State for the Middle East, Lord Moyne, who, together with his chauffeur, Corporal Fuller, was murdered by two members of the Stern Gang, a particularly vicious Jewish terror group, in November 1944. This had nothing to do with Egyptian politics and when the killers were caught red-handed the Egyptian authorities were only too pleased to put them on trial and hang them.[3]

But the newly arrived Edward O'Farrell, driving for the first time to the Gezira Sporting Club for lunch before boarding the Wagons Lits to Assouan for Christmas, was only vaguely aware of these menacing political under-currents. He recalls:

I remember ... the colour of the flowers and the shrubs, the brightness of the sunshine and the blueness of the sky. At the door (of the Club) Generals and Air Marshals were arriving, pennants flying on their car bonnets, ADCs saluting ... It all felt marvellous but it was the *fin de siècle* of Empire.

That evening, with my uncle and aunt, I boarded a train at Bab el Luk station for Assouan ... There was dinner before retiring to single compartments and being lulled to sleep by the rhythm of the train on the track. In the morning the sun was shining and over the sandstone cliffs lay the desert stretching to the Red Sea. In the foreground was a fertile strip beside the Nile where *durra* (maize) and palm trees grew ...

Then there was Assouan and the Cataract Hotel ... Few people today, accustomed to the brash metallic convenience of Hiltons and Sheratons, can have any concept of the luxurious elegance of such a hotel. The staff were dressed in immaculate, white *gallabayahs*, with red cummerbunds and tarbooshes on their heads. If there was sand on your shoes when you came back from a walk, a boy with a feather duster would whisk it off before you went through the front door ...

On Christmas Eve, my uncle and I walked down to the Post Office to send telegrams of good wishes to our families. Afterwards we called into a Greek store whose proprietor was an old friend [of my uncle]. He offered us very good French brandy and divulged huge volumes of gossip and information, all of which was incomprehensible to me. While we were so engaged, word apparently went round the local population that Keown-Boyd Pasha was in town[4] and as we walked back to the hotel the street was lined with people. They extended their hands in warm affection and cries of '*Ya Basha!*' rang in the air.

A year or two later, during a similar Christmas holiday in Upper Egypt, a lunch party in honour of K-B was given by a local dignitary in the vicinity of Luxor. The male members of the family and Dr Courtney Pochin, a well-known Cairo GP, were also invited. Before setting out from the hotel, Pochin delivered a stern lecture to the youngest guest, a truculent youth in his teens. 'Now then, Henry, under no circumstances are you to touch the water – you'll get typhoid, dysentery and every other disease under the sun – d'you understand? Anyway, there'll be *gazooza* [bottled fizzy lemonade] and you can drink that.'

The lunch, sumptuous, lengthy and highly spiced included course after course of lamb, turkey, chicken, pigeon, *kuftas* (rissoles) and fish, grilled, fried, roasted and boiled; mountains of savoury rice, succulent vegetables and salads (also forbidden unless known to have been washed in permanganate of soda), rounded off with sweetmeats and sticky cakes – only the *gazooza* was lacking – while in front of each place was a glistening jug of apparently clear, iced water. Maddened with thirst, the rebellious youth filled his glass from one of these, and staring the infuriated but speechless Dr Pochin straight in the eye, swallowed it in one gulp. A veil will be drawn over the good doctor's remarks in the car on the way back to the hotel but the miscreant has lived to tell the tale.

One prominent victim of the assassin's bullet, Sir Amin Osman Pasha, the Anglophile Wafdist politician who was murdered in 1946, was the unluckiest of men as his assailant was half blind and usually unsuccessful in his attempts at murder.

The son of a wealthy Maadi resident and apparently inspired by hatred of his British neighbours (he does not seem to have been connected to any known terrorist organisation), Hussein Tewfik Ahmed embarked upon his career as a terrorist at the age of fifteen in 1940, stealing army motor-cycles and setting fire to garages in the Maadi area.

Later he graduated to violence against the person by attacking, together with his brother Said and another relation, a British officer with a club. However, the blow to the back of the head was a feeble one and when the officer bellowed, 'You bloody buggers!' the youths panicked and fled. On another occasion he nearly attacked a friend of his father, presumably owing to his poor eyesight, who happened to look like an Englishman.

The police were well aware of his activities but were inclined to be indulgent, his father being a respected citizen. This was at best a mistake and at worst criminal as the boy was clearly a psychopath and a potential murderer. At his trial it emerged that he had fired at and wounded a Lance-Corporal Mills (or Miller) less than two months before the murder of Amin Osman. Nor is it inconceivable that he was responsible for the two unsolved murders at Maadi mentioned above.

For one reason or another – perhaps his family connections or because his victim was known to be pro-British – he was not executed and eventually died in 1978.[5]

The perennial disagreements confronting the British and Egyptian governments had, for obvious reasons, been shelved for the duration of the war. Now these questions, principally the continued presence of British troops in Cairo and Alexandria and the future of the Sudan, were re-opened. Over the next few years successive British and Egyptian Governments tried to negotiate settlements to these issues.

Looking back, it is hard to understand why, on the one hand, the British did not immediately withdraw their forces to the Canal, as had been agreed under the 1936 Treaty and was recommended by the C-in-C Middle East, General Paget, immediately after the war, as soon as any foreign threat to Egypt had been lifted and, on the other, why the Egyptians persisted so vehemently in their claim to the Sudan.

In March 1946 Lord Wavell, then Viceroy of India wrote to Delaney of Reuter's:

> For some reason the Foreign Office have never been able to handle Egyptian affairs with sympathy or tact ... I have never quite understood why we could not have withdrawn our troops from Cairo and Alexandria soon after the end of the war, at any rate from Kasr el Nil Barracks where their presence was always an irritation ... I cannot believe there was any necessity for keeping fighting troops in the middle of Cairo. I understand that the local military authorities were quite willing that they should move out.[6]

By the time this problem had eventually been resolved and the troops withdrawn to the Canal Zone, it was too late. The damage had been done and the Egyptians were determined upon nothing less than total British military evacuation from Egypt. One suggestion, which was probably never given serious consideration but might well have been an acceptable compromise, was a Sovereign Base at Gaza (such as exist today in Cyprus) which was administered by Egypt but was not an integral of the country itself, within rapid striking distance of the Canal but out of sight of the population of Egypt proper and thus, hopefully, out of mind.[7]

Meanwhile the Egyptian obsession with the Sudan persisted. Why they (or anyone else) should have imagined the Sudanese would ever have tolerated that Egyptian rule after their experience of the past is extraordinary. Furthermore, as we have already observed, the Sudan was regarded with fear and loathing by ordinary Egyptians, a place of exile and death. Nevertheless, it was an article of faith to which the Egyptian ruling classes, from successive Heads of State downwards, clung up to the moment when the Sudan was declared independent on 1 January 1956. However, perhaps surprisingly, Egypt's claim seems to have been supported, to some extent, by Keown-Boyd. Writing to a British Government Minister just before the 1952 Revolution, he urged in forceful terms: '... recognise Farouk as King of the Sudan and tie him up with all the promises you have made to the Sudanese about self-government.'[8]

As had so often been the case in the past, these intractable problems had little or no effect on individual Anglo-Egyptian friendships. This is exemplified by the success of the Oxford and Cambridge Dinner held at the Mohamed Ali Club at a time of considerable tension in 1950 to which we have referred in an earlier chapter.[9]

But a new ingredient had by now been added to the Egyptian cocktail – the Americans.

Until their entry into the war in 1941 the Americans had shown little interest in Egypt but in 1946 they upgraded their Cairo Legation to Embassy status and their Minister to Ambassador. From the British point of view they could not have chosen a better man. Somerville Pinkney Tuck, known to his friends as Kippy, had come to Egypt as a small child when his father was appointed a judge in the Mixed Courts. Brought up in a cosmopolitan atmosphere and surrounded by friends and playmates of many nationalities, the young Tucks were by no means typically American. They would spend their holidays in England and Europe and two of Kippy's brothers served in the British Army in the First World War with distinction, while his sister married a British officer.[10]

From 1913 to 1919 and again from 1921 to 1922 Kippy had held various diplomatic posts in Egypt and returned there in 1944 as Minister. He was not the man to rock the British boat. However, on his retirement in 1948, when, incidentally, he joined the Board of the Suez Canal Company, he was replaced by an Irish American diplomat, Jefferson Caffery, who held very different views to his predecessor. Described elsewhere as 'a discreet homosexual',[11] it is unlikely that any degree of discretion would have fooled the gossips of Cairo, a city in which everyone knows everything about everybody.

At any rate, we can be sure that his activities, both diplomatic and sexual, were well known to the British Embassy as his chauffeur was an ex-policeman, a Sudanese, who would meet regularly with his former chief, a retired British officer of the Cairo City Police, for a *mazbout* (Turkish coffee) and a yarn about old times – and no doubt present times as well.[12] Of course, if the British Embassy knew what Caffery was up to then so did the Russians as the Counsellor and Head of Chancery was none other than Donald MacLean, the notorious Russian spy!

Be that as it may, the British community believed that Caffery was encouraging dissident elements, especially in the army, and was busily undermining Britain's position in Egypt and the monarchy. Understandably the Americans had little confidence in Farouk and believed that stability lay in promoting some other form of government. However, it is most unlikely that, in their naivety, they either desired or foresaw the anti-western military dictatorship that was to replace the ancient regime, although the meddlesome activities of the CIA probably helped to bring this about.[13]

Since 1925 when it lost its British regimental officers and Sudanese troops, the quality of the Egyptian Army had deteriorated rapidly and by the time the first Arab-Israeli war of 1948 broke out, although greatly enlarged, it was useless as a fighting force. Poorly equipped and badly led, it was defeated by an army which was little more than a Home Guard. Deeply humiliated, many junior officers blamed not only their seniors and the politicians but also the King himself – especially as he was suspected of involvement in corrupt arms deals and the purchase of defective weaponry.

Meanwhile the politicians had returned to their old pre-war game of proving their impeccably anti-British credentials.

Nahas, who returned to power in 1950, and the Wafd had long ago abandoned their wartime 'pact' with the British, had unilaterally abrogated the 1936 Treaty and were encouraging terrorist attacks, often supported by the local police, on the Canal garrison, including servicemen's families – an almost unheard of departure from the norm in Egypt. When a British nun, Sister Anthony, and several soldiers were

killed in rioting at Ismailia in January 1952, the GOC, General Sir
George (Bobby) Erskine, demanded the disarming and withdrawal from
the Canal Zone of the auxiliary police. Not only was the demand ignored
but the Egyptian Government threatened further attacks on British
targets.

As a result, on 25 January 1952, when a company of auxiliaries
refused to evacuate a building in Ismailia known as the Bureau Sanitaire,
which they were using as a headquarters, they were surrounded by
British troops with tanks. Being left with no means of escape and on
receiving orders from the Minister of the Interior in Cairo by telephone
to stand their ground, the policemen decided to fight it out with the
result that over forty were killed and many others wounded.[14]

General Erskine had made two fundamental and inexcusable errors.
He had not ensured that the telephone lines to Cairo were cut and he
did not allow time and a suitable point of exit, after the initial bursts
of fire by his troops, for the policemen either to surrender or to evacuate
the building in safety.

The diplomat, Sir Thomas Rapp, visiting the scene on the same day,
noted that

> The corpses had been removed but the blood and brains were still
> scattered about the ruins ... yet what sickened me most was the conviction
> that something had gone wrong and that the bloodshed had been
> unnecessary ... Psychologically it had certainly been a blunder ...
> without an escape route [the Egyptian soldier] will fight to the death. It
> had been foolish moreover to attack so early in the morning when all the
> senior officers – no tough characters like their men – were comfortably
> in bed elsewhere ... It had been unnecessary to give so peremptory an
> ultimatum, time for reflection and parleying would have resulted in
> peaceful submission.

Rapp continues,

> The reaction in Cairo to this gory episode was immediate. The Wafd
> had sown the wind and now they were to reap the whirlwind ... the next
> day came to be known as Black Saturday. In former times, when passions
> were inflamed in Cairo and Alexandria, well-known gang leaders and
> criminal elements were temporarily taken care of by the police. On this
> occasion, on the contrary, they were organised and reinforced by
> subversive and extremist organisations, each promoting disorder for its
> own ends. Far from attempting moreover to nip trouble in the bud the
> Wafd government initially hoped to profit by a violent demonstration of
> protest, little realising that it would involve their own fate ... For several
> hours the centre of Cairo was given over to the rioters who destroyed,
> burnt and murdered at will. British buildings were the first objective but

xenophobia in general led to a rapid extension of the range of their assaults until the Government, in fear of British armed intervention, finally called in Egyptian troops to quell the rioters. Among the premises attacked and burnt to the ground was the Turf Club ... Worst of all nine of its members, including my friend Joseph Boyer, the Canadian Trade Commissioner, were brutally murdered by the mob.[15]

Another target was one of Cairo's most famous landmarks, Shepheard's Hotel, which was gutted and a number of its guests and staff burnt to death. But it is significant that no attempt was made to attack residential areas such as Zamalek on Gezira Island or Heliopolis where most British families lived. Presumably the organisers, whomsoever they may have been, judged that this would have led inevitably to the arrival of British troops.

On the question of British military intervention there was some confusion. According to Rapp, staff officers and the embassy had worked out plans to protect British lives in the event of serious rioting but had 'over-insured ... by underestimating the effect of the shock action of disciplined troops on an unco-ordinated opposition', whatever that may mean, and had overestimated the time required for troops from the Canal Zone to reach Cairo and Alexandria. Even so, General Erskine apparently decided that he had insufficient troops to deploy for riot control in the major cities and maintain security in the Canal Zone at the same time, informing the Foreign Secretary, Sir Anthony Eden, accordingly. Eden's reply was that the lives and property of British civilians were to be given priority. But, it would appear, the rioting had been brought under control by the Egyptian Army before the GOC had time to carry out his instructions. Rapp sums up by saying, 'So the question never had to be thrashed out whether the politicians had set the soldiers an impossible task or whether General Erskine's actions and dispositions were at fault.'

The balance of probability lies with the latter conclusion but Erskine's miscalculations may have been all to the good. The explosion of violence in Cairo erupted with such speed that the arrival of British troops on the streets would probably have been too late to prevent the worst outrages and might well have led to greater spilling of Egyptian blood and therefore even deeper resentment.

Responsibility for this outburst of mayhem has never been satisfactorily apportioned – it was too well organised to be spontaneous and there may even have been Eastern Block involvement – but an enquiry set up by the British Embassy made little or no progress, while Egyptian Government investigations, if any, were to be overtaken by events.

Farouk took the opportunity to sack Nahas, whom he had always

All that remained of Shepheard's Hotel after the 1952 riots.

disliked, and appoint his old friend Ali Maher as Prime Minister but he did not last and was replaced by the respected Hilali Pasha whose government was described as 'a good clean lot'.[16] Nevertheless, this was the death rattle of a generally corrupt, sleazy and incompetent political establishment, over which presided the grotesquely obese figure of a monarch who was destroying himself and his dynasty with overindulgence and neglect of his duty as a Head of State.

Soon he and the House of Mohamed Ali were to be swept away, almost certainly forever. But, as Professor Elie Kedourie has put it so succinctly. '... If Fuad and Faruq, Zaghloul and Nahas chastised the Egyptians with whips, their successors, after the downfall of the monarchy, were to chastise them with scorpions.'[17]

CHAPTER 16

The Traitor

I N THE LATE 1940s the British Embassy in Cairo – still known to
some of the older generation as The Residency – retained many of
the trappings of imperial might. A huge staff, diplomatic and domestic,
was presided over by the Ambassador, Sir Ronald Campbell, on the
one hand and his valet and lifelong companion, the aptly named Charles
Butler,[1] on the other. Only the British Army Guard at the gates and
the military ADCs had gone.

Sir Ronald's principal assistants were Edwin Chapman-Andrews, the
Minister, and Donald MacLean, Head of Chancellery. The Embassy
building, idyllically situated on the Nile at Garden City and dating
from the days of Cromer, also housed the Middle East Office under
a senior diplomat, Sir John Troutbeck. Although no longer the fief
of a Minister of State, this remained the centre for British policy

Members of the British Embassy staff being presented to King Farouk by the
Ambassador Sir Ronald Campbell, *c*.1950.

implementation throughout the area. The whole set-up was regarded by the Foreign Office, under the robust (except in health) Ernest Bevin, as of lesser importance only to Washington and Moscow, especially as Campbell had worked closely with Bevin, every conservative Englishman's favourite Labour minister, in the immediate post-war period as his deputy on the Council of Foreign Ministers, and the two men held each other in the highest regard.

Fleets of gleaming limousines, the flagship of which was the Ambassador's black and yellow Rolls, slid in and out of the Embassy gates, bearing grave-faced diplomats to crucial conferences and vital negotiations with Egyptian ministers.

Magnificent balls, dinners and receptions were held in the spacious ballroom; invitations to lavish garden-parties on appropriate occasions (King's Birthday etc) were much sought after: hundreds of guests impeccably served by a team of perfectly trained Berberin *suffragis* under the watchful eye of Charles.

It may all have been something of a delusion as British power and influence was rapidly melting away, but it was nonetheless dazzling for Sir Ronald's eighteen-year-old nephew Colin, newly arrived from a grim post-war Scotland and the harsh regime of Gordonstoun School for an extended Christmas holiday in 1948.

Landing at Port Said from the SS *Orcades* he found himself whisked off by the British Consul and his wife to a sumptuous dinner at the Cercle Français 'particularly appreciated by someone who had endured nine years of rationing at home'.

There followed weeks which

> ... were like a dream; parties, nightclubs, first serious girlfriend, intrigue, gossip and a glorious almost vice-regal safari to Luxor and Aswan ... and a marvellous visit to a Senussi [sic] chieftain's desert encampment where the Ambassadorial convoy was greeted by a troop of thirty tribal horsemen who met us a mile from our destination firing their rifles in the air and whooping encouragement as we arrived to be met by their chieftain.

The inevitable refreshments offered included sweet tea and sheeps' eyes which Campbell managed to swallow by closing his own eyes and 'thinking not of England but of oysters'.

The duck shooting season at Ekiad was in full swing and Campbell enjoyed the kind of unforgettable sporting experience described in an earlier chapter. He was also introduced to the cosmopolitan world of Egyptian society, so soon to be swept away.

> Prince Mohamed Ali, the fervently pro-British uncle of King Farouk who came every year to sign the [Embassy] book on King George VI's

birthday; the business tycoon Aboud ... married to an Aberdonian lady; sandy haired Turkish noblemen resident in Cairo since the days of their Ottoman ancestors. Then there were the old British expatriate families [and] ex-chiefs of police such as Fitzpatrick Pasha and Giles Bey, held in high regard by both Egyptians and Europeans. Sir Alexander Keown-Boyd and Sir Teddy Peel were legends in their time.

Young Colin made many friends among the (to him, demi-gods) of the Embassy staff. The First Secretary Lees Mayall, the one-legged Michael Maude and his beautiful wife ('who tended to stray a little') and, above all, Donald MacLean who

> ... had very soon become one of my top heroes. He and his American wife Melinda were the vital ingredients to any successful party. a glamorous couple, they radiated laughter and enjoyment and were the greatest fun to be with. I remember saying to my uncle how no late party nor sortie to the Champagne Club was complete without Donald MacLean. My uncle replied that despite these all night marathons Donald was the brightest and most talented of the Embassy staff.[2]

It should be borne in mind that the MacLeans were newly arrived in Egypt at the time of Colin's holiday and the darker side of his character had not yet openly manifested itself, but it was not long before another acquaintance was to observe that 'Donald ... was developing a deep dislike for Egypt', while, more or less at the same time, his social behaviour and self-control were beginning to deteriorate.[3]

However, MacLean's young admirer did detect signs that all was not entirely as it appeared on the surface. In the first place, the rebelliousness and anarchic indiscipline of their two small sons was 'a flaw in the MacLean couple's apparent perfection'. At the time Campbell attributed this to their American upbringing (the Macleans had come to Cairo from Washington) but 'later events suggested to me that it may have been a sign that their parents' jollity and seeming closeness cloaked a deeply disturbed and troubled life that may have been instinctively detected by those small boys.'[4]

As their father was sexually ambidextrous, drunk to the point of dipsomania and probably already aware, via his well-placed co-traitor Philby, that the security net was beginning, very slowly, to close around him, Colin's observation may be fairly near the mark. Furthermore, we know now that his Soviet controllers paid far less attention to him while he was in Egypt than had previously been the case, thus exacerbating his sense of isolation and fear of betrayal.[5]

Another event, which occurred after lunch one day at the Macleans', also aroused surprise and a certain dismay in the impressionable mind of the eighteen-year-old. Looking out over the roofs of Zamalek (the

Macleans lived in a house recently vacated by the Keown–Boyds) he noticed some shabby one-storey huts in a fenced compound, which, presumably, did not have the appearance of native dwellings. 'What are those, Donald?' he asked. 'Oh,' was the reply, 'they are the married quarters of the Soviet Embassy junior staff.' 'They must look over here and see what fun we are all having and long to join us in the West!' said Colin. 'As I said it ... a strange thing happened. I saw an expression I had never seen before on Donald's face, a grimace of extreme irritation, which was not entirely justified by the banality of my remark. He said nothing and we walked back into the house in silence, thought no deeper about it but it made me sad that obviously Donald thought less of me than before.'[6]

MacLean's biographer, Robert Cecil, expresses the opinion that his subject was also disturbed by the extremes of rich and poor which were so apparent in Egypt and that this too may have affected his behaviour and contributed towards his eventual 'break-down'.[7] However, we should take this theory with a pinch of salt. There is no evidence that he ever showed the smallest respect or consideration for the few working-class Egyptians whom he encountered – rather, as we shall see, to the contrary. Indeed, he may well have relished the thought that their condition would hasten the inevitable Communist, or at least Socialist, revolution – and in this he was not mistaken.

It is well known that MacLean and others were recruited as 'trainee' spies by the NKVD (forerunner of the KGB) at Cambridge in the 1930s. In 1935 he had joined the Foreign Office, presumably on NKVD instructions, passing the interview with little difficulty. We need not be concerned here with the details of his remarkably successful career both as a diplomat and a spy up to his arrival in Egypt, except to remind ourselves that it was during his Washington period from 1944 to 1948 that he was able to inflict the maximum damage upon the West for the benefit of Stalinist Russia, particularly in the field of atomic secrecy.[8]

To some extent MacLean remains an enigma and the reasons for his treachery are still unclear. The only point in his favour is that, although never well off, he does not seem to have worked for money. Presumably, at least at first, ideology was his motivation, but he was an intelligent man and it is hard to believe that this could have survived revelation of the true horrors of the Soviet regime and the unparalleled ruthlessness of the brutal organisation whose slave he had become. Perhaps conviction was replaced by fear – fear of betrayal or even death. In any case, it matters little and the principal point of interest in his story is that he got away with it for so long.

His behaviour by the summer of 1949 had become the talk of Cairo. One of his most notorious escapades was a *felucca* (river sailing boat) trip up the Nile to the suburb of Helouan where a late dinner was to be prepared for the Macleans and their party of about ten, including the First Secretary Lees Mayall and his wife, by an English family called Tyrrell-Martin who lived there.[9]

It seems that either the wind was in the wrong direction or the time required to reach their destination had been underestimated. Whatever the case, there was plenty of booze on board the vessel and this was not spared, especially by MacLean who roundly abused the *rais* (captain) and Melinda for whatever real or imagined faults he could find in their organisation of the expedition.

On eventual arrival around midnight at the Helouan landing stage, the party was confronted by a *ghaffir* (watchman) who, armed with an ancient shotgun, no doubt pronounced the word most beloved of all Egyptian policemen and security staff – '*Mamnu!*' ('Forbidden') – whereupon MacLean proceeded to wrest the weapon from the man's grasp while Mayall, fearing bloodshed, attempted to restrain him. The astonished *ghaffir* and the rest of the MacLean party were then treated to the undignified spectacle of two senior diplomats, both tall, powerfully built men, locked in combat and rolling down the bank towards the river. In the course of the struggle Mayall's leg was broken and, incredibly, he was left lying on the riverbank for the rest of the night watched over by another diplomat called Scott-Fox before being removed to hospital in the morning.

An unrepentant MacLean spent the next day, Sunday, sunbathing and then reported on the Monday to the Embassy's summer quarters in Alexandria. There he explained to the Ambassador that Mayall had met with a 'mishap', the nature of which he did not, apparently, disclose. Later, it seems, Sir Ronald questioned Mayall, but, as MacLean's biographer puts it, '... did not persist in his enquiry, in the face of Mayall's loyal reticence, and made no report to the Foreign Office.'[10]

The diplomatic ranks had closed and, whatever havoc MacLean was to wreak for the remainder of his Egyptian posting, they were to remain so.

However, by May 1950 the MacLean boil had come to a head. In April to his household in Zamalek was added a drunken journalist called Philip Toynbee, an ideal boozing companion for Donald. On 26 April he and Toynbee '... tumbled into a two-day trough together ...' in the course of which MacLean hit one of his reputed boyfriends, the notorious homosexual Eddie Gathorne-Hardy, and 'hurled glass after glass against the wall'. Then again, on 4 May, the two plunged into a further orgy of alcoholic destruction in the course of which, after drinking six bottles of gin, they broke into a flat occupied by two girls from the American

Embassy and smashed it to smithereens. Fortunately the girls were not at home as MacLean was indiscriminate in his sexual tastes and it is improbable that Toynbee would have been a restraining influence – indeed he seems to have joined whole-heartedly in the devastation. 'Donald,' he reported later, 'raises a large mirror above his head and crashes it into the bath, when to my amazement and delight, the bath breaks in two while the mirror remains intact.'[11]

This was enough for Melinda who, having kicked Toynbee out of her house, formed up to the Ambassador and demanded that Donald be sent home for psychiatric treatment to which Sir Ronald Campbell agreed. It is not clear whether he would have taken this step on his own initiative – for whatever reason, complaints from the American Ambassador, Jefferson Caffery, following MacLean's latest outrage, seem to have been curiously muted – and to the end of his long life Sir Ronald remained silent on the subject of his trusted but treacherous subordinate. He retired from the Diplomatic Service in the same year to become a director of the Royal Bank of Scotland and lived at his home in Haddington, served by the faithful Charles, until his death in 1983 at the age of ninety-two.[12]

Robert Cecil, himself a diplomat, ruminates with diplomatic circumspection on the roll of Charles in the MacLean affair.

> The importance of this issue [Campbell's failure to file a report on MacLean] justifies some investigation for Campbell's reason for acting as he did. Those who served with him in the later stages of his distinguished career knew that at these posts an efficient and faithful servant, against whom he would not have a word spoken, accompanied him. It was widely believed, rightly or wrongly, that this man had homosexual proclivities. Campbell was a much respected and long-serving member of the Diplomatic Service and it is not suggested that there was any impropriety in his relations with his manservant ... however, it may well be that [Campbell] came to adopt a defensive attitude which predisposed him to ignore all stories about the private lives of his staff, whether diplomatic or domestic.

The reader must be left to draw his own conclusions from these remarks.[13]

Melinda's motives are also unclear. According to all accounts she loved Cairo and thrived on its social whirl. Furthermore. it seems she had acquired a rich Egyptian lover and should have been most unwilling to leave. As she had been aware of his treachery since their marriage in 1940,[14] we may speculate that the NKVD, through their Cairo resident, may have prevailed upon her to initiate the move in order to save a valued agent who was likely to be of far greater use to them elsewhere.

Under Foreign Office rules a member 'cured' of a psychiatric disorder or mental breakdown must be treated in exactly the same way as one fully recovered from a physical illness and thus retained in the Service.

Be all that as it may, MacLean left Cairo for good by air on 11 May, apparently unaccompanied by any adverse report from Sir Ronald. As MacLean's biographer puts it, 'No aspect of this strange story is stranger than the behaviour of Campbell,' which, notwithstanding his remarks on the subject of Charles quoted above, is likely now to remain forever unexplained.[15]

But inexplicable behaviour on the part of officialdom does not end at this point in the MacLean saga. On arrival in England he is not immediately interviewed by some High Mandarins of the Foreign Office but eventually meets George Middleton, the head of Personnel, for lunch, when he is told that an appointment has been made for him to see a psychiatrist regularly used by the Foreign Office called Dr Wilson.

However, after one examination by the good doctor, who recommends that he enter a clinic, which he declines to do, he is then allowed by the Foreign Office (and at its expense) to undergo a course of treatment by one Dr Erna Rosenbaum who, it seems, may well have been recommended to him by the NKVD![16]

MacLean's remarkable recovery from his probably simulated breakdown; his appointment to the American Desk at the Foreign Office; his defection with Burgess and his subsequent rather miserable existence in Russia, examples of 'the truth being stranger than fiction', are outside the compass of this book but perhaps the last word in this bizarre story should be left to some of those who knew him and thought he was their friend.

Some thirty years after his memorable Egyptian holiday, Colin Campbell recognised an old Cairo acquaintance in the street in London. Major Tim Fisher, a former Assistant Military Attaché at the Embassy and now a businessman, had recently returned from Moscow where he had met a group of young British diplomats who offered to take him to see MacLean. 'He declined the offer,' says Campbell, '... but was shaken by the obvious unawareness of these young men that Donald had betrayed his many friends and admirers as much as he had betrayed his country ...'[17]

CHAPTER 17

Nasser and Suez – The Last Act

T HE BLOODLESS REVOLUTION which brought the Free Officers to power on 23 July 1952 ended the monarchy, the parliamentary party system and any pretence of political freedom in Egypt.

The removal of the King was handled in the most civilised manner. Farouk abdicated in favour of his infant son a few days later and was allowed to sail away into exile on his yacht. One way or another, he was provided with sufficient funds to keep him in comfort for the rest of his life. He died in Rome of gluttony in 1965 aged forty-five.

The driving force behind the revolution was el Kaimakam (Lieutenant Colonel) Gamal Abdel Nasser and a group of youngish middle-ranking officers, most of whom had been associated with such extremist movements as the Muslim Brotherhood or Young Egypt. Some of them, Anwar Sadat for example, had played an actively anti-British and pro-German role during the Second World War and, once having disposed of the monarchy, their principal objective was to rid Egypt of all residual traces of the British Occupation.

The monarchy was officially abolished about a year after Farouk's departure and, as a figurehead, the Free Officers appointed a genial and avuncular half-Sudanese general, Mohamed Neguib, as President but within a couple of years he had outlived his usefulness, was framed with complicity in a plot to assassinate Nasser, deposed and placed under house arrest. Nasser took over the Presidency as, of course, he ha intended from the outset.

For the first four years of the revolutionary regime Egypt coasted along quite quietly, at least so far as external affairs were concerned. Perhaps surprisingly, by October 1954 an agreement providing for the withdrawal of all British troops from Egypt within twenty months and the 'civilianisation' of the Canal Zone had been signed.

Significantly, both parties had also agreed to uphold the 1888 Convention which had neutralised (Cromer's word) the Suez Canal until 1968 when it would come under Egyptian control. In fact the British

President Gamal
Abdul Nasser
making his historic
speech at
Alexandria in July
1956, announcing
the nationalisation
of the Suez Canal.

withdrew all combat troops well before the deadline on 31 March 1956 and her military installations and stores were left in the care of British civilian technicians. By coincidence the last British troops to leave Egypt were a battalion of the Grenadier Guards and a squadron of the Life Guards, both regiments which had landed with Wolseley in 1882.[1]

On 2 April *The Times* remarked, 'This was hardly an occasion for pomp but it seems regrettable that such an era in British military annals should have been concluded so unobtrusively, almost in the manner of the Arab folding his tent and stealing away.' However, in the case of the Welsh Guards, who had left a few weeks earlier, its 'tent' was actually burnt down. Writes Brigadier Michael Lee, a subaltern at that time:

> Shortly before leaving, the Welsh Guards Officers' Mess was badly damaged by fire caused by an electrical fault. This was the one and only properly constructed mess in the whole area. The incident infuriated the Egyptian authorities whose Army was about to occupy the barracks.
>
> A Court of Enquiry was therefore convened with the second-in command of the Irish Guards appointed as President. The enquiry quite properly exonerated the [Welsh] Battalion from any guilt but the incoming Egyptians remained suspicious and angry.

Nor, one imagines, would their suspicions have been allayed when a Welsh Guardsman was observed boarding the troop-ship wearing an Egyptian fireman's helmet![2]

Perhaps it was only to be expected that nearly three-quarters of a century of military occupation should have ended in an atmosphere of some bitterness but at least the withdrawal was conducted with dignity, which was not to be the case in Aden a few years later.

The dismal story of the Suez Crisis has been told many times and has been analysed over and over again by historians, by some of the main participants in their memoirs and by their biographers. No need, therefore, to repeat the sad saga in detail here but the basic elements of the event which, more than any other, demonstrated the reduced status of the world's two great former imperial powers, Britain and France, cannot be shirked.

Incensed by Nasser's flirtation with the Soviet Union and his arms deal with the Czechs, in July 1956 the United States, Britain and the World Bank withdrew their financial support for the construction of Nasser's pet project, the Assouan High Dam. Although there were mixed views as to the economic and agricultural benefits to Egypt of the dam, the project was of great political and diplomatic significance and the decision, a snub to Nasser's pride and prestige, was a serious error of judgement on the part of the Americans without whom the other two potential participants could not proceed.

Whether or not the Russians were genuinely prepared at the time to take over the financing of the dam is uncertain but Nasser was, in any case, loth to be pushed too deeply into their debt. Furthermore, he wanted vengeance against the West and – ever an opportunist – seized the chance to grab a rich prize, thus killing two birds with one stone. In a speech at Alexandria on 26 July 1956 he announced the nationalisation of the Suez Canal Company (which was registered in Egypt) and, ipso facto, of the Suez Canal itself and its revenues of about £E3 million per month. This, he told his frenziedly cheering audience, would finance the dam and just about everything else.

At first the entire western world was outraged by what was seen as an act of international banditry but there was little unity of purpose. The countries at greatest risk from the dangerous whims of a capricious dictator were those of Western Europe, two thirds of whose oil supplies passed through the Suez Canal, but only Britain and France were in a position to take immediate remedial action and this they failed to do.

The Iraqi Prime Minister, the anglophile Nuri Said, happened to be at a Downing Street dinner party when the news was announced and advised his British counterpart, Sir Anthony Eden, 'Hit them, hit them now and hit them hard!³ Had they the military assets in place, that is to say in Cyprus and Malta, the Anglo-French might have taken his advice – indeed a swift *coup de main* using the Royal Navy and 1,200 Royal Marines was, rather half-heartedly, suggested by the First Sea Lord, Admiral the Earl Mountbatten, but turned down as too risky.⁴

Eden had taken a personal dislike to Nasser, regarding him as a second Mussolini and, whatever the legal niceties, his nationalisation of the Canal as an act of aggression. At this stage most of the British public and politicians agreed with him. The French, who held Nasser at least partly responsible for the bloody and costly rebellion in Algeria, loathed him and saw the perfect opportunity to knock him off his perch. Emotionally too, the nationalisation of the Canal, built by a Frenchman, had been even more galling to the Prime Minister, Guy Mollet, and his government than it was to Eden and his, especially as Nasser had used the code-name De Lesseps as the signal for the seizure of the offices and installations of La Compagnie du Canal de Suez.

Months of diplomatic wrangling over a possible peaceful solution followed and it was not until October that the Anglo-French assault force was ready. But still, to the fury of the French, the British hesitated, seeking a legitimate excuse to invade Egypt, seize the Canal and, with luck, topple Nasser. To satisfy this need the French, after intensive negotiations with the Israelis, came up with what became known as the Sèvres Protocol.

Under this secret plan the Israelis were to invade Egyptian Sinai (which they were eager to do anyway), whereupon the Anglo-French were to issue an ultimatum giving both sides twelve hours to stop fighting and withdraw ten miles from the Canal on pain of Anglo-French intervention. It was agreed that the Israelis, having smashed the Egyptian forces in Sinai, would accept the ultimatum, and it was assumed, correctly, that the Egyptians would not.

With some reluctance Eden accepted this plan and the Israeli attack was launched on 29 October. On the following day the ultimatum was issued, complied with by the Israelis, who had another twelve hours to continue their rout of the Egyptian army and their penetration into Sinai. The Egyptian Air Force was almost totally destroyed on the ground by the RAF and Anglo-French ground forces, spearheaded by paratroops and marines who landed by air and sea at Port Said and Port Fuad on 5–6 November 1956.

The initial operation was a rapid and complete success. Only the 3rd Battalion Parachute Regiment encountered any serious resistance (in a cemetery)⁵ and, bearing in mind that opposed landings are the most hazardous of all military operations, Anglo-French casualties were extremely light, amounting to thirty-one dead and one hundred and thirty wounded. After several confused announcements and denials of surrender, Port Said and Port Fuad came under full Allied control by the evening of 6 November. Then, to the dismay of the commanders and troops on the ground, London (reluctantly followed by Paris) ordered a ceasefire at midnight. Later the Allied commander, General Stockwell, gave it as his opinion that his men were within forty-eight hours of occupying the whole length of the Canal,[6] placing the British and French Governments in a strong negotiating position and perhaps fatally weakening Nasser's grip on Egypt.

After all he had been through to get to this point, Eden's decision was an extraordinary one, but, sick, exhausted and under heavy pressure from the Americans, the United Nations, some members of his own Cabinet and alarmed by a run on sterling, he had finally lost his nerve. By Christmas a UN force had taken over the Anglo-French 'peace-keeping' role on the Canal and Nasser, by default, had won a stunning and conclusive victory. Eden's career was in ruins and he resigned in January 1957.

The political careers of several junior ministers were also at an end. The last survivor of these, Sir Douglas Dodds-Parker, recalls:

> On 30th October the Foreign Secretary [Selwyn Lloyd] made a Statement to the Commons denying any foreknowledge of the Israeli attack. He left the next day for the UN, remaining there until the Xmas Recess, never facing Commons Questions again. That day I was informed by the best source that the attack had been 'colluded'. With Lord Reading and four other junior ministers I choose to ignore this ... to try to save what was possible for the Country's and the Party's good name. Little did we realise that the pressure would continue for ten weeks non-stop without a word of guidance or encouragement from any Cabinet Minister or anyone else. It ceased only with the resignation of the Prime Minister, when all other appointments fell vacant. None of the junior ministers who had held the line was re-appointed or given any explanation, then or ever since. Discussing it with WSC [Churchill] months later he said he had never known junior ministers being put in such a position and being so treated in consequence.[7]

Incidentally, the Egyptians had managed to take one British prisoner. In the course of patrolling the streets of Port Said Second Lieutenant A. G. Moorhouse of the West Yorkshire Regiment became separated from his men and was seized by *fedayin* (guerrillas or commandos). In a successful attempt to prevent him being found by search parties, his captors hid him in a box or cupboard where he suffocated. Even at the this distance in time it is hard to imagine this unfortunate young man's last hours without a shiver of horror. Cramped and stifling in his tiny prison, he may have heard the sounds of the troops searching for him within yards of his place of concealment, perhaps even the homely Yorkshire voices of the men of his own regiment.[8]

Vain, petulant, rather affected in manner and speech and, arguably, never up to the job of Prime Minister ('I don't think Anthony can do it,' Churchill is said to have murmured on the eve of handing over the Premiership)[9] Sir Anthony Eden (later the Earl of Avon) was not a sympathetic figure but he is deserving of some sympathy.

In Nasser he recognised all the hallmarks of a totalitarian dictator against the likes of whom he had struggled throughout his political career. His feelings and fears were perhaps most clearly expressed by one of his most fervent supporters, the Permanent Under-Secretary at the Foreign Office, Sir Ivone Kirkpatrick.

> If we sit back whilst Nasser consolidates his position and gradually acquires control of the oil-bearing countries, he can and is, according to our information, resolved to wreck us. If Middle East oil is denied us for a year or two, our gold reserves will disappear. If our gold reserves disappear, the sterling area disintegrates. If the sterling area disintegrates and we have no reserves, we shall not be able to maintain a force in Germany or anywhere else.[10]

Unfortunately Eden was unable to impress the Americans with this point of view. President Eisenhower (in the throes of an election campaign) and Secretary of State Dulles, much as they disliked and distrusted the Egyptian dictator, saw in Eden's policy an attempt to re-establish 'Imperialism'. Furthermore, the nationalisation of the Suez Canal was considerably less of an economic threat to the United States than it was to Britain (its single largest user) and France. Indeed, the American oil companies might well benefit from the disruption of Middle Eastern supplies to western Europe and Dulles was not without connections in the oil industry. That said, the behaviour of the US administration during and after the Anglo-French landings was nearer to that of an enemy than of a friend and ally. It was clear then (as it is clear now) that the Special Relationship was a fine thing – so long as the Brits did as they were told.

As for domestic opposition, some of Eden's cabinet colleagues had little stomach for the fight, while his Chancellor of the Exchequer, Harold Macmillan, who succeeded him as Prime Minister, has been accused of cynical opportunism, hoping to dislodge Eden for his own political profit. Certainly he seems to have given strong backing to the military option in the early days of the crisis, vehemently changing his tune when the going got rough and pressure on sterling mounted, urging surrender to American and Security Council demands for a cease-fire.[11]

On the military side, his service chiefs, sorely tried by political dithering, were not of one mind. Mountbatten, despite his early suggestion of a swift – and, with hindsight, possibly viable – *coup de main*, was a man of liberal, even socialistic, views, and did not favour military operations against Third World nations. On the other hand, the Chief of the Imperial General Staff, General (later Field Marshal) Sir Gerald Templer, had no such inhibitions and the two not infrequently quarrelled, a state of affairs probably exacerbated by the absence on sick leave of the Chairman of the Chiefs of Staff, Marshal of the RAF Sir William Dickson.[12]

It should also be borne in mind that these men, politicians and service chiefs alike, were of a generation which had spent years fighting the finest martial races in the world – Germans, Turks and Japanese – in two World Wars and were haunted by memories of such disasters as Gallipoli, Dieppe and Arnhem. Therefore their approach to war, even against the most insignificant of opponents, was ultra cautious and they greatly overestimated the defensive capability of the ill-led and badly trained Egyptian Army. Thus to unpreparedness at the beginning of the crisis were added hesitation, frequent changes of plan and exaggeration of the numbers of men and quantities of matériel required for the operation.

Most Conservative MPs and almost all grass-roots party members were staunchly behind the Prime Minister. Nevertheless there were a few dissidents, including the Foreign Office Minister Anthony Nutting who resigned. With a few exceptions, the Labour Party opposed the invasion which, of course, it had every right to do, but the behaviour of its leader, Hugh Gaitskill, was despicable and, in the opinion of some, treasonable. Having supported the Government in the early days of the crisis, later he changed his tune and broadcast a virulent attack on Eden and his policy after British forces had been committed to action on foreign soil.

The public at large was divided, perhaps as never before or since over a matter of foreign policy, but not necessarily on class or party lines. Many of the working class, hundreds of thousands of whom had served in the Middle East either during the two World Wars or as peacetime National Servicemen and were never averse to a bit of 'wog-bashing', backed Eden, while the so-called intelligentsia were mainly against him. Later there was to be much sanctimonious criticism on moral grounds of the 'collusion' between the Anglo-French and the

Israelis – although why temporary allies should not co-operate in a *ruse de guerre* on the age-old basis of 'my enemy's enemy is my friend' is unclear. However, the Sèvres Protocol was a serious diplomatic miscalculation as the involvement of Israel made it impossible for even the most anti-Nasserite Arab regimes to give so much as tacit support to the Anglo-French action.

But the most obvious weakness in Anglo-French strategy was the apparent lack of any long- or even medium-term policy for the future governance of Egypt once the Canal had been repossessed. Presumably Nasser was to be overthrown, but what was to be done with him? Was he to be killed, imprisoned or exiled? Doubtless the first would have been desirable but almost impossible to implement without causing even greater international uproar than had already been aroused. Imprisonment too would have been fraught with difficulty. Who would try him and on what charges, and where would he be held? Exile would have been the only viable alternative but that would have allowed him to continue his 'anti-imperialist' struggle from afar. And who was to govern in his place? Was the monarchy under an infant king to be restored? Certainly there could be no question of restoring Farouk. Who was to form the government? The old, discredited politicians perhaps, living in constant fear of their lives? Apparently low-level talks had been held outside Egypt with potential candidates with suitably anti-British – but also anti-Nasserite – credentials but little or nothing had come of them.

Were there to be garrisons in Cairo and Alexandria as well as on the Canal? Templer had estimated that eight divisions and five hundred military government officers would be required to police Egypt. No doubt he produced this exaggerated figure, unsustainable by the British and French armies combined, in order to persuade the politicians of the impracticality of an Occupation – or rather Re-Occupation – of the interior of the country. Perhaps fortunately, the situation wherein all these questions would have had to be addressed and solutions found never arose.

Eden emerges as a figure from Greek tragedy, abandoned by his friends and destroyed by an evil opponent. He had rendered considerable services to his country and to western civilisation in the past and deserved better than that he should be remembered only for the Suez catastrophe. In 1999 a number of historians, politicians and 'commentators', when asked by the BBC to rank Britain's twentieth-century prime ministers in order of merit, placed Eden at the bottom of the list, below even such relative nonentities as A. J. Balfour and Bonar Law.[13] Whether this reflects Eden's true worth or simply the prejudices of the 'sample' is a matter of opinion.

The Prime Minister, Sir Anthony Eden, leaving 10 Downing Street to hand in his resignation to the Queen following the Suez débâcle of 1956.

Curiously, none of his senior colleagues or allies suffered the venomous excoriation which was heaped upon him then and since. His French counterpart, Guy Mollet, survived unscathed, as did the two Foreign Ministers involved, Selwyn Lloyd and Christian Pineau. As for the Israeli leaders, principally Ben Gurion and Moshe Dayan, they were, and were to remain, regarded as national heroes. Most irksome of all for Eden and, indeed, for those who supported his policy, was the survival for another fourteen destructive years of his chief tormentor, Gamal Abdel Nasser, as a kind of Third World demigod.

A cunning and devious tyrant, Nasser has been treated with remarkable indulgence by posterity. By the time he died in 1970 the extent of the damage he had inflicted upon his own country and upon the Arab world as a whole, some of which has never been repaired, can hardly be overestimated.

An ethnic cleanser before the expression had been coined, he drove out of Egypt virtually the entire foreign community: for example, the Greek population which had numbered some 140,000 before the 1952 revolution was reduced during the Nasserite era to about 3,000.[14] The Italians, though smaller in number, suffered a similar fate. The Jews, probably some 25,000 of them, either fled or were deported.[15]

His economic policies, including large scale nationalisation and bungled land reform, destroyed the value of the Egyptian pound, ruined industries and stifled enterprise, while many talented young Egyptians voted with their feet to escape an oppressive and corrupt police state. Above all, as a war leader he was an unmitigated disaster, plunging his country into reckless adventures in the Yemen and against Israel at the cost of thousands of lives and untold treasure.

However, he possessed four important assets (in addition to a sense of humour, without which an Egyptian is yet to be born), which outweighed all his shortcomings and ensured his political survival. Firstly, he was an Egyptian of the Egyptians, untainted by the Turkish or Albanian blood of the old ruling class and the first to govern Egypt for thousands of years. Secondly, after 1956, his people saw him as the man who had given the British the great and final *khazook*[16] impalement). Thirdly, he controlled a large and efficient secret police apparatus, which reported to him on the activities of friends and foes alike, carrying out killings, arrests and tortures at his behest. The ability of this force to extract confessions and information from suspects was legendary.

It seems that one day an anonymous but undoubtedly important mummy was unearthed by Egyptologists. However, the greatest experts were unable to identify the body. When this was reported to Nasser he summoned the Chief of the Mabahis (Investigation Branch of the Secret Police) and ordered him to take charge of the case. On the following day, the Chief, somewhat dishevelled and weary but his face glowing with satisfaction, reported back to Nasser with complete details of the name, age, date and dynasty of the mummy. Even Nasser was impressed and asked how this information had been obtained.

'*Ya Rais* (O Leader)', came the reply, 'he talked!'

Fourthly, and perhaps to his enemies his most damaging asset, was that powerful and effective radio propaganda medium, the Voice of the Arabs, which would have excited the admiration of Dr Goebbels had he been alive to hear it. Spewing forth an endless stream of lies, distortions and vituperation against Imperialists, Colonialists, Zionists and any Arab rulers, especially kings, who dared to defy or disagree with Nasser, this heady barrage helped to bring about, among other disasters, bloody revolution in Iraq where King Faisal and his Prime Minister Nuri Said were brutally murdered in 1958 to be succeeded by a series of ruthless tyrants who have misruled that unhappy country to this day; several attempts on the life of King Hussein of Jordon; Britain's chaotic abandonment of Aden to a Communist regime; and civil war in the Yemen. Ultimately, however, most such events rebounded upon Egypt and by the time Nasser departed the scene the Arab world was more divided than ever.

He was also fortunate in the timing of his appearance on the world stage. Anti-imperialism and decolonisation were the watchwords of the era, while men like Nehru, Sukarno and their 'non-aligned' guru, Marshal Tito, embraced him as a brother. The old imperial powers ran helplessly before this tide, resisting here and there but fighting a losing battle, while the United States and the Soviet Union (the world's largest surviving empire) vied with each to prove their impeccably anti-imperialist credentials. Third World leaders were adept at playing one Superpower off against the other and were wont to punish the less generous or accommodating with petulant acts of revenge. Thus Nasser's nationalisation of the Suez Canal was intended as much to chastise the Americans for their refusal to finance his pet project, the Assouan High Dam, as to bait the British and French or to acquire its revenues.

Some years later, a 'senior Nasserite' told Sir Douglas Dodds-Parker that, as the Suez Canal would have reverted to Egypt (under the 1888 Convention) in 1968 anyway, it was felt that 'Anthony Eden was a good diplomat and would understand', but had Winston Churchill still been in power they would not have tried it on in the first place! [17]

Forgotten in all this were the ultimate victims of the Suez fiasco, the British (and French) residents of Egypt.

During the height of the crisis and invasion many expected, at best, to be arrested and interned or, at worst, to be massacred by rampaging mobs. Except in the case of the Canal Zone technicians, who were held for a time in 'protective custody', neither of these things happened. Determined to give the Allies no excuse to seize Cairo, Alexandria and the interior of Egypt, Nasser ordered a total clampdown on all public demonstrations and, if there was any disorder, it was nipped in the bud.

Thus, paradoxically and temporarily, the foreign communities benefited from residence in a police state. In any case, unlike 1919 and 1952, there seemed to be little resentment on the part of 'the man in the street' against British or French civilians who could mingle with the Cairo crowds unmolested with the RAF zooming about overhead.

Certainly, as had always been the case at times of crisis, most Anglo-Egyptian friendships remained unimpaired. while domestic servants, mostly Sudanese and therefore naturally suspicious of Egyptian intentions, would offer to hide their employers in their own homes.

However, within a few weeks of the cessation of hostilities in November 1956, the majority of British residents had been expelled at a few days' notice with what they stood up in and one suitcase; their assets, including their personal possessions, were sequestrated or nationalised. These people included a number of Maltese and Cypriots (in those days still British subjects), most of whom had been born in Egypt and knew no other home: shopkeepers, garage owners, mechanics, skilled artisans and the like. A community of some 13,000 souls, which had developed over the past three-quarters of a century and more, virtually ceased to exist.

Deportation is not a pleasant experience but it can have its lighter side. On 17 November 1956, among the first batch of deportees to fly out from the newly re-opened Cairo Airport on a KLM flight to Amsterdam were such sinister characters as the Right Reverend Francis Johnston, Anglican Bishop in Egypt, the Middle East Representative of a leading tea company, and the present author (probably mistaken for his father who had died two years before). Customs examination was rigorous but the Bishop arrived in the departure lounge with his face wreathed in smiles. 'After thirty years in Egypt,' he announced, 'I have at last persuaded a Moslem to open the Bible. The customs officer went through it page by page to see if I had any codes or secret messages concealed therein!'

The author's experience was rather more nerve-racking. Shortly before take-off he was tapped on the shoulder by a policeman (was the Bishop's hand raised in silent blessing?) and conducted to the airport commandant's office. The commandant, an Egyptian Air Force general, rose from behind his desk with his hand outstretched. ' Mr Keown-Boyd, I apologise for troubling you, but Jays Pasha [a retired British officer of the Egyptian Police who was himself later deported] told me you were leaving for Europe today and I would be very grateful if you would post this letter when you get to England. As you can see, it is to my daughter who is at school there, just to let her know that her mother and I are all right!'

A handful of elderly British residents were either overlooked or ignored by Egyptian officialdom: a few retired nannies eking out their meagre savings in cheap pensions and ex-police constables or old soldiers who had married locally and become absorbed into the indigenous population. These lingered on for a few years until time caught up with them, but there can be none left today. Indeed, there must be many more Egyptians living in the United Kingdom at the beginning of the new century than there are British in Egypt.

After the initial payout of an 'ex-gratia' loan from the British Government, amounting to a small percentage of their Egyptian assets and repayable against recovery of those assets, the dispossessed, many of them elderly, found themselves at the mercy of a bureaucratic blocking mechanism known as the Foreign Compensation Commission. The Egyptian Section of this agency, financed, we were to learn later, by its victims, was staffed at that time by Mummies excavated from the Valley of the Mandarins in Whitehall and (partially) resuscitated. Over the dreaded portals of its Kingsway offices should have been inscribed Dante's famous epigram: 'All Hope Abandon Ye Who Enter Here!'

To what an extent the former British community was able to recover its assets in Egypt in one form or another over the years which followed, it is impossible to say, especially as no total figure for the value of British property there seems ever to have been calculated – or, at least, agreed. Some went to their graves after years of struggle with nothing more to show for their efforts than a debit (the balance of their ex-gratia loans) on their account with the FCC. Others, luckier or more resourceful, reached private arrangements in Egypt, but probably the majority found that their assets had been either so misappropriated or mismanaged by their Egyptian sequestrators that there was little left, their problems having been exacerbated by the Nasserite regime's refusal to grant entry visas to former British residents.

At no time were any retaliatory steps taken against Egypt by the British. For example, the very considerable Egyptian sterling balances held in London could have been used to compensate the British community for its losses and to resettle those with no other home but Egypt. But, rightly or wrongly, this was not done, principally on the grounds that such action would lead to loss of confidence on the part of other foreign holders of sterling.

When the prominent banker Olaf Hambro heard that the Government intended to compensate the former British residents by public subscription (an idea which seems to have been dropped), he wrote furiously to *The Times*:

> Surely the most absurd and monstrous appeal that has ever been made to the generosity of the British public is the appeal to help the people who have been expelled from Egypt by Nasser. The expulsion is illegal under the Geneva Convention and also inhuman. These people are mostly friends of the Egyptian people and have for years been helping Egypt. There is no suggestion that they have been engaged in any political activity ... their only sin is that they are British subjects ...

This is the last straw in a series of humiliating agreements by successive governments in this country since the decision to evacuate the Canal Zone was made when whole installations costing millions of the British tax-payers' money were given away, to say nothing of defending them from German and Italian occupation. Surely it is time that this sort of charity should stop and that Nasser himself should pay? [18]

The final settlement eventually negotiated (if such a verb is appropriate in the circumstances) with the Egyptian Government by the Foreign Office proved, in its own words, 'sufficient to pay only a small percentage of adjudicated claims.' [19] Therefore we may safely assume that, in furtherance of its policy of propitiating Egypt, the Foreign Office concluded that the dwindling band of former British residents could be thrown to the wolves and that no one would notice that they had been devoured. It was right. One of their few champions, Lord Killearn, who used to speak up for them from time to time in the House of Lords, died in 1964 and there was no one to take up the torch. Perhaps today, in an era when compensation is doled out on the grand scale to the deserving and undeserving (often murderers and terrorists) alike, the Anglo-Egyptians might have fared better (See Appendix F).

Now few Egyptians remain who remember, for better or for worse, the British Occupation. The old quarrels and the old triumphs and defeats have passed into a history which is of little interest to the vast majority. Perhaps it is better so, as whatever mutual resentment there may once have been has faded with the memory and there are few British footprints in the sands of Egypt.

Afterthought

A S WE KNOW, 'the past is another country,' and nowhere more so than the United Kingdom. But the most significant changes, with the exception of the creation of the Welfare State and various technological advances, have occurred since 1956 rather than during the period covered by this book.

Between 1882 and 1956 Britain remained one of the great maritime and industrial powers. At the time of the Suez crisis, with 19.5 million gross tons of shipping flying the Red Duster, she operated the second largest (after the United States) merchant fleet in the world. By 1999 this had been reduced to 4.5.

In 1956 much of the Empire, despite the loss of the Indian sub-continent, remained intact. The White Ensign fluttered over the Seven Seas and numerous British Army garrisons straddled the globe. The Ruling Class ruled: an Old Etonian Prime Minister, Gladstone, had invaded Egypt in 1882 and an Old Etonian Prime Minister, Eden, evacuated Egypt in 1956: a Marquess of Salisbury replaced Gladstone as Prime Minister in 1885 and a Marquess of Salisbury sat in Eden's cabinet in 1956.

In 1956 the Monarchy enjoyed even greater public support, deference and respect than it had in 1882. The population of the United Kingdom was largely homogenetic and most people thought of themselves as primarily British and secondly as English, Scots, Welsh and Northern Irish. The nation's right to rule herself and to make and obey her own laws was unquestioned; indeed, any diminution of that inheritance was unimaginable. Two World Wars had been fought to retain it.

Thus for that three-quarters of a century the status quo was more or less maintained. Today, however, less than fifty years later, the United Kingdom is in the process of disintegration and its disparate parts threatened with absorption into a European super-state of dubious democratic credentials. Not to put too fine a point on it, the nation is threatened with a supra-national dictatorship masquerading as a union of free states.

National identity, especially that of the English population, has been diluted by waves of immigration, much of it in recent times illegal but unchecked. The people are bemused and demoralised by the tyranny of Political Correctness. A stream of squalid, even perverted, filth is the 'cultural' diet served up by television. Patriotism has become the prerogative of the football hooligan and the National Front thug.

The Monarchy is subjected to the minutest media scrutiny and the grossest intrusion. Its future is endangered by constant carping criticism and the barely concealed hostility of a largely foreign-owned press. It receives little, if any, support from the political establishment. The former Ruling Class has disappeared from public life altogether; the abolition of the right of most hereditary peers to sit in the House of Lords a *coup de grâce*.

Britain's industrial base and mercantile fleet are unrecognisably reduced, partly as a result of the loss of the huge trading block, the British Empire. Her agriculture, bullied, harassed and trammelled in every way by red tape and health-obsessed bureaucracy, is in a permanent state of crisis. Even her currency is threatened with abolition, while the use of her traditional weights and measures is regarded a subversive and subject to heavy penalties.

The species of mankind which exercised Britain's ill-defined authority over Egypt is extinct. There are no Cromers, Allenbys or Lloyds. The mould is broken and the formula lost. Perhaps it would be difficult to find a role for them today but the world is the poorer for their passing.

On the other hand, despite burgeoning population growth and dependence on foreign aid, Egypt has undergone no such metamorphosis and has demonstrated a remarkable stability for the past thirty years. Since the death of Nasser in 1970 she has had only two rulers, Presidents Sadat and Mubarak, both pragmatic statesmen who have steered their country away from Nasserite socialism and contributed immensely to the atmosphere of relative peace which exists in the Middle East today – one of them, Sadat, paying with his life for his courage and initiative. Domestic terrorism, of a particularly vicious variety, has been handled with a firmness and resolution which successive British governments failed notably to display in their dealings with the IRA.

There is no threat to Egypt's independence and her future, whatever difficulties may lie ahead for her, is less uncertain than that of the uninvited guest who came for a short visit and rather outstayed his welcome – for all the improvements he may have made to the household while he was there.

The British are long gone from Egypt and are forgotten, but it was not everyone who was glad to see them go.

After an absence of nearly twenty years, the present author returned to Cairo in the 1970s and had occasion to call on a member of the British Embassy staff. Asked to wait in the office of an elderly Coptic clerk, he enquired of that gentleman, for the sake of breaking the silence, 'How long have you been at the Embassy?' 'Over thirty years,' was the reply. 'You must have seen many changes in that time?' 'No, not changes – but the End of the World!'

Notes and References

Notes to Background

1. Sir Alexander Keown-Boyd's letter to Henry Hopkinson (Lord Colyton), 15 April 1952.
2. Khaled Fahmy, *All the Pasha's Men* (CUP, 1997).
3. Earl of Cromer, *Modern Egypt*, Vol. I (Macmillan: London, 1908).
4. John O. Udall, *The Nile in Darkness* (Michael Russell: Norwich, 1998).
5. Fahmy, *op. cit.*

Notes to Chapter 1, Enter the British

1. Cromer, *Modern Egypt*, Vol. I.
2. Clara Boyle, *Boyle of Cairo* (Titus Wilson: Kendal, 1965).
3. Cromer, *op. cit.*
4. Michael Barthorp, *War on the Nile* (Blandford: Poole, 1984).
5. Cromer, *op. cit.*
6. *Ibid.*
7. Grenfell Papers, Middle East Centre, Oxford.
8. *Battles of the Nineteenth Century* (Cassell & Co., 1896), Vol. I, pp. 195–204.
9. Barthorp, *op. cit.*
10. Cromer, *op. cit.*
11. Charles Coles, *Recollections and Reflections* (St Catherine's Press: London, 1918).
12. Peter Mansfield, *The British in Egypt* (Weidenfeld & Nicolson: London, 1971).

Notes to Chapter 2, The Early Days

1. Cromer, *op. cit.*
2. Henry Keown-Boyd, *A Good Dusting* (Leo Cooper: London, 1986).
3. Anne Baker, *A Question of Honour* (Pen & Sword/Leo Cooper: London, 1996).
4. Keown-Boyd, *A Good Dusting*.
5. Cromer, *op. cit.*
6. Julian Symons, *England's Pride* (Hamish Hamilton: London, 1965).
7. Information from Miss Lucinda Romilly (great-niece).
8. Henry Keown-Boyd, *Soldiers of the Nile* (Thornbury Publications, 1996).
9. Keown-Boyd, *Soldiers of the Nile*.
10. Andrew Haggard, *Under Crescent and Star* (William Blackwood: London, 1895).
11. *Ibid.*
12. Major General Hon. E. Montagu-Stuart-Wortley, Diary (unpublished), Green Jackets Museum, Winchester.

13. Keown-Boyd, *A Good Dusting*.
14. Philip Magnus, *Kitchener – Portrait of an Imperialist* (John Murray: London, 1958).
15. Coles, *Recollections and Reflections*.
16. El Lewa D. Baker Pasha, *The European Constable in Egypt* (Alexandria, 1944).

Notes to Chapter 3, A Place in the Sun

1. Rapp Papers, Middle East Centre, Oxford.
2. *The Sphinx Magazine*, Jubilee Number, 1943.
3. Membership list provided by Edward O'Farrell.
4. Sir Percival Marling, Rifleman and Hussar (London, 1931).
5. Grenfell Papers.
6. C.S. Jarvis, *The Back Garden of Allah* (John Murray: London, 1939).
7. Delany Papers, Middle East Centre, Oxford.
8. Duncan Doolittle, *A Soldiers' Hero* (Ananwan Publishing: USA, 1991).
9. K.D.D. Henderson, *Set Under Authority* (Castle Cary Press, 1987).
10. Henry Keown-Boyd, *Soldiers of the Nile*.
11. Grenfell Papers.
12. J.E. Marshall, *The Egyptian Enigma* (John Murray: London, 1928); Gladys Peto, *Egypt of the Sojourner* (J.M. Dent: London, 1928).
13. Documents supplied by Alwyn Jennings-Bramly (grandson).
14. Samir Rafaat, letter to the author, 1999.
15. E.W.C. Sandes, *The Royal Engineers in Egypt and the Sudan* (Institution of Royal Engineers: Chatham, 1937).
16. Boyle, *Boyle of Cairo*.
17. Adrian Carton de Wiart, *Happy Odyssey* (London, 1950).
18. PRO, FO141/787.
19. Peto, *Egypt of the Sojourner*.
20. Margaret Forster, *Daphne Du Maurier* (Arrow: London, 1994).
21. Grenfell Papers.
22. *Egyptian Gazette*, Cairo 1908, provided by Mrs E. Vernon Hart.
23. Mrs E. Vernon Hart to the author.
24. Cairo press reports provided by Mrs E. Vernon Hart.
25. El Lewa George Naldrett-Jays conversation with the author. In the early years of the twentieth century the pay of a European Constable was about £E5 per month (El Lewa D. Baker Pasha, *The European Police Constable in Egypt* (Alexandria, 1944)).
26. The Marquess of Anglesey, *History of the British Cavalry*, Vol. 5 (Leo Cooper: London, 1994).
27. Sarah Searight Lush to the author.

Notes to Chapter 4, The Anglo-Egyptian Sudan

1. C.S. Jarvis, *Oriental Spotlight* (John Murray: London, 1937).
2. Keown-Boyd, *A Good Dusting*.
3. Grenfell Papers.
4. Keown-Boyd, *A Good Dusting*.
5. Winston S. Churchill, *The River War* (Eyre & Spottiswoode: London, 1899).
6. Keown-Boyd, *A Good Dusting*.
7. Grenfell Papers.
8. Churchill, *The River War*, Appendix.

9. Sir Harold MacMichael, *Sudan Political Service 1899–1956* (Oxonian Press: Oxford, 1956).
10. Jarvis, *Oriental Spotlight*.
11. *Who Was Who*.
12. Maurice Lush, *A Life of Service*, edited by A.J.M. Lush (Private publication, 1992).
13. Keown-Boyd, *A Good Dusting*.
14. Magnus, *Kitchener – Portrait of an Imperialist*.
15. Lord Edward Cecil, *The Leisure of an Egyptian Official* (Hodder & Stoughton: London, 1921).
16. Magnus, *Kitchener – Portrait of an Imperialist*.

Notes to Chapter 5, Sporting Egypt

1. Stationery Office, Wilfrid Blunt's *Egyptian Garden/Fox Hunting in Cairo*, 1901 (re-issued 1999).
2. J. Wentworth Day, 'Sport in Egypt', *Country Life* (London, 1938).
3. Grenfell Papers.
4. Lawrence Grafftey-Smith, *Bright Levant* (John Murray: London, 1970).
5. David Mackenzie to author, *Who Was Who*, Lloyd's Register.
6. Samir Rafaat, *Maadi 1904–62* (Palm Press: Cairo 1994).
7. Trefor Ellis Evans, *Mission to Egypt, 1934–46* (University of Wales Press, 1971).
8. Richard Giles conversation with author.
9. C.S. Jarvis, *Three Deserts* (John Murray: London, 1936).
10. Evans, *Mission to Egypt, 1934–46*.
11. Keown-Boyd, *A Good Dusting*.
12. *Daily Telegraph*, 20 May 1999.
13. Grenfell Papers.
14. *Ibid*.

Notes to Chapter 6, Denshawi

1. *The Times*, 15–18 June 1906.
2. *Ibid*.
3. *Ibid*.
4. Sue Limb and Peter Cordingly, *Captain Oates* (William Batsford: London, 1982).
5. *The Times*, 24–28 June 1906.
6. *Petit Bleu*, 4 July 1906.
7. *Illustrated London News*, 14 July 1906.
8. Bernard Shaw to *The Times*, 7 July 1906; also Preface to his book, *John Bull's Other Island*.
9. Peter Mellini, *Sir Eldon Gorst – The Overshadowed Pro-Consul* (Stanford University, 1977).
10. Marshall, *The Egyptian Enigma*.
11. Lord Lloyd, *Egypt since Cromer*, Vol. 1 (MacMillan: London, 1932).
12. *The Times*.
13. *Ibid*.
14. Lloyd, *Egypt since Cromer*, Vol. 1.

Notes to Chapter 7, After Cromer

1. Peter Mellini, *Sir Eldon Gorst, The Overshadowed Pro-Consul* (Cambridge University Press, 1997).

  2. Lloyd, *Egypt since Cromer*, Vol. 1.
  3. Samir Rafaat in the *Egyptian Mall*, 30 March 1996.
  4. Theo Klat (*Old Victorian*), letter to the author, May 1999.
  5. Various documents provided by Lillian Ireland.
  6. Colonel W.F. Stirling, *Safety Last* (Hollis & Carter: London, 1953).
  7. Violet Milner Papers, Bodleian Library, Oxford.
  8. Magnus, *Kitchener – Portrait of an Imperialist*.
  9. Grenfell Papers.
 10. Mellini, *Sir Eldon Gorst*.
 11. Mary Repington (Garstin), *Thanks for the Memory* (Constable: London, 1938; *Dictionary of National Biography*.
 12. Lloyd, *Egypt since Cromer*, Vol. 2.
 13. Magnus, *Kitchener*; Marshall, *The Egyptian Enigma*.
 14. Keown-Boyd, *Soldiers of the Nile*.
 15. Hatfield Archives, Hatfield House.
 16. Violet Milner Papers.
 17. *Ibid*.
 18. Keown-Boyd, *Soldiers of the Nile*.
 19. Cecil, *The Leisure of an Egyptian Official*.
 20. Violet Milner Papers.

Notes to Chapter 8, War and its Aftermath

  1. Trevor Royle, *The Kitchener Enigma* (Michael Joseph: London, 1985).
  2. G.E. Badcock, *History of Transport of the Egyptian Expeditionary Force*.
  3. Jarvis, *Back Garden of Allah*.
  4. *The Guards Magazine*, Spring 1998.
  5. Violet Milner Papers.
  6. Jarvis, *Back Garden of Allah*.
  7. Grafftey-Smith, *Bright Levant*.
  8. Violet Milner Papers.
  9. Mrs Ruth Maudslay conversation with the author.
 10. Ronald Wingate, *Wingate of the Sudan* (London, 1955).
 11. Grenfell Papers.
 12. Elle Kedourie, *Politics in the Middle East* (Oxford University Press, 1992).
 13. Lloyd, *Egypt since Cromer*, Vol. 2.
 14. Cromer, *Modern Egypt*, Vol. 2.
 15. Alexander Keown-Boyd to his parents, September 1918.
 16. Sir Alexander Keown-Boyd conversation with the author.
 17. Grafftey-Smith, *Bright Levant*.
 18. Sir Alexander Keown-Boyd conversation with the author.
 19. Brian Gardner, *Allenby* (Cassell & Co.: London, 1965).

Notes to Chapter 9, Revolution

  1. P.G. Elgood, *Transit of Egypt* (London, 1928).
  2. Major-General Sir Rudolf Slatin Pasha, a prisoner of the Mahdists for many years, became a Moslem during his captivity but reverted to Christianity when he escaped to Egypt. He was appointed Inspector-General of the Anglo-Egyptian Sudan but, as an Austrian citizen, had to resign in 1914. (See Richard Hill, *Slatin Pasha* (Oxford University Press, 1965).
  3. Sir Douglas Dodds-Parker to the author.

4. Not to be confused with the Egyptian administrator and writer Major C.S. Jarvis.
5. Derek Hopwood, *Tales of Empire – The British in the Middle East* (I.B. Tauris: London, 1989.
6. Grafftey-Smith, *Bright Levant*.
7. Jarvis, *Back Garden of Allah*.
8. Grafftey-Smith, *Bright Levant*.
9. *The Times*, 12 April 1919.
10. Lawrence James, *Imperial Warrior* (Weidenfeld & Nicolson: London, 1993).
11. *The Times*, 16 April 1919.
12. Elgood, *Transit of Egypt*.
13. Grafftey-Smith, *Bright Levant*.
14. *Dictionary of National Biography*.
15. Keown-Boyd, *Soldiers of the Nile*.
16. *Who Was Who*.
17. Grafftey-Smith, *Bright Levant*.
18. Lloyd, *Egypt Since Cromer*, Vol. 2.
19. Copies of reports in the author's possession.
20. *Ibid.*
21. Mary Joan Innes, *In Egyptian Service – British Officials in Egypt 1911–36* (PhD thesis, Oxford, 1986).

Notes to Chapter 10, Assassination

1. Russell Papers, Middle East Centre.
2. Sir Sydney Smith, *Mostly Murder* (London, 1958).
3. *Ibid.*
4. *Ibid.*
5. Russell Papers.
6. Keown-Boyd. *Soldiers of the Nile*; *Who Was Who*.
7. PRO, FO141/502.
8. Various biographies of Allenby; Grafftey-Smith, *Bright Levant*.
9. PRO.
10. Black Watch Regimental Secretary to author, 1999.
11. PRO.
12. James, *Imperial Warrior*.
13. Nevile Henderson, *Water under the Bridges* (London, 1943).
14. PRO.
15. Gwynne, C.W., *Imperial Policing* (London, 1934).
16. Keown-Boyd, *Soldiers of the Nile*.
17. Henderson, *Water under the Bridges*.
18. Field Marshal Viscount Wavell, *Allenby in Egypt* (George Harrop: London, 1943). Lawrence James, *Imperial Warrior*. Brian Gardner, *Allenby*.
19. Nicholas Reeves, *The Complete Tutankhamoun* (Thames & Hudson: London, 1990).
20. Carnarvon Archive, Highclere Castle.
21. Soon after Carnarvon's death Almina married an impecunious former Guards officer called (inaptly) 'Tiger' Dennistoun and became involved in a sensational law suit with his former wife. Several of the leading Silks of the day were involved and the case afforded the public much salacious entertainment. See H. Mongomery Hyde, *The Life of Lord Birkett* (World Books, 1964).
22. Reeves, *The Complete Tutankhamoun*.

Notes to Chapter 11, Detective Story

1. Thomas Russell, *Egyptian Service* (London, 1946).
2. M.E. Yapp, *Politics and Diplomacy in Egypt – Diaries of Sir Miles Lampson, 1935–37* (Oxford University Press, 1997).
3. Innes, *In Egyptian Service – British Officials in Egypt, 1911–36.*
4. *Ibid.*
5. Yapp, *Politics and Diplomacy in Egypt.*
6. Grafftey-Smith, *Bright Levant*; Innes, *In Egyptian Service.*
7. Russell, *Egyptian Service.*
8. PRO, FO141/502.
9. PRO.
10. Russell Papers.
11. *Ibid.*
12. *Ibid.*
13. *Ibid.*
14. *Ibid.*
15. *Ibid.*
16. Grafftey-Smith, *Bright Levant.*
17. Sydney Smith, *Mostly Murder.*
18. Russell Papers.
19. Grafftey-Smith, *Bright Levant.*
20. Sydney Smith, *Mostly Murder.*
21. PRO, FO141/503.
22. Russell Papers.
23. PRO, FO141/493.
24. PRO, FO141/787.
25. Sir Anthony Kershaw to the author 1999.
26. PRO, FO141/493 and Lloyd, *Egypt since Cromer*, Vol. 2.
27. Lloyd, *Egypt since Cromer*, Vol. 2.
28. PRO, FO141/493.
29. *The Times*, 1 March 1929.
30. Sydney Smith, *Mostly Murder*; *Who Was Who.*
31. PRO, FO141/502.
32. Sydney Smith, *Mostly Murder.*
33. PRO, FO141/787.

Notes to Chapter 12, A Distinguished Australian

1. PRO, FO141/522.
2. Much of the rest of this chapter is based on *Fred: An Australian Hero* by Peter Sekuless, University of Queensland Press, 1981
3. Dan Parsons' letter to the author 1998.

Notes to Chapter 13, The Last Pro-Consuls

1. Marshall, *The Egyptian Enigma.*
2. Grafftey-Smith, *Bright Levant.*
3. Delany Papers.
4. John Charmley, *Lord Lloyd and the Decline of the British Empire* (Weidenfeld & Nicolson: London, 1987).
5. *Ibid.*
6. Grafftey-Smith, *Bright Levant.*

7. Delany Papers.
8. Grafftey-Smith, *Bright Levant*.
9. Charmley, *Lord Lloyd*.
10. Lloyd, *Egypt since Cromer*, Vol. 1.
11. *Who Was Who*.
12. *The Times*, 28 December 1954.
13. *Who Was Who*.
14. HM Stationery Office, *Treaty of Alliance*, London, 26 August 1936.
15. Innes, *In Egyptian Service*.
16. Yapp, *Politics and Diplomacy in Egypt*.
17. *Who Was Who*.
18. Walter Lucas conversation with the author.
19. Andy Hurst (son) to the author.
20. Grenfell Papers.
21. Grafftey-Smith (who promotes Crosbie to the rank of Sergeant), *Bright Levant*.
22. *Ibid*.

Notes to Chapter 14, Uneasy Allies

1. Colonel E. Windsor Clive (quoting General Sir Arthur Smith) conversation with the author.
2. Letter in the author's possession.
3. Artemis Cooper, *Cairo in the War* (Hamish Hamilton: London, 1989).
4. *Ibid*.
5. Author's conversation with the (alleged) driver of the armoured-car, later Chief of the Addis Ababa Fire Brigade, *c*. 1960.
6. Ahmed Hassanein, *Lost Oasis* (London, 1926).
7. Adel M. Sabit, *A King Betrayed* (Quartet Books: London, 1989).
8. Ian Weston-Smith, a friend and brother officer of the late Harold Morrison, conversation with the author.
9. Sabit, *A King Betrayed*.
10. Cooper, *Cairo in the War*.
11. Mansfield, *The British in Egypt*.
12. Joan Keown-Boyd to her mother, 1940.
13. Rafaat, *Maadi, 1904–62*.
14. The Countess of Ranfurly, *To War with Whitaker* (William Heinemann: London, 1994).
15. *Ibid*.
16. Michael Dewar in *Churchill's Generals*, edited by John Keegan (Weidenfeld & Nicolson: London, 1991.
17. Brigadier Dudley Clarke, *The Eleventh at War* (Michael Joseph: London, 1952).
18. Sir Rennie Maudslay conversation with the author.
19. David Keown-Boyd conversation with the author.
20. Richard Casey, an Australian, had replaced Oliver Lyttelton as Minister of State in the Middle East Office.
21. Ranfurly, *To War with Whitaker*.

Notes to Chapter 15, Happy Days Are Here Again

1. Edward O'Farrell to the author.
2. Afaf Lutfi Al-Sayyid Marsot, *A Short History of Modern Egypt* (Cambridge University Press, 1985).

3. Cooper, *Cairo in the War*.
4. Keown-Boyd was not a Pasha (few non-Egyptian civilians were, apart from senior police officers), but most men of standing in Egypt were referred to and addressed by that title. As there is no P in the Arabic alphabet it is pronounced *Basha*.
5. Rafaat, *Maadi, 1904–62*.
6. Delany Papers.
7. Sir Alexander Keown-Boyd conversation with the author.
8. Keown-Boyd to Hopkinson.
9. Rapp Papers.
10. Carola Mills, *Brown Shoes* (Private Publication, 1964).
11. Antony Beevor and Artemis Cooper, *Paris after the Liberation* (Hamish Hamilton: London, 1994).
12. David Keown-Boyd to the author.
13. W. Scott Lucas, *Divided We Stand* (Hodder & Stoughton: London, 1991).
14. Rapp Papers.
15. *Ibid.*
16. Keown-Boyd to Hopkinson.
17. Elie Kedourie, *Politics in the Middle East* (Oxford University Press, 1992).

Notes to Chapter 16, The Traitor

1. Colin Campbell to the author.
2. *Ibid.*
3. Robert Cecil, *A Divided Life* (The Bodley Head: London, 1988).
4. Colin Campbell to the author.
5. Cecil: Christopher Andrew and Vasihi Mitrokhin, *The Mitrokin Archive* (Allen Lane: London, 1999).
6. Colin Campbell to the author.
7. Cecil.
8. *Ibid.*
9. Edward O'Farrell to the author.
10. Cecil.
11. Colin Campbell to the author.
12. *Ibid.*
13. Cecil.
14. *The Mitrokin Archive*.
15. Cecil.
16. *Ibid.*
17. Colin Campbell, confirmed by Tim Fisher.

Notes to Chapter 17, Nasser and Suez – The Last Act

1. Mansfield, *The British in Egypt*.
2. Michael Lee to the author.
3. Scott Lucas, *Divided We Stand*.
4. *Ibid.*
5. Peter Harcleode, *Para! Fifty Years of the Parachute Regiment* (1996).
6. Scott Lucas, *Divided We Stand*.
7. Dodds-Parker to the author.
8. *Illustrated London News*, 22 December 1956.
9. Quoted in BBC *Reputations* programme, 6 June 2000.
10. Scott Lucas, *Divided We Stand*.

11. Scott Lucas, *Divided We Stand*; Robert Rhodes James, *Anthony Eden* (Weidenfeld & Nicolson: London, 1986); John Cloake, *Templer* (Harrop: London, 1985).

12. *Ibid.*

13. Quoted in *Daily Telegraph*, December 1999.

14. Greek Community Records, Alexandria.

15. *The Times*, 18 November 1956.

16. The *khazook* was a particularly barbaric form of execution, probably invented by the Ottoman Turks, by which the condemned man was impaled upon a sharp stake in such a way that he remained alive in frightful agony for hours, even days, before dying. The practice seems to have been discontinued by about the middle of the nineteenth century, but the word is still used in Turkey and Egypt to describe an especially painful event suffered by an individual or nation.

17. Dodds-Parker to the author.

18. *The Times*, 14 December 1956.

19. Letter from the Under Secretary of State at the FCO to the author, 2 February 1983.

APPENDIX A

Rulers of Egypt, 1882–1956

Khedive Tewfik	(1879–92)
Khedive Abbas II Hilmi	(1892–1914)
Sultan Hussein	(1914–17)
King Fuad I	(1917–36)
King Farouk	(1936–52)
King Fuad II (infant son of Farouk, ruled only in name)	(1952–53)
President Mohamed Neguib	(1953–54)
President Gamal Abdel Nasser	(1954–70)

British Agents, High Commissioners and Ambassadors in Egypt, 1882–1956

Sir Edward Malet	(1882–83)
Earl of Cromer (Sir Evelyn Baring)	(1883–1907)
Sir Eldon Gorst	(1907–11)
Field Marshal Earl Kitchener	(1911–14)
Sir Henry McMahon (First British High Commissioner)	(1914–17)
General Sir Reginald Wingate	(1917–19)
Field Marshal Viscount Allenby	(1919–25)
Lord Lloyd	(1925–29)
Sir Percy Loraine	(1929–33)
Lord Killearn (Sir Miles Lampson)	(1933–46)

Lord Killearn was the first British Ambassador to Egypt 1936–46

Sir Ronald Campbell	(1946–50)
Sir Ralph Stevenson	(1950–55)
Sir Humphrey Trevelyan	(1955–56)

Sirdars of the Egyptian Army

Field Marshal Sir Evelyn Wood   (1882–86)

Field Marshal Lord Grenfell   (1886–92)

Field Marshal Earl Kitchener   (1892–99)

General Sir Reginald Wingate   (1899–1917)

Major General Sir Lee Stack   (1917–24)

The last three were also Governor-Generals of the Sudan

Inspector-General of the Egyptian Army

Major General Sir Charlton Spinks   (1925–36)

APPENDIX B

Mutiny of Albanian Troops

An extract from the diary of Lt F.B. de Sales la Terriere, 18th Hussars and Egyptian Cavalry – Summer 1884. (By kind permission of I.C. de Sales la Terriere. Esq.)

The much vaunted Turkish [sic] Battalion under Grant [Major H.F. Grant, 4th Hussars], Surtees [Lt H.C. Surtees, Coldstream Guards] and Besant [Lt W.H. Besant, Norfolk Regt.] was ordered on service and then the fun began.

The Mahdi movement was then developing pretty freely and it was pretty evident that Egyptian troops would be engaged if an English expedition did not come out.

I knew these so-called Turks having had a few foisted on us in the cavalry and knew what unmitigated scoundrels and undisciplined ruffians they were, nothing but the sweepings of the ports of the Levant. However, it was one of the deceptions of the Egyptian Army that they were a fine and trustworthy body of men. However, when told to prepare for active service about 80 out of 300 bolted that night and were never heard of again including the guard on the gate ... Grant, Surtees and Besant kept guard at the gate with loaded revolvers to prevent the rest of the 'Turks' bolting too as soon as they heard of it and marched the remainder off to Boulaq Dacroor (Cairo) Station at daylight, some more deserted on the way but they got most of them to the station and myself and Teddy Bartellot [Lt E.M. Bartellot, Royal Fusiliers][1] hearing of this determined to go to the station to see if we could help at all. We met one deserter on the way whom we knocked down and jumped on and took back and on arrival at the station found old Grant and Surtees mounting guard on their own guard at the gate to prevent the whole lot going off.

It was a truly melancholy sight and positively wicked that British officers should ever have been asked to command such troops. Teddy Bartellot and I relieved old Grant and Surtees at the gate while they went and got something to eat and to show what thorough curs they were they didn't dare to run though we only had our walking sticks with us.

Eventually something over 200 of them were got onto the train and as the train moved they all proceeded to fire off their rifles out of the windows and it was a mercy no one was hit!

On arrival at Assiout this festive battalion further disported themselves by breaking out into open mutiny refusing to go on board and turning on their officers ... one party of them got a boat and crossed the river and Grant went across alone and hunted them out of a house that they had taken up a position in, shot two and made the rest lay down their arms. For the rest about 80 remained loyal not even having the pluck to mutiny, some were induced to come back and about 30 were made prisoners of and the rest filtered off and were never heard of again.

I was a member of the General Court Martial that tried them. Nine were condemned to death, but seven were committed (commuted?) to Penal Servitude for life the remainder got periods from ten years to six months.

The shooting parade was a ghastly business in the cold grey dawn at the back of the Cavalry Barracks at Abbassiyeh. The prisoners were tied in chairs with their backs to the firing party after having their court martials and sentences read to the whole of the Egyptian troops in Turkish by Zohrab and Egyptian (Arabic) by Mucktar.[2] The firing party consisted of 10 Blacks, 10 Turks, and 10 Egyptians and couldn't have been done better as they shot their heads clean off being only 9 paces distant. The prisoners were wonderfully plucky to the last, asked for a glass of water and declared they died at peace with all men. I was there on the Staff and the Sirdar (Major General Sir Evelyn Wood, VC) was most awfully affected by the business. Keggie Slade (Captain F.G. Slade. RA) had the arrangements to make and did it all first class.

Thus ended the mutiny of the Turks though for a long time Teddy Bartellot couldn't be persuaded not to run in any respectable Turk he could find about the streets of Cairo on suspicion of being a deserter. No real efforts were made to catch those who had escaped as they were only too glad to get rid of them at any price and their taking would have necessitated more CMs.

Author's notes

1. There was some doubt about Bartellot's sanity. His violent nature came to the attention of his superiors during the Gordon Relief Expedition when he shot dead an Adeni camel-driver, who, he claimed, had hit him with a stick. He did not complete his two-year contract with the Egyptian Army but the explorer Stanley put him in command of his rear party during the Emin Rescue Expedition. He flogged his men constantly, one of whom died under this punishment, and was accused of kicking his servant to death. Eventually, in July 1888, he was murdered by a follower of Tippoo Tib, the notorious Arab slaver.
2. Zohrab and Mucktar were Ottoman officers attached to the Egyptian Army.

Zohrab, an Armenian, was Wolseley's interpreter and intelligence officer during the Gordon Relief Expedition. He was highly regarded by Wolseley, promoted to Lewa (Major General), made a Pasha and later knighted.

APPENDIX C

The Capitulations, Mixed Courts and Consular Courts

Extract from *The Egyptian Enigma* by J.E. Marshall

'Capitulations' is the name given by Europeans to those concessions which secured from the early Sultans of Turkey extra-territorial rights to foreigners residing there (Ottoman Empire) ... They are unilateral and non-terminable, but liable to modification by subsequent treaties. Primarily they were intended to make possible for Christians to trade and reside in the territories of the Ottoman Empire by safe-guarding them against any forms of injustice or ill-usage, to which, as foreigners of a different religion, they might otherwise have been subjected. The Capitulations granted to Great Britain date back to a very early period ... Nearly all the other Great Powers obtained similar concessions from the Porte at one time or another in the course of the last 400 years.

It is in virtue of these unilateral treaties with the Porte that Capitulations exist in Egypt ... In Egypt the rights conferred on foreigners by the Capitulations, apart from certain commercial concessions, included: immunity from personal taxation without the consent of their Governments; inviolability of domicile and protection from arbitrary arrest; and exemption from the jurisdiction of the local courts. Since the creation of the Mixed Tribunals in 1876, the practical effects of the last-mentioned privilege are that no legislation applicable to foreigners can be enforced without the consent of the capitulatory powers, and that civil jurisdiction in cases between Europeans and natives or between Europeans of different nationality is exercised by the Mixed Courts, while criminal jurisdiction over Europeans and jurisdiction in civil cases between Europeans of the same nationality is exercised by the Consular Courts applying the laws of their own countries. The only internal taxes to which foreigners are at present liable are house and land tax.

APPENDIX D

'Free Elections in Egypt 1930' (Anon.) attached to an official report to the Residency on the 1930 Elections

To lighten this somewhat heavy note, let me describe to you once more what really happens in a 'free election' under a 'neutral Government' in Egypt. You will recognise some of the characters in this sketch, but I have changed their names[1] so as not to be too personal.

In a certain constituency of Egypt there were three candidates: 1. Mohamed Bey Mukh, Liberal Constitutionalist: 2. Eissa Pasha el Ghani, Ittihadist[2] and 3. Dr Abdu Makar, Wafdist. The first two were big men of the place owning many hundreds of *feddans* in the four villages forming the constituency, the last a doctor from Alexandria.

When the electoral lists were drawn up and the election decree issued, Mohamed Bey Mukh gave a tea-party at his country house coming down from Cairo and missing an evening at the Mohamed Ali Club for the express purpose. He invited the four Omdahs of the four villages. Ahmed Wessikh of Kom el Gilla, Mohamed Bey Maarass of Kimam el Zift, Hanaf I Bakshish of Hosh el Boyagieyeh and Hussein Afrit el Din of Kafr el Barabra. There was an excellent spread with tea, cakes, lemonade and ices from Groppi's in Cairo and a Greek waiter in European dress clothes. When the Omdahs had well eaten and drunk, Mohamed Bey gave them a lengthy address on the principles of the Liberal Party, pointed out the advantages which would accrue to them generally if he were elected and his party came to power, cast a few veiled aspersions on the King and a few hints about the greed of foreigners and ended by saying that in front of each man under the saucer would be found a little present as a memory of a very nice party. Under the saucers the Omdahs found each an envelope containing a note for £E100 which they placed in their pockets. They were given to understand that if Mohamed Bey were successful in the elections there would be another party and more similar notes. They also understood that the Ford cars on the farms were at the disposal of electors and that in case of success, bills for taxi hire would be footed by the candidate. They left with expressions of esteem and satisfaction.

Shortly afterwards Eissa Pasha el Ghani who had come to reside on his estate for a few weeks gave a dinner party to the four Omdahs. There were whole sheep, turkeys, pigeons, *bamia*, *mulkhia*, rice and sweets. The Omdahs ate their fill and after ablution sat and talked pleasantly in the *salamlik*. There was one chorus of '*Yehia el Malik*'[3] and a little chat about the elections. Each Omdah withdrew for a space with the Pasha into his office, where he learned that rumours were going about that a certain Bey had tried to bribe the Omdahs of Kom el Gilla, Kimam el Zift, Hosh el Boyagieyeh and Kafr el Barabra, but that these honest gentlemen had of course refused his advances – times were hard and out of pure kindness of heart the Pasha would like to make it up to them for their loss and slipped notes for £E200 into the hand of each and, of course, if it so happened that the Pasha were elected to Parliament, further similar aid would be forthcoming and any little expenses they might have in the course of the election would be met without question.

The Omdahs went on their way rejoicing.

The next day Ahmed el Wessikh, Omdah of Kom el Gilla, received a letter from a Bey in Cairo of great Wafdist distinction recalling to him the fact that the Bey's aunt's first husband's third cousin was married to the Omda's second wife's fourth cousin and recommending to his care Dr Abdu Makkar, the Wafd candidate, who would shortly be visiting the district. The Omdah replied that in view of the close relationship with the Bey and of his excellent position he would be delighted to entertain Dr Abdu Makkar, but that in view of the strong political feeling in the village of Kom el Gilla he thought it would be best for Dr Makkar to visit him at night. Next day Dr Makkar arrived and under cover of night called on the Omdah. After greetings and long discussion of relationship, Dr Makkar mentioned the great possibilities that awaited the eminent Bey in Cairo if a Wafdist majority were obtained in Parliament. He went on to mention some recent government appointments in particular the promotion of Hassan Bey Abdel to a high post in the Public Security Department. A friend of the Doctor in the Ministry of the Interior had told him that Abdel Bey had called for the papers of a case in which the Omda of Kom el Gilla was related to have caused the disappearance of a school boy who had been corrupted by a certain great man of the village. 'Oh', said the Omda, 'but that case was filed away three years ago by the Criminal Investigation Officer.' 'Yes,' said the doctor, 'it is surprising what an effect two turkeys and five pounds of butter will have on an Investigation Officer. But sometimes even an officer's findings may be upset by the appearance of a new witness and Abdel Bey when he sent for the papers spoke of a new witness, but, of course, if my party came to power and the Omda of Kom el Gilla had assisted in the victory, nothing more would be heard of the case.' 'I quite understand,' said the Omda, 'that it would be very convenient if my relative became a Minister in the new cabinet.' 'Yes,' said the doctor, 'and perhaps it would help if I were to meet your colleague Mohamed Bey Maarass, the Omda of Kimam el Zift.' The meeting was accordingly arranged for the next day.

To cut a long story short, Dr Makkar met the Omda of Kimam el Zift and referred to a case in which some brigands who had committed murder in the course of their highway robbery had mysteriously disappeared. He was then passed on to Hanafi Effendi Bakshish, Omda of Hosh el Boyagieyeh, who owned some land at the end of a canal to which irrigation water could only reach if the other owners on the way were cut short. The Irrigation Inspector of the region was much in need of a loan. From this conversation an Introduction to the Omda of Kafr el Barabra resulted. This Omda's name had for some years been on the list of persons recommended for the grade of Bey. The doctor had a relation who, if a Wafdist Government were returned, would certainly bring the necessary influence to bear. Hassan Effendi explained that his villagers were very obstinate in their political creed but this was got over by the doctor who explained that the Assistant to the Chief Police Officer was a great friend of his and that if the Omda would arrange on the Election Day for a crime to take place in the village, the Police Officer would see to it that the matter assumed such importance that none of the villagers would be able to go to the polling place, except those chosen by the Omda. The rest would all be concerned in the investigation.

After these interviews the four Omdas, after deep thought and long consultation, became extremely active. It is needless to relate how each of them summoned Zeid and Amr and expounded to them the virtues of Dr Makkar and either by uncupboarding some family skeleton or by the gift of half a dollar, persuaded them to the virtues of the Wafd. But one conversation is worth recording: Mohamed Bey Maarass. Omda of Kom el Zift, summoned a certain farmer called Hassan el Tayeb and when the farmer stood before him the following conversation ensued:

'May your day be happy, oh Hassan.' 'May your day be happy and blessed, oh Excellency.' 'That is a nice field of maize you have, oh Hassan.' 'It promises well, oh Bey.' 'That is a fine young buffalo that turns your water-wheel, oh Hassan.' 'It is better than others, oh Excellency.' 'Your daughter Fatima is well grown, oh Hassan, she is plump and comely and should bring a good dowry.' 'There have been worse looking girls, oh Bey.' 'Happy are you, oh Hassan, but if you are to enjoy the fruits of your labours it is necessary that Dr Makkar should be elected to represent us in the Parliament.' 'And who, oh Bey, is this Dr Makkar?"He is a friend of a near relation of my friend the Omda of Hom el Gilla and a most powerful man. He is the choice of the Wafd.' 'But I am the man of Eissa Pasha. My father was his manager of a farm and four years ago when times were bad Eissa Pasha gave me £E5 to pay my taxes and save my property and family and asked for no repayment.' 'Yes, oh Hassan, but what would the £E5 profit you now if your field of maize were burnt one dark night and your buffalo were hamstrung and your daughter raped by my large blackguard, Allagabu, and there were witnesses to prove that she consented, nay, lured him on. Think, oh Hassan! 'I have thought, oh Bey, and I find that Dr Makkar is the true representative of the people.' It is well', said the Omda, 'but forget not your daughter when the automobile takes you to the place where votes are recorded.' 'You are a powerful man,' replied Hassan.

On the day of the polling, the Ford cars of Mohamed Bey Mukh, the taxis paid for by Eissa Pasha and other cars conveyed to the place of polling Hassan el Tayeb and others, who gave their votes for Dr Makkar, who was duly returned as member for that constituency. The Omdas were each £E300 richer and he who had sworn by the triple divorce to return Mohamed Bey Mukh was absolved of his oath because he was not married and Dr Makkar was true to his word and Lieutenant Abdel Razzek who investigated the case of the crime in Kafr el Barabra, in due course, was promoted to the rank of Captain, the Constitution was preserved and the people were free.

Notes

1. Some of the names of the personalities and villages are a play on impolite Arabic words.
2. The King's Party
3. 'Long live the King!'

APPENDIX E

Egyptian Army Operations under British Officers in the Anglo-Egyptian Sudan 1899–1921 for which the Khedive's Sudan Medals 1896 and 1908 were awarded

The Battle of Gedid or Urn Dibaykarat on 27th November 1899 at which the Khalifa Abdullahi was finally defeated and killed by a force under Miralai Wingate (future Sirdar and Governor-General of the Sudan).

Exploratory operations in Bahr el Ghazal Province under Miralai Sparkes including Sudd clearance work in 1902.

Also in 1902 the Shambe Field Force under Miralai Stack (future Sirdar and Governor-General of the Sudan) was mounted to punish the Agar Dinka tribe after a District Inspector, Bimbashi Scott-Barbour, and fourteen of his men had been lured into a trap and murdered.

Expedition to Gebel Jerok on the Sudan-Abyssinian border against a notorious slave-raider called Ibrahim Wad Mahmoud under Miralai Gorringe. Mahmoud was captured.

The Nyam-Nyam or Zande expedition of 1904–05 under Miralai Boulnois against the recalcitrant King Yambio of the Zande. Yambio was killed, as was an Egyptian Army doctor, Bimbashi Haymes.

Operations in the Nuba Mountains in 1905 following an attack on Talodi by the Abu Rufas tribe in which the Egyptian Mamur (Sub-Governor) and thirty-one soldiers were killed. The town was retaken by 500 men of the Camel Corps and infantry under Miralai O'Connell, Governor of Kordofan Province.

In April 1908 a British official of the Sudan Political Service, Colin Scott-Moncrieff (son of Sir Colin, former Director of the Egyptian Irrigation Department), and an Egyptian officer were murdered by rebels under a prominent Mahdist called Wad Habuba in Blue Nile Province. An Egyptian Army force under the Provincial Governor, Miralai Dickinson, captured Wad Habuba after some stiff resistance in which Dickinson was wounded. Wad Habuba was hanged.

In November 1908 the Governor of Kordofan Province, Kaimakam Lloyd, mounted an expedition against certain clans in the Nyima Hills 'which had refused to make their peace with the government'. The troops were commanded by Kaimakam Lempriere who was at loggerheads with Lloyd and the outcome seems to have been inconclusive.

Operations against Chief Ashwol of the Atwot Dinka who had shown 'a truculent attitude towards the government' were carried out by Kaimakam Harvey from February to April 1910. Perhaps surprisingly, his force was assisted by the Aliab Dinka, a section of the same tribe, and Chief Ashwol was captured.

Also in 1910, for reasons which are unclear, a major operation under Lewa Asser Pasha, Adjutant-General of the Egyptian Army, was mounted against Mek (Chief) Gedeil of Gebel Tagoi in Kordofan Province. However, the Mek escaped, returned in the following year and killed the man who had been appointed in his place! But his triumph was short-lived as a few months later he was captured, tried and hanged.

In 1912 a disastrous expedition was launched against the Adonga Anuak tribe in the southeastern Sudan on the Abyssinian border. This tribe had been trafficking in arms and raiding its neighbours, the Nuer. The OC Troops, Kaimakam Leveson, seriously underestimated the fighting capabilities of the Adonga and suffered the heaviest casualties ever inflicted upon the Egyptian Army during the Condominium era: five officers, two of them British (Bimbashis Kinahan and Lichtenberg) and forty-two Other Ranks killed with little or nothing achieved. For reasons best known to the Anglo-Egyptian authorities, Leveson was awarded the DSO.

From December 1913 to June 1914 a force under Bimbashi Fairbairn was employed in operations against Chief Machar Diu of the Zeraf Nuer in Upper Nile Province. Diu had failed to pay nominal tribute to the government, had attacked parties laying telegraph lines and raided neighbouring Dinka cattle camps. Having failed to capture Diu after several months of floundering about in the swamps Fairbairn withdrew empty-handed, but Diu was killed in a raid on the Bor Dinka soon afterwards.

In March 1914 Bimbashi Romilly (Winston Churchill's brother-in-law) with a contingent of Camel Corps was despatched to punish the Sabai and Mandal Nubas for raiding their Arab neighbours and refusing to pay taxes. Romilly imposed a fine of rifles, which had to be extracted from the Nubas by force.

It was believed in March 1915 that one Fiki (Holy Man) Ali and his followers, inhabitants of the Miri Hills, were about to attack the District HQ at Kadugli in the Nuba Mountains. Ali refused to meet the Provincial Governor to discuss the matter and troops were sent to arrest him. His stronghold was occupied and he was eventually arrested but escaped after having been sentenced to death. In November he and eight of his brothers gave themselves up and his death sentence was commuted to banishment.

Between December 1915 and March 1916 military expeditions under Kaimakam Percy-Smith were sent to the remote Imatong and Lafite Mountains of Mongalla Province. The objectives are unclear and may have been of an exploratory nature as little was known of the area at that time.

In March 1916 the British Government decided that the semi-autonomous sultanate of Darfur in western Sudan should be annexed to the Condominium for fear that the Sultan Ali Dinar was coming under Turkish influence. An Egyptian Army force of 2,000 men under Miralai Kelly, supported by a British machine-gun company (Royal Warwicks), an ASC MT unit and a flight of the

Royal Flying Corps, invaded the province and defeated the Sultan's warriors at Beringia near the capital, El Fasher. This may have been the last occasion on which British commanded troops 'formed square'. The Sultan escaped but a patrol under Kaimakam Huddleston (future Governor-General of the Sudan) caught up with him at Guiba where he was killed by a stray bullet.

Persistent requests from the Bor Dinka of Mongalla Province for protection against the Lau Nuer, coupled with an attack on a patrol of the 9th Sudanese in which an officer and six men were killed, led to intervention by three patrols under the overall command of Kaimakam Bayly in March 1917. In the course of these operations Bimbashi Heinekey-Buxton was severely wounded by a spearman whom he managed to kill with his sword! The patrols withdrew after a small garrison had been established at Nyerol.

In April 1917 the District Commissioner of Dilling, Bimbashi Hutton, was killed in a raid on a rebellious chief called Agabna in the Nyima Hills. With the onset of the rainy season punitive operations were postponed until November but then mounted on an unusually large scale when a mixed force of over 3,000 men under Miralai L.K. Smith surrounded the area. By the end of February 1918 Agabna and his witch-doctor Kilbun had been captured with 2,000 of their followers. The two leaders were sentenced to death and executed.

Among those implicated in the murder of Bimbashi Scott-Barbour in 1902 (see above) was one Malwal Matiang of the Atwot Dinka who had managed to escape the attentions of the Shambe Field Force. In May 1917 he re-emerged to attack a medical officer and his police escort as well as a government cattle camp on the Naam River (near where Scott-Barbour and his men had been killed). Little action was taken until early in 1918 when an operation under Miralai Darwall was mounted during which Bimbashi Lawton died of wounds received in action. In May Matiang and his brothers and followers surrendered after suffering heavy casualties and the confiscation of thousands of head of cattle.

Raids by the Garjak Nuer, a warlike people who inhabit a remote area of the Upper Nile near the Abyssinian border, on their peaceful neighbours, the Burun, led to intervention by the Egyptian Army from December 1919 to April 1920. Two columns, under Kaimakams Bacon and Cobden, were employed and Bacon and two other British officers were wounded in the course of operations. However, by the end of April Bacon felt able to report 'that the authority of the Government had been completely re-established' – which is most unlikely to have been the case!

One of the most sensational events of the Condominium era occurred on 8 December 1919. Several months earlier the Aliab Dinka and their (temporary) allies, the Northern Mandari, had risen against the government, murdering telegraph linesmen and police. A strong patrol of the Equatorial Battalion of the Egyptian Army under Kaimakam White accompanied by the Governor of Mongalla Province, Miralai Stigand, was ambushed in long grass by the Aliab. In the confused fighting Stigand, White, Yuzbashi Saad Osman and twenty-four Other Ranks and carriers were killed. The four surviving British officers, under Bimbashi Roberts VC (one of the most highly decorated officers of the Great War), managed to rally their companies and drive off the enemy. Following this humiliation the prestige of the government was at stake and a massive punitive operation under Miralai Darwall was mounted in the course of which hundreds of tribesmen were killed, thousands of head of cattle seized and numerous villages burnt.

In September 1921 religious insurgents (they probably objected to paying taxes as well), inspired by the Fiki Abdullahi el Suheina, attacked the District HQ Nyala (Darfur) and overran it, killing the District Commissioner, Tennent McNeill, and Bimbashi Chown of the Egyptian Army Veterinary Department. However, a brave and skilful counter-attack by men of the Western Arab Corps under Yuzbashi Bilal Rizq, heavily outnumbered, drove off the insurgents and killed the Fiki in the process. For this exploit Rizq was awarded the DSO. Later a patrol under Kaimakam Grigg accounted for a number of the rebels and rounded up the remaining ringleaders.

Although this was the last operation for which a Khedive's Sudan Medal was awarded, at least three more British officers and an NCO were to die violently while serving with the Egyptian Army. In 1922 Kaimakam Corrall was killed in action against the Ingassana tribe of Fung Province; the Sirdar, Sir Lee Stack, was assassinated in Cairo and Bimbashi Carlyle and Sergeant Renshaw of the Medical Department were killed by mutineers in Khartoum in 1924.

APPENDIX F

British Assets in Egypt –
Letter to the Daily Telegraph

13th January 1985

The Editor
The Daily Telegraph

Sir,

HMG's indifference to the plight of British subjects with assets blocked or seized by foreign governments, highlighted in your columns by Mr Cunningham and Mr Smith, is scandalous and former British residents in Rhodesia are unlikely to be treated any better than have been, for example, the former British residents of Egypt.

  Negotiations with foreign powers in these matters are carried on by the Foreign Office, to which body the pre-emptive cringe has become a way of life. The Foreign Office negotiators' only concern is to go through the motions of representing the interests of those who have been deprived of their property without offending or incommoding the relevant foreign government in any way.

The story of the conduct of the Foreign Office and the Foreign Compensation Commission towards the 'ex-Egyptians' since the Suez debacle of 1956 would fill a long (and pretty boring) book. It is one of delay, prevarication, incompetence, duplicity and ignorance. To give one example, at a meeting a few years ago between the writer and a Minister of State at the Foreign Office, an official in attendance let slip, to the Minister's obvious irritation and discomfort, that the British negotiators of the so-called settlement between Great Britain and Egypt on the question of nationalised British assets did not even know how much money they were negotiating about! [1]

There is little doubt that they entered these negotiations with instructions to conclude them with the minimum of fuss and on Egypt's terms.[2] Later there followed a devious exercise on the part of the Foreign Compensation Commission by which claimants for a share in the tiny sum which had been agreed with the Egyptians were required to fill out huge forms, involving a great deal of research, setting out their claims. These claims, rigorously and arbitrarily reduced by the FCC, were credited to the claimants' accounts against the loans, representing a small percentage of their assets, which they had received from HMG as refugees in the 1950s.

I am willing to bet that thirty years from now (although I am unlikely to be around to collect my winnings) the 'ex-Rhodesians' will still be whistling for their money just as many ex-Egyptians are nearly thirty years after Suez.

Yours faithfully
Henry Keown-Boyd

Notes

1–2. In correspondence subsequent to the meeting these points were disputed by the Minister concerned.

Selected Bibliography

Barthorp, Michael, *War on the Nile*, 1984
Cecil, Lord Edward, *The Leisure of an Egyptian Official*, 1921
Cecil, Robert, *A Divided Life*, 1988
Charmley, John, *Lord Lloyd*, 1987
Churchill, Winston S., *The River War*, 1899
Coles, Charles, *Recollections and Reflections*, 1918
Cooper, Artemis, *Cairo in the War*, 1989
Cromer, The Earl of, *Modern Egypt*, 1907
De Wiart, Carton, *Happy Odyssey*, 1950
Dictionary of National Biography
Elgood, P.G., *Egypt in Transit*, 1928
Evans, Trefor, *Mission to Egypt 1934–46*, 1971
Fahmy, Khaled, *All the Pasha's Men*, 1997
Grafftey-Smith, Sir Lawrence, *Bright Levant*, 1973
Henderson, K.D.D., *Set Under Authority*, 1987
James, Lawrence, *Imperial Warrior*, 1993
Jarvis, C.S., *Oriental Spotlight*, 1937
Jarvis, C.S., *Back Garden of Allah*, 1939
Kedourie, Eli, *Politics in the Middle East*, 1992
Keown-Boyd, Henry, *A Good Dusting*, 1986
Keown-Boyd, Henry, *Soldiers of the Nile*, 1996
Lloyd, Lord, *Egypt since Cromer*, 1933
MacMichael, Sir Harold, *Sudan Political Service*, 1956
Magnus, Philip, *Kitchener – Portrait of an Imperialist*, 1958
Mansfield, Peter, *The British in Egypt*, 1971
Marshall. J.E., *The Egyptian Enigma*, 1928
Marsot, Afaf Lutfi al Sayyid, *A Short History of Modern Egypt*, 1985
Mellini, Peter, *Sir Eldon Gorst, The Overshadowed Pro-Consul*, 1997
Pollock, John, *Kitchener*, 1998
Rafaat, Samir, *Maadi*, 1995
Reeves, Nicholas, *The Complete Tutankhamoun*, 1997
Rhodes James, Robert, *Anthony Eden*, 1986
Royle, Trevor, *The Kitchener Enigma*, 1985
Russell, Sir Thomas, *Egyptian Service*, 1949
Sabit, Adel, *A King Betrayed*, 1989
Sandes, E.W.C., *The Royal Engineers in Egypt and the Sudan*, 1937

Scott Lucas, W., *Divided We Stand*, 1991

Seth, Ronald, *Russell Pasha*, 1966

Smith, Sir Sydney, *Mostly Murder*, 1958

Wavell, Field Marshal Viscount, *Allenby in Egypt*, 1943

Wentworth Day. J., *Sport in Egypt*, 1938

Who's Who (*Who Was Who*)

Wingate, Ronald, *Wingate of the Sudan*, 1955

Yapp, M.E. (ed.), *Politics and Diplomacy in Egypt* (Diaries of Sir Miles Lampson 1935–37), 1997

Principal Unpublished Sources

Middle East Centre, St Antony's College, Oxford

Bodleian Library, Oxford

Public Record Office, Kew

Personal recollections of some of those mentioned in Acknowledgements and others now deceased

Author's recollections and documents in his possession

Index

Page numbers in *italic* type denote illustrations